Praise for

One Girl vs. A Nation Asleep

"This is a non-fiction narrative filled with remarkable adventures and feats of fearless courage side-by-side with rich inspiration and manifest conviction and told with incisive and engaging writing—a very rare combination. You will laugh cry, think and ponder. Highly recommended."
—**DR. GEORGE GRANT,** Pastor and professor, who holds three doctorates and prolific author of more than seventy books in the areas of history, biography, politics, literature, and social criticism. His books include *Killer Angel, Third Time Around, Changing of the Guard, In the Shadow of Plenty, The Last Crusader, Courage* and *Character of Theodore Roosevelt.*

"When warriors speak the conversation is different. This book reveals the heart of a true warrior—one who fights for all that is good and noble. Anne issues a clarion wake-up call to all who cherish the freedoms of Western Civilization and seek to pass them on to the next generation. 'There's some good in this world, Mr. Frodo… and it's worth fighting for.' Thank you, Anne, for beautifully compelling readers to rise and enter the arena."
—**DR. MATTHEW NOCAS,** author and speaker

"Reading Anne Odendhal is not a passive experience. It is a pilgrimage through values we assumed were foundational—faith, family, responsibility, and reverence for divine order in civic life. With an unmistakably Christian Conservative perspective, Anne doesn't just share ideas, she bears witness to truths that history is desperate to forget.

Her narrative has a firm stance on moral clarity, unapologetically elevating biblical principles above popular sentiment. She challenges the reader not to settle for lukewarm neutrality and reminds us, through both her commentary and character analysis, that every public decision is rooted in spiritual consequence. Nothing in governance is morally neutral.

Silence can be complicit, especially when it permits or perpetuates injustice. Her work will equip and challenge you with truth and grace to rattle the gates of complacency."

—**JIM QUICK,** Director, North Carolina Faith & Freedom Coalition

"I benefited from and recommend reading this book of interesting, pivotal periods in the U.S. It is enlightening to read a first-hand account, and I am sure others will gain insights.

It is good to know how Anne stood up to change in public education policies. It seems silly to me, that an atheist-initiated court mandate can stop Americans from practicing religious freedom."

—**DR. PO-WING THAM,** Pastor & missionary 譚保榮博士

"Anne Odendhal grabs our hearts and takes us in detail back to the days of bell bottoms, free spirits and the introduction to reckless lifestyles! Her impeccable awareness of morality and the political atmosphere at such a young age brings us full circle to the destruction and distortion we see today. Her independence and willingness to stand alone for righteousness' sake will leave you with many questions about yourself and where to go from here. Her book *One Girl vs. A Nation Asleep* is truly a precious gem discovered in a dark world."

—**JALISE MIDDLETON,** January 6th American political hostage

"Anne Odendhal shares real life experiences and observations through up close vignettes of the chaotic changes in our culture during the last 60+ years. While many of us moved through the motions without question, Anne walked us through her thoughts, challenges, emotions, and lessons she learned. Even as a child, God had placed in her an innate sense of good and evil compelled by an intense drive for taking a bold stand while persuading others: pastors, leaders, as well as lay people, to understand biblical mandates, forsake complacency, and carry them out in obedience and glory to God. I encourage everyone to read Anne Odendhal's book and take the challenge in bringing back biblical principles into our culture for today and following generations."

—**JILL COWARD,** Former NC State Director,
Concerned Women for America

"*One Girl vs. A Nation Asleep* is more than a book—it's a testimony. Anne Odendhal writes with honesty, courage, and a heart anchored in faith. As we celebrate 250 years of our Constitutional Republic and the 1700th anniversary of the Nicene Creed, her words remind us that our personal journeys are woven into God's greater story. Anne stirs gratitude for the past, clarity for the present, and hope for the future. This book will inspire anyone seeking to live faithfully in these historic times."
—**STANLEY L. COFER,** Founder & President, Texas Minority Coalition

"This is about a woman who is a nonconformist, a passive and active resister, and a world changer. When they took prayer and Bible reading out of her school, she was the only one to object. She was a pioneer in the homeschooling movement, and other things such as natural and alternative health. She started the second and third pregnancy centers to exist, modeled after the first one started by Christian Action Council in Washington, DC. She'd likely have been aborted if it had been legal. Her becoming a Christian is how faith started in my family. She is the reason I want to change the world. She is my mom."
—**JOANNA CHANDLER,** Center for Bioethical Reform, activist, speaker, writer, author's daughter

"As a public-school educator for 42 years, I encourage teachers—especially those in history, social studies, and government/civics—to use this book as a classroom resource.

It offers students a vivid, firsthand look at America's cultural and political changes through Anne's eyes and experiences around the world—bringing history to life in a way textbooks can't."
—**BETH STOKES**

"Theologian/philosopher Dr. Francis A. Schaeffer addressed the significance of each individual in a world of billions of people, an issue that plagues every honest person in every generation—'...I am such a small person, limited in talents, energy, psychological strength, or knowledge that what I do is not important.'

Schaeffer insisted there are No Little People, (and) No Little Places. Anne's book demonstrates that 'with God nothing is accidental nor incidental, and no experience is ever wasted.' What one chooses to do with the life that he/she has been handed makes all the difference! Anne has chosen wisely; that not only makes her significant, but it also makes her a hero! Read her book!"

— **CDR THOMAS BRAITHWAITE,** Chaplain Corps US

This is the story of a woman who values her vote at its real price, who understands the inestimable ripple effect of just one voice crying in the wilderness. This book is more than the tale of a little girl who stood when everyone sat; the book you hold in your hands is physical proof of the one-in-a-thousand woman who still stands against the evils in our nation.

Unaware of the dangers of deceit, device, and damnation, this country is sleeping, snoozing, slumbering and sawing logs. But God's justice is imminent and it's time to speak up for changes that can save souls.

I've been reminded often that by learning from the past we can avoid its mistakes. If that is so, then the content in these next pages is not only a chronology of the past for the past's sake: it is a gift to the future—mine, yours, and that of the United States of America."

— **NOAH BALLARD,** a young author, artist, and YouTuber. (NoahBallard.com)

"I am honored to be a part of Anne's book and see how a simple thing like flower bulbs can cause someone to think about generations of family life. Her book brings a unique historical perspective to our world today, told in the first-person perspective we can all relate to."

—CHRIS WIESINGER, "The Bulb Hunter",
Author of *Heirloom Bulbs for Today*

"A courageous voice and sane wakeup call for each individual, family and nation."
—MARK GUNGOR, Pastor and CEO of Laugh Your Way America. A sought-after international speaker and author of the best-selling book *Laugh Your Way to a Better Marriage*, is known for using humor and insight to strengthen marriages and families worldwide. His popular video series Singles & Stinking Thinking offers practical, laugh-out-loud guidance for navigating relationships and preparing for marriage.

"Anne and I became fast friends in 1975 as roommates at Covenant Theological Seminary. I urged her numerous times to author a book about her tumultuous, daring, creative life of service. She has done it! Admirably."

—CAROL BRAITHWAITE, Vision Impairment Therapist

"A powerful and deeply human narrative, this book is an insightful wake-up call that connects personal experience with the profound forces that have shaped modern society.

Anne expertly weaves her personal story of childhood abandonment and faith with a broader analysis of significant societal shifts in post-war America. With depth and honesty, she reflects on the intersection of faith, culture, and identity—from the removal of God from schools to the rise of media and the Civil Rights movement.

Too many have forgotten the history of atheist Madalyn Murray and how Baltimore became ground zero for a pivotal shift in our nation. Since 1963, we've seen a steady decline in moral grounding. This book is right on time to influence real change."

—KIM KLACIK

"One Girl vs. A Nation Asleep: Awakening the Soul of America' is a thoughtful read for an intimate look at the nuances unique to understanding the dramatic changes this generation experienced and facilitated. It is a contemplative account of life through a changing America, told with conviction, honesty and a well thought out perspective.

Anne blends her story with reflections on American culture and its foundation. Through vivid storytelling, she takes readers from her childhood in Baltimore to her involvement in activism, her risky experiences smuggling Bibles into China, and the discovery of herself along the way, leading the reader to laugh along."

—TONYA LESSLEY

"One Girl vs. A Nation Asleep delivers a powerful call to reclaim faith, truth, and moral courage as the foundation for America's soul. This inspiring book reveals how individual conviction can awaken a nation."

—MARIE BECKER

"From the very first paragraph, the words draw you in with a quiet intensity. The author's intentionality behind what was written creates a meaningful and most enjoyable experience."

—SARAH HARKEY

"Anne brings an authentic 'up close and personal' experience to the social, political, and spiritual journey of our country. She is articulate and specific in chronicling the decades of American change. She offers a voice of hope and triumph for the future of our country. Well written with much for the reader to ponder. Highly recommended!"

—THEA BARBATO, Long time friend, avid reader, fellow artist, author, and kindred spirit.

Anne Odendhal has been a warrior for life, liberty, and truth for decades. Her story is an inspiration to me, and I know it will stir you as well.

—FLETCHER ARMSTRONG, Southeast Director, Center for Bio-Ethical Reform

"Anne's writing is fascinating and beautifully written. Each vignette makes me want to keep reading. Her narrative encompasses the ways that social history shapes people's physical, cognitive, emotional, social, and moral changes. The mixture of facts and ideas is enjoyable and informative. Well done!"

—NANCY FURZE

"Anne Odendhal's book offers a clear, concise perspective on life during America's moral decline and sexual revolution. Live it with her as she vividly conveys the emotions of her experiences. I highly recommend this book to those of any age seeking an intimate, firsthand view of how this transformative era shaped present-day America."

—MARY BARNETT

Anne's book is a warm, personal account of a patriotic, courageous American Christian woman. Her reflections about growing up during a turbulent time in America will inform and inspire readers of all ages. Anne took a principled stand at an early age. Throughout her life, she has tirelessly sought to urge our country to return to God and to our nation's biblically informed roots."

—KATHLEEN R.

"If you seek truth, raw, unabashed, well-articulated truth from a deeply personal experience, read Anne's book! I have known her for 15 years. She always gives her all! This is not just a book but her passionate life journey scanning pivotal years of American 20th - 21st century history and societal change in conjunction with deep personal traumas and miracles that fueled her Faith. Anne brings history to life in a way that few are committed to doing. Her love for others is incredibly great! Readers will be inspired, challenged, and awed by her resilience and better yet possibly, be led to join her battle cry for freedom and discover the longed-for answer to the soul-searching quest for genuine peace and rest."

—KIM WELBORN

"Anne writes straight from the heart. Her truth and vulnerability show from page to page, and it was humbling and a blessing to read. 'One Girl vs a Nation Asleep' is an honest look at a woman of strength and character. Her passion for her family, our nation, and life, shine through. I recommend this book to all who seek a riveting account of courage and conviction."

—ABAGAIL NEZELEK, songwriter

"I have had the privilege of knowing Anne both professionally and socially for many years, and over that time I witnessed her undergoing several major life challenging experiences. Through everything I have always known her to remain totally grounded in the Almighty. Her steadfastness in her beliefs is truly inspirational, especially given the ongoing assaults on our culture. Her life is a living testament to the fact that our American culture and our Christian values are worth fighting for. Read her book!"

—DAVID MCPHERSON

"Anne Odendhal's book is an important read for anyone wanting to understand the American cultural experience. There's hope that gives light to our times."

—DR. TIMOTHY EDWARDS, author

"I have known Anne for more than a decade and look forward to the success of her book. Her knowledge of history and current affairs is extensive, and her insight and intellect shine through every page. If ever there was a good book to read of epic depth, it would be this one! Great things are coming soon."

—SCOTT BROOME

One Girl *vs.*
A Nation Asleep

Awakening the Soul of America

ANNE ODENDHAL

MAVEN
Publishing Media

ONE GIRL VS. A NATION ASLEEP
Copyright © 2026 by Anne Odendhal
All rights reserved.

No part of this book may be reproduced, stored in a retrieval system, or transmitted in any form or by any means—electronic, mechanical, photocopying, recording, or otherwise—without prior written permission from the publisher, except for brief quotations used in reviews or scholarly works.

Paperback: 979-8-9938166-0-9
Hardcover: 979-8-9938166-4-7
eBook: 979-8-9938166-5-4

Cover design: Anne Odendhal
Interior design and layout: Mark Karis
Author photo: © Anne Odendhal

Published by Maven Publishing Media
www.MavenPublishingMedia.com

This book is a work of historical, cultural, and personal narrative. Real events are described as remembered by the author. Historical references, dates, and quotations are used in accordance with fair-use standards.

Printed in the United States of America

To my Lord and Savior, Jesus Christ, and to my husband, Shawn, who both demonstrate unconditional love to me.

Thank you to the wonderful and special people who have prayed for me and helped me through life in this fallen, broken, beautiful world—many of whom I long to see again in heaven, as they are already there.

To my children, who have been precious gifts from God. And to their spouses.

To my stepdaughters, each an unexpected and delightful blessing along with their spouses.

And to my grandchildren, future great-grandchildren, and all the generations yet to come—I love you, and I pray for you continually.

"Some truths wait in silence until history itself demands to be told."
—ANNE ODENDHAL

In Honor of

The 250th anniversary of the United States of America, my beloved Constitutional Republic.

The 1700th anniversary of the Council of Nicea (325 A.D.), who penned the most widely confessed expression of the Christian faith, The Nicene Creed (one Lord, one faith, one gospel).

"The Ruler of the kings of the earth." Revelation 1:5

Contents

Prologue: I Can't See You Anymore 1

PART I: BREAKING THE SILENCE
1 Introduction 7
2 Why me? 11
3 The Making of a Writer 17

PART II: ROOTS OF INHERITANCE
4 Hasselbarth, German Immigrants 25
5 Mildred 28
6 Tuberculosis 31
7 Baltimore, 1950s—Life in Mildred's House 34
8 Christmas at Mildred's House 37
9 Eleanor and Her Mother 40
10 Men Lost to War 46
11 Domestic Abuse 51
12 Annapolis and Marv 59
13 Russian—German Wedding 63
14 No Christmas Baby 69
15 Bring Me My Baby 71
16 Alcoholism: The Potential Robber 73
17 My Parents 77
18 Grandmother Mildred—Love and Dedication 80

19	Grandmother Anna—Enterprising Role Model	83
20	Color Blind	85
21	Art of Ironing & Where Are the Sidewalks?	88
22	Lexington Market	92

PART III: CAUGHT IN THE CULTURAL CROSSFIRE

23	Brides of Dracula & Light	99
24	Prejudices against Flowers and People	104
25	Great Gran	110
26	Flower	118
27	Cultural Taboo	120
28	Waking Myself: School Buses and RX Drawers	123
29	Latchkey	126
30	Nature or Nurture?	129
31	Towers of Jello	132
32	Penpals: The Outward Reach for Connection	136
33	Possessions Can Own Us	139
34	American Dark Dive Day	141
35	The Murray Chronicles: The House That Took Prayer From America	147
36	Assassinations and Aftershocks of 1963	157
37	The Beatles—When the Ground First Shifted	160
38	The Teachers Who Shape Us	164
39	Vietnam	172
40	Woodstock Nation	175
41	Planned Barrenhood and Slippery Slopes	181
42	Love Hunger	188

PART IV: RESTORING WHAT WAS LOST

43	Truth Seeking	195
44	Robbing God	208
45	Cannot Have Children?	212
46	Teaching Freedom: A Journey Through Fear, Family, and Home	217
47	Multigenerational Divorce	229
48	A New Name	233
49	Non-Profits, Civics, Vocations	238
50	Diving into Fear	250
51	Smoke in the Air, Sugar in the Cupboards	254
52	Mortality	265
53	The Tribute	269
54	Finding My Father	274
55	O America!	287
56	Social Insecurity	291
57	My Husband	294
58	Commission	297

Reflection and Discussion Questions 301
Appendix 323
Notes 327
About the Author 333
Author Resources/Continuing the Journey 335

Prologue

I Can't See You Anymore

Photo Marv took of Eleanor

It was early spring and Eleanor had something important to tell Marv one weekend when they were together. Ever since the wonderful Christmas dance and the other events with Marv at the Naval Academy, their relationship had escalated to a serious, intimate level. All who knew them knew they were in love and assumed they were heading for marriage when Marv, the midshipman, graduated in June.

That Saturday, the air was filled with all the early signs of spring. Eleanor was so full of emotions that she felt she might burst. She didn't know whether to be happy or afraid. For days, she had rehearsed in her mind exactly what to say to Marv, but nothing seemed exactly right. Bottom line was that she just had to tell him plainly that she was expecting a baby—his baby.

The restaurant was half-empty, the kind of place where conversations floated between the clink of silverware and the muted hum of traffic outside. Eleanor stirred her coffee without drinking it, her eyes tracing the thin wisp of steam that curled and vanished. Marv sat across from her, immaculate in his crisp white shirt, the faint scent of sea salt and starch still clinging to him.

Eleanor was working up her courage to "spill the beans" to Marv after they had lunch together. Sitting together at a table, sharing a meal is such an effective way to speak the thoughts of one's heart, along with news, events, and anything that enters one's mind. During the entire meal, Eleanor was uneasy but did an excellent job of concealing her nervousness. She had rehearsed what she wanted to say a hundred times. The words were heavy in her throat. "Just tell him," she thought. "Tell him before it's too late."

Just as she had nearly mustered the courage, he reached into his pocket and placed a small, wrapped box on the table. "An early birthday gift," he said, smiling without joy. "I wanted to give it to you now because… I won't be able to see you on your birthday."

The air around them thickened. She blinked once, twice, searching his face for a clue that this was a joke. "What do you mean?" she asked, her voice smaller than she intended.

Marv looked down, his jaw tightening. "I'm graduating soon. Orders will come any day. I can't see you anymore, Eleanor."

For a moment, the world stopped moving. The din of the restaurant faded to silence, replaced by the slow, deafening pulse in her ears. She tried to speak, but nothing came out.

He looked up once, then looked away again, as if bracing for a

Prologue: I Can't See You Anymore

blow. "You've been wonderful. You deserve—"

Eleanor felt a large lump in her throat and didn't know if she could swallow at all. It felt like she was in a dream or movie, and nothing that was happening could be real. Her mind started racing, her head swaying; she felt like she might faint in a sea of fire. Eleanor sat there across the table from Marv, feeling frozen to the chair. Her legs were so heavy that they could not move. She forced one hand to pick up her purse and clutched it close to her body.

Marv sat silently across from her, looking forlorn but resolved. He had said what he needed to say, and there was nothing more worth saying. After long minutes of painful, agonizing silence, Eleanor—holding onto her purse for dear life—rose to her feet and pushed back her chair from the table. The last thing she wanted to do was leave and be without Marv.

She didn't hear the rest. The words dissolved into noise. She picked up her purse, her hands trembling, and forced herself to stand. Her legs felt numb, detached, but she walked anyway—past the counter, past the couple laughing in the booth by the window, past the door that released her into the raw chill of the afternoon.

Outside, sunlight fractured across the windshields of parked cars. She stood on the sidewalk, disoriented, the traffic rushing by like water. The small box was still in her hand. She couldn't remember opening it.

The walk to the bus stop felt endless. Each step scraped against disbelief. "He can't mean it. Not after everything." She thought of the Christmas Ball—the music, the way he had looked at her under the strings of lights, his hand steady at the small of her back. For a year, she had measured time by Marv's visits—the letters, the weekends and the quiet certainty of belonging.

A bus hissed, then stopped beside her. She climbed aboard, found a seat by the window, and stared out as the city moved past in blurs of brick and motion. Her reflection in the glass looked foreign, like someone watching her own life from a distance.

In the space between one heartbeat and the next, everything she believed about the future had changed. The rhythm of the tires on asphalt became the only sound anchoring her to the present.

Eleanor knew she was carrying Marv's baby. The realization that she and her baby were walking away from devastating rejection felt unbearable. The forces of darkness were already after her conceived-out-of-wedlock baby. Was this baby set apart for destruction? Abortion was illegal, but it could be done in places like New York City.

She pondered whether Johns Hopkins Hospital, right there in Baltimore, might somehow provide an illegal abortion. Marv was from New York City and might have been glad to pay her way there so she could have a procedure. If there was no way he wanted to marry her, there'd be no way he'd want the child either.

Outside, the city gave way to quiet streets and rows of houses fading in the early dusk. Eleanor sat very still, the unopened box in her lap, and she whispered into the window's reflection, "What now?"

No one answered.

The bus rolled on.

Eleanor was alone. Tears fell from her eyes like a faucet where the shut-off valve was broken. As the tears continued gliding down her cheeks, even her dress became wet. "Oh God, what am I going to do?"

Eleanor could never remember what it was that Marv gave her for a birthday present. Marv never contacted her again, and Eleanor never saw or spoke to him again. He did not know he was a father. Eleanor never told anyone until thirty-six years later.

Every story of life begins with both loss and promise. One young woman's heartbreak became a doorway through which history and destiny would walk.

From the pain of one spring afternoon would emerge the pulse of a greater story—about truth, memory, courage, and the unseen hand that turns endings into beginnings.

Part I

Breaking the Silence

1

Introduction

Mavens have grit and determination. They question everything. Mavens want proof and facts and need to be persuaded by more than opinion. I'm sure there are times when others see me as opinionated. I prefer to view myself as a person of strength and conviction. I am slow to embrace an idea or a doctrine, but when I understand it, I embrace it wholeheartedly. I love learning and understanding ideas, research, and perspectives.

When mavens are knocked down (as they inevitably will be), tough as it may be, they get up; they bounce back, repeatedly.

Endurance is a lifestyle. Mavens are resolute, decisive, persistent, courageous, dauntless, and spirited. A maven is a specialist, an expert, or a connoisseur that is adept at something. Usually they are a nonconformist, a passive and active resistor, and a potential world changer.

I hesitated about describing myself as a maven. It's just an aspiration, but maven means expertise. I am knowledgeable about my own life and my time in history. I have firsthand insight into a wide variety of subjects, particularly about being born, growing up, and living in the U.S.A. I am the best expert on my life history. I am knowledgeable about the history of my country, especially over the last three quarters of a century. I've lived up close and personal through vast changes in my country.

My lifelong passion for learning contributes to my growing expertise in certain areas. Delusional though it may be, in better moments, I think of myself as something of a Renaissance woman. Buried in the business of everyday living, I've long neglected to share even a fraction of my own history with anyone, including my own children.

I love English language and literacy. Learning excites me, especially in areas such as Biblical, financial, theology, holistic preventive health, fitness, history, civics, the arts, science, writing, public speaking, and teaching. I am an award-winning artist thanks to a friend who persuaded me to enter paintings in shows with art gallery judges or curators.

I have always liked nonfiction and fiction. The book 1984 by George Orwell rattled my being years ago and still does. If you have not read 1984, I suggest you read and re-read it.

I was a girl born in the United States of America and grew up in Baltimore, Maryland, near the U.S.A. federal capital, Washington D.C., where I often went. I acquired layer upon layer of love and respect for my nation. I love the U.S.A. It is my Home.

My life is like a long love affair with the U.S.A., the Beloved

Introduction

Republic. I pray and work to see that this Republic never changes for the worse in my lifetime or for future generations. We have the best Constitution in the world, it explains what the government cannot do to citizens. When upheld, our Constitution protects citizens from tyranny. The U.S.A. Constitution brilliantly focuses on the rights and privileges of the governed—its citizens.

I've meant to write this book for years. My own children, who, like me, are descendants of immigrants, may never be interested in this story. Still, I think that documenting my real-life "living museum" of growing up and living in America is worth telling. As my own hourglass has precious little sand remaining on the upper side, I'd better get it done before it is all lost to history's ash heaps.

I believe in ancestral treasures. We each reside on the backside of a senseless and complicated tapestry. We see threads, knots, tears, and fading colors, but we struggle to find beauty amidst the chaos. How can we peek around to the tapestry front and glimpse the answers? Don't we long for clarity, meaning, purpose, brightness, and beauty? They show up on the front side of our life tapestry. If only we can glimpse it, we might see realities, facts, and truths.

Our post-industrialized culture is entirely fragmented, especially when held up against mankind's history. Strong relationships and family connections are rapidly disappearing. Parents, grandparents, and great-grandparents are essential living textbooks. How else do younger generations find their moorings?

Permanent relationship anchors can equip us to successfully navigate life and the dying process.

How did those before you live and handle life experiences amidst noteworthy events, challenges, successes, losses, and aging? How and when has God worked in our lives? How has faith gotten us through?

Observing by doing life together is ideal. I wish for more of it and always have. Reading records of momentous events and important pieces of my family history is helpful for understanding how I got to be me. Recording stories contributes to future generations.

Each life is a textbook for those yet to come.

I am factually documenting history. Factual reporting is a skill I developed as a technical writer and a decades-long freelance journalist. Mixed in are thoughts, feelings, and opinions. The historical events are authentic.

My life has been, and still is, like an abstract painting. I continue learning to make sense of it. I'm piecing together a positive rhyme or reason, giving credit to why I was born.

I've spent a lifetime observing, learning, and recording the world around me. Every writer at some point reaches a moment where reflection turns into responsibility. For me, that moment arrived with a simple but pressing question: Why me? Why should I be the one to tell this story, to document what I've seen and lived? That question—persistent, humbling, and insistent—became the spark that opened the next chapter.

2

Why me?

"Regardless of how large, your vision is too small."
—THOMAS CHALMERS

"Creativity Takes Courage,"
—HENRI MATISSE

Bravery is required to express oneself. Sharing new ideas means being vulnerable to potential judgment, criticism, or even rejection. Courage involves overcoming fear of failure or rejection to put one's work out into the world. Courage allows one to take risks, think outside the box, and authenticate creative pursuits.

Ask your unasked questions. Ask to listen. Do you ever wish you'd thought of asking questions of relatives, friends, and even strangers, but you never thought of doing it when you had a chance? It's easy to miss opportunities when those with information are alive.

I long to interview people I knew and loved, now that it is too late. When my grandparents and parents were around, I was too busy and self-focused to realize that their stories were an integral part of my history, my story, and the American story.

One theme in my own history is feeling repeatedly urged or compelled towards various endeavors but allowing the tyranny of the urgent to snag me from acting. Anyone else? .... Ever?

Writing nonfiction means truth-telling. Whether one is a journalist, historian, or technical writer, the documentation should be honest and factual. The journalist inherently bears an ethical and professional obligation to report the facts without bias or personal agenda. Otherwise, it is not journalism.

A historian's main job is to provide facts. The current cancerous plague of historical revisionism is nothing more than altering truth to suit one's own presuppositions. Scandalously depriving young and upcoming generations of facts is manipulative, disgraceful, and public lying.

Modern American journalism has so veered from the exacting standards of objective reporting that I sometimes think we need term limits for journalists. It is increasingly difficult to find a media professional who cares more about reporting facts than promoting an agenda. The twisting, churning, and selective storytelling are so out of hand that we need a revival of ethics among media professionals.

Now, with social media, people can finally speak their minds without the censorship that has long strangled American media, print, radio, and television broadcasting.

> "Americans have witnessed a concerted and widespread effort to rewrite our Nation's history, replacing objective facts with a distorted narrative driven by ideology rather than truth."
> —**PRESIDENT DONALD J. TRUMP**, March 27, 2025

Why me?

It grieves me to imagine people in other countries forming opinions about American citizens based on newspapers or the often-worthless television programs and Hollywood films. To those in other nations, please—don't believe that the United States is what you see on a screen.

We live ordinary lives and seek to be good, honest, hardworking citizens and caring family people. I've heard story after story about visitors who, once they travel around and meet real Americans, discover who we truly are. Not to brag, but Americans are still prone to generosity and compassion. There is little evil intent in helping people who have no way to repay. Time and again, Americans are known for this.

I intend to tell the truth about the people who set the stage for my life. There were men—but more often women—who helped form the backdrop of my childhood. I will distinguish clearly when I am writing historical facts and when I am sharing personal reflections.

I am an unashamed, loyal, patriotic lover of my country. I cry when I hear our national anthem. I know we are far from perfect, but like loving one's imperfect family, I love my imperfect yet beautiful country. I love many other countries too—especially those I've visited or long to visit—but there's no place like home.

There was even one time I came back to the U.S. and seriously considered kissing the ground after stepping off the plane. Clearly, I am an American woman writing about life in America. I take my liberty to be authentic about both the good and the bad.

I intend to tell the truth, but not to downgrade or tear down. Any fool can look for what's wrong and highlight it with a big yellow marker. What little imagination it takes to focus only on the negative, to squawk and complain! The human condition is such that finger-pointing so often circles back to the complainer. We are joint strugglers on life's stage—no one escapes trials, tears, or regrets. While we are here, let's be accepting and less judgmental.

My professional experience includes working as a senior technical writer and editor. At least one vice president of a global corporation—whose name most would recognize—once read my work on a plane and wrote afterward to say my user manual was the best documentation he had ever read. I was assigned to oversee its translation into seven languages other than English.

My writing has a reputation for making complex ideas simple—what I call demystifying the complex. I figured if I could make it understandable to myself, then others in the non-technical world could grasp it too. Technical capability and skillful communication are entirely different animals.

Good technical writing means transforming what programmers and systems analysts convey into language that is accessible and accurate. I loved the work and the challenge—it resembled sorting, organizing, and assembling complex puzzle pieces into a concise, beautiful story.

Freelance journalism became a perpetual side gig spanning decades—from newspaper editorials and opinion pieces to digital magazine features. It was harder than technical writing, since I was crafting the written piece entirely myself, without charts or code or data from brilliant programmers.

I drafted stories on public, civic, and cultural events. I interviewed legislators about bills they hoped to see become law. I also covered health and civic issues. I wrote for newspapers and magazines—first print, later digital—for the modest pay and occasional "exposure." Journalism is tough; it can win friends and make enemies.

I invested hours attending events, conducting interviews, writing, and editing with no guarantee of publication. No publishing, no pay. I worked for two weekly papers that operated on that model—paid if published, with extra pay for front-page features.

Amazingly, my articles were always published, sometimes even on the front page. I often handled photojournalism to accompany the text. Being a member of the press gave me access to the inner

Why me?

circles—special badges, front-row seating, and candid interviews. It was fun, hard work, and low pay.

Book writing, however, has been a different kind of challenge. Despite the consistent prompting, prodding, and compelling reminders, I often argued with the call. Many urged me to "show and tell" my stories. Yet the deeper nudge—the one that felt divine—was harder to ignore. If it is God who asks me to write, then rehearsing a long list of reasons why it's too hard is unacceptable.

I share this arduous process because it may relate to the struggles many of us face. Is it God mysteriously moving and speaking, or merely my own inventive mind and emotions? Is that You, or me, talking, God?

How do we handle uncertainty about who's speaking? Is it divine leading or imagination? I concluded long ago that if I sense a call to action, I should first make sure it's not wrong, immoral, or against God's commands. Then it's better to move ahead in faith than to shrink back in fear. Apprehension is normal, but the mistake is letting fear stop us.

If I felt capable of doing every good thing I'm called to do, I might do nothing at all. No path is ever completely smooth or obstacle-free. Isn't faith always part of stepping out and forward for what is good and right? I aim to step out in faith when compelled toward the good. But the book!?

The wonder is that, while the inner voice has been persistent, it has also been patient. God is patient—but He did resort to extreme efforts to persuade Jonah to heed His call! I've been wearied, disgruntled, and argumentative. "Can't You pick someone else to take up causes and step out into controversy?" That's one of my favorite rebuttals. "Clearly, You can see I'm too tired, too worn, too old, too busy, too isolated, too ignored, too heartbroken, too stripped of life." I laugh at my melodrama now and thank God for His patience with me.

I have always been asked to write this book in the same place—

during worship. Strange, I know. At first, I thought my mind was wandering. Eventually, I realized it was a calling.

I finally stopped arguing with excuses. God can find others to fill the roles we refuse, but laying down my excuses and saying yes has been indescribably freeing. It became obvious that no one else stood in my shoes. My unique "reading" of history might yet serve others—if it increases hope, reduces fear, and helps someone else escape loneliness.

The call to write no longer felt optional. It became part of my obedience—a way to testify, to connect, and to make sense of the times I had lived through. If God gives us words, perhaps He also gives us the courage to share them.

And so, the making of a writer began.

3

The Making of a Writer

How books, calling, and courage found their voice.

"I write to discover what I know."
—FLANNERY O'CONNOR

"We read to know we are not alone."
—C. S. LEWIS

Books have always been my teachers and my friends, yet they also became mirrors—quietly challenging me to add my own voice to the chorus of writers I admired. Reading filled the lonely places, but writing demanded something more: courage.

Though I've spent years writing technical manuals and journalism pieces, this is my first full-length book—and it feels like the most personal assignment of all. Writing about one's own country and conscience is different from reporting facts for someone else's deadline.

BOOKS AS COMPANIONS

Literacy is a hallmark of civilization. President Harry S. Truman allegedly said, "Not all readers are leaders, but all leaders are readers." You've no doubt seen a plethora of "top ten" book lists published by presidents, renowned CEOs, and successful entrepreneurs.

A book is a companion that is always there. It doesn't leave us alone. A book is there with us when everyone else is gone. Books guide us, instruct us, inform us, inspire us, and make us laugh. Unlike previous times throughout history, books are available to nearly everyone. Literacy is an incredible blessing.

Wrestling with writing—and why to do it at all—brought me back to why I have so often read what others write. Reading is one of the finest escapes from loneliness. As an only child of an only child, there were days and nights of being isolated. Reading connected me closely with others, allowing me to enter their hearts and minds. Books have been my consolation. Books have been, and still are, my treasured friends.

Reading others' thoughts and ideas is important because people matter. We are *Imago Dei*—wonderfully made in the image of God. We can glean so much from interacting with ideas. When you write it down, someone else can understand what you truly mean. Readers can learn from our failures and mistakes, and from what we discovered in the process. One person's writing can affect another's life, family, and even a nation.

Unsupervised for significant periods, I was forced into self-reliance and independence. Discovering the world of books became an escape from isolation and an act of self-preservation. It also became a form of positive self-care that never left me.

While in college, I read *Escape from Loneliness* by Dr. Paul Tournier. He painted a compelling picture of what life can be like in genuine community with others. Books, I realized, are often where that community begins.

The school library and public libraries were favorite spots—an endless feast of journeys into other times, places, and ideas. My mother, ever thoughtful, purchased a child's illustrated encyclopedia set, which I pored over for hours after school, often taking notes.

One time, I brought home a school library book titled *Bugs, Insects and Such*. I don't know what got into me to select it, but I learned the difference between bugs and insects. The sophistication of these tiny creatures impressed me—so intricately designed by an obviously intelligent Designer. I still love butterflies, bees, ladybugs, and fireflies. Now, as a plant-a-holic, I choose flowers that attract pollinators and birds.

Another book that deeply marked me was *My Side of the Mountain* by Jean George. I daydreamed long hours about imitating the runaway lifestyle of Sam Gribley, who left the city to live in a hollowed hemlock tree in the Catskills. His independence and simplicity captivated me.

Like Sam, my urban life surrounded by concrete sidewalks left me yearning for adventure in creation, apart from all things manmade. My love for nature grew when I became a Girl Scout in Baltimore Troop #10. Scouting opened new worlds—woods, forests, wildlife, natural crafts, and life outside the urban jungle.

Later, while earning my B.A. in English and Education at the University of Maryland, Baltimore County (UMBC), I discovered *Living the Good Life* by Helen and Scott Nearing. After studying I would reward myself by reading about the Nearings' escape to a Vermont farm and their self-sufficient lifestyle.

The Nearings reminded me of the Schaeffers in Huemoz, Switzerland, whose God-led experiment became known as *L'Abri Fellowship* ("The Shelter"). The Schaeffers opened their home to counterculture seekers from around the world. I was privileged to live there in the early 1970s.

I admired the Nearings' self-sufficiency but not their socialism. Scott Nearing was part of the Communist Party which to me was a tragic irony. Communism is a Christian counterfeit, promising what only true Christianity can deliver. It is a brilliantly deceptive heresy, alluring because it mimics the Kingdom's ideals while rejecting its King. Only Christianity, applied to every aspect of life, offers "liberty and justice for all."

I devoured learning of every kind. I drew dinosaurs in little homemade books and wrote by hand with pencils and fountain pens that leaked and blotted. Decades later, my fascination with and research about dinosaurs led me to believe they lived alongside humans—that Noah even brought baby dinosaurs onto the Ark. None of us can know for sure; still, I love thinking about it.

I read avidly and wrote my own stories. Biographies, especially about baseball players were my favorites. Babe Ruth fascinated me because he, too, was from Baltimore. His determination to rise above hardship inspired me. I also loved reading about Mickey Mantle, who replaced Joe DiMaggio in center field for the Yankees and worked hard to become a legend in his own right.

Baseball became part of my childhood fabric. Baltimore's Memorial Stadium was our city's pride, home to the Orioles and the heartbeat of neighborhood life. I was there the year they won the World Series, defeating the mighty Yankees. My mother's boyfriend had season tickets for us, and I kept scorecards by hand. "K" means a strikeout. I learned the rules, the rhythms, and the etiquette—back then, fans did not boo or mock players. Fans may not have agreed with the umpire's decision, but deference for his official position prevailed. It was a more civil, respectful culture, one I miss dearly.

Lacrosse later captured my heart when my son played. The speed and skill of the game enthralled me—so much that if you blinked, you missed a play. Sports, like books, taught me discipline, endurance, and joy. Long before it became a modern field sport, lacrosse was a deeply rooted tradition among the Native American tribes. It was more than recreation—it was training for warriors and, at times, a substitute for war itself. Rival tribes might play for days across vast stretches of land, their contests fierce, physical, and at times deadly. What began as a contest of courage and community would one day evolve into America's oldest—and perhaps most genuinely American—sport.

That same spirit of courage—choosing conviction over comfort—has often shaped the people who've influenced me most. Whether on a playing field or in the field of faith, courage demands endurance, self-sacrifice, and the will to do what's right when it costs something.

AM I NUTS?

One of my favorite people is Elisabeth Elliot, the young widow of missionary Jim Elliot, who was killed with four others by the Waorani or Auca Indians in Ecuador in 1956. She later wrote:

> "The Aucas were a fierce group whom no one had succeeded in meeting without being killed. Our daughter, Valerie, was ten months old when Jim was killed. I remained there for two years."
> —ELISABETH ELLIOT, *Through Gates of Splendor*

Elisabeth's life and writings about womanhood and the making of a home deeply influenced me. During my early years of motherhood and homeschooling, we corresponded by old-fashioned snail mail. Elisabeth became my mentor from afar.

Her childhood and family life were the opposite of mine—stable, structured, loving. I envied that security and dreamed of offering it to my children. Like my grandmother and mother, I didn't always make the best choices, and some circumstances were beyond my control. Still, I longed to create the kind of home Elisabeth described.

I loved her calm voice on her daily radio program when my children were small. Writing, she once confessed, was her hardest task. She advised many aspiring writers:

"Don't be a writer if you can get out of it! It's a solitary job...

A writer must be some kind of nut to stick with it. But if, like the psalmist, you say, 'My heart was hot within me, while I was musing the fire burned,' then perhaps you will have to write." Her words resonated with me.

I, too, have wrestled with that fire that will not go out. Writing was never my main career, yet it has been a persistent calling.

Before I could tell America's story, I needed to understand the beginnings of mine.. Every voice has an echo, and mine was shaped by those who came before me—immigrants who crossed an ocean with little more than faith, hope, and courage. Their story became the foundation of mine.

Part II

Roots of Inheritance

4

Hasselbarth, German Immigrants

"They left what they knew for what they hoped."
— ANONYMOUS

The late 1800s was a time of massive immigration to the United States. Baltimore had grown into the second-largest port of entry—after New York—for newcomers to the New World. The majority were Germans, who made up more than half of the foreign-born residents of Baltimore. Many came seeking opportunity as craftsmen in the city's expanding manufacturing industries.

Mr. and Mrs. George Hasselbarth voyaged from Germany across the Atlantic and stepped onto the shores of their new homeland. They established themselves as part of the German Lutheran community. The reasons for their emigration are lost to unrecorded history. I can only imagine the courage required to pack what little one could, then board a ship to an unknown world, and face the dangers of the voyage. Some ships never made it across. The hope of a better life was the dream that propelled them forward.

Below are photographs of my two great-grandparents, who immigrated from Germany to America. My mother always marveled that people in those old pictures never smiled. In early photography, posing required remaining still for several seconds, so photographers advised their subjects to maintain a calm "at repose" expression to avoid blurring.

This was a time when those who immigrated to America came seeking a brighter future. Though they retained much of their cultural heritage, customs, and cuisine—whether German, Irish, Italian, Dutch, or others—they eagerly and proudly became Americans. They were grateful for the hope of improving their lives and those of their children. Characterized by hard work and perseverance, they expected little and gave much.

Immigrants instilled a strong work ethic in their children, who later endured the Great Depression and World War II. That same ethic was passed to their Baby-Boomer descendants, including me.

My German great-grandmother

New American citizens learned English and adapted to their lives in a new culture. How different this is from today, when some immigrants wish to live as if they never left the countries of their origin. Why come to America if not to become part of her? If I were to move to another nation, I would be expected to learn its language and respect its customs—not the other way around. I yearn for the day when our government finally makes English the official language of the United States.

My German great-grandfather

My great-grandparents, the Hasselbarths, had five children who grew up on the cement sidewalks and city streets of Baltimore. The adult sons became steelworkers at the Bethlehem Steel factory, one of the region's industrial giants. I assume they came in part, for greater vocational and economic opportunity. Most women were homemakers, but for my grandmother, working outside the home was a necessity. She worked in a seamstress factory to support her orphaned siblings and later her daughter when she became a single mother. Abandoned by her husband, my grandmother, Mildred, was a single mother long before there were many like her.

5

Mildred

Mildred with baby Eleanor

For reasons lost to time, both of my great-grandparents, Hasselbarth, died prematurely. The causes of their deaths are unknown. They left behind five children to fend for themselves. The eldest, Mildred Hasselbarth, became the de facto parent to her younger siblings—Annette (who later married George Seymour) and her three brothers, George, Henry, and Frank.

Mildred was barely an adult herself, yet she shouldered full responsibility for her family. Their Baltimore neighborhood was lined with narrow row houses, marble steps that were polished bright, and treeless sidewalks stretching in every direction—a cement world with little softness.

She found steady work in a factory, sewing zippers into men's trousers. The routine was unrelenting, day after day, year after year. She did it well. Somehow, she managed both her full-time job and the household duties: cooking, cleaning, and ensuring her siblings attended school. It was an enormous task during the Great Depression, when jobs vanished and families struggled to survive.

Mildred later met and married an Irish Scottish merchant marine named Reedy. While her sister Annette was still in elementary school, Mildred gave birth to her only child, Eleanor Elizabeth Reedy—my mother.

Mildred was the unquestioned matriarch, practical and decisive. Eleanor grew up close to her Aunt Annette, who was more like a sister since they were nearly the same age.

Mildred's marriage, however, was stormy and brief. Her husband vanished when Eleanor was a baby, never to return. He left no trace—no letters, no visits, or even a rumor. Mildred destroyed the few mementos that he had left behind, determined to erase his memory from their lives. Eleanor grew up with only a faint photograph and a surname: Reedy.

Decades later, I began my own quiet investigation to help my mother uncover her father's story. Using old phone directories and long-distance calls on a corded phone, I searched for any remaining relatives. Eventually, I located his nephew in Virginia, who warmly welcomed my mother as family. Eleanor even traveled to meet them, forming a bond through letters in the years that followed.

At last, we learned what had happened: her father had died while serving in the Merchant Marines. His body was buried at sea.

Mildred's story was one of quiet endurance—an uncelebrated

heroism born of necessity. Her daughter Eleanor would carry that same strength forward, but also the ache of unanswered questions and buried memories. The struggles of one generation often shape the choices of the next, and in my mother's life, the pattern of independence and loss repeated itself in ways neither of us could have foreseen.

6

Tuberculosis

> "The illness did not only take the sick. It rearranged the lives of the well."
>
> **—ANONYMOUS**

The sudden deaths of Mildred's parents left her in charge of all the family responsibilities. Her older brother, Henry, wanted to help but could not as he was far from Baltimore—living high in the Maryland mountains at the Maryland State Tuberculosis Sanatorium.

Henry had traveled by railway to the hospital, built in 1907 just south of the Pennsylvania border in Sabillasville, Maryland. From the railway station, a horse-drawn carriage carried him to the sanatorium, where he remained for months until he was finally strong enough to return home. The state later converted the hospital into a boys' reform school in 1965.

Bed rest, nutritious meals, light exercise, and fresh mountain air were the main prescriptions for recovery. These facilities resembled the health resorts in their appearance, but their patients were gravely ill and isolated from all family and community. Some never returned to their homes. Called the "White Plague" or "Romantic Disease," tuberculosis inspired both dread and fascination in earlier centuries.

Mildred's sister, Annette, later contracted TB and was quarantined as well. Sanatorium stays often lasted many months; the recovery process was painfully slow. My family's relatives were among those who slept outdoors on screened porches, seeking the curative power of the cold, clean air deep in the western Maryland mountains.

Tuberculosis (TB) is caused by the bacterium *Mycobacterium tuberculosis*. It primarily attacks the lungs but can also affect the kidneys, spine, or brain. Untreated, TB can be fatal—and once, it was the leading cause of death in the United States.

> "If the importance of a disease for mankind is measured from the number of fatalities which are due to it, then tuberculosis must be considered much more important than those most feared infectious diseases, plague, cholera, and the like. Statistics have shown that one-seventh of all humans die of tuberculosis."
> — *Die Ätiologie der Tuberculose*, Robert Koch (1882)

> "At the beginning of the 20th century, tuberculosis (TB) was one of the UK's most urgent health problems. After the establishment in the 1880s that the disease was contagious, TB was made a 'notifiable disease' in Britain; there were campaigns to stop spitting in public places, and the infected poor were pressured to enter sanatoria that resembled prisons; the sanatoria for the middle and upper classes offered excellent care and constant medical attention. Whatever the purported benefits of the fresh air and labor in the sanatoria, even under the best conditions, 50 percent of those who entered were dead within five years (1916)."
> —Wikipedia summary of historical tuberculosis accounts

"Antibiotics developed in the 1940s were effective in treating TB. Hopes that the disease could be eliminated were dashed in the 1980s with the rise of drug-resistant strains. Responding to the resurgence of tuberculosis, the World Health Organization issued a declaration of a global health emergency in 1993. Every year, nearly half a million new cases of multidrug-resistant tuberculosis (MDR-TB) are estimated to occur worldwide."
—Wikipedia summary of World Health Organization records

Who could have imagined that the humble discovery of antibiotics would save so many lives? Though at times overprescribed, antibiotics became one of the most profound medical advances in human history—turning a dreaded disease of despair into one of hope and survival.

7

Baltimore, 1950s—
Life in Mildred's House

Mildred remarried when my mother, Eleanor, was eight years old

My earliest memories of Mildred's house are of narrow spaces, careful steps, and an unspoken need to stay alert.

Mildred remarried a man named George, a popular family name. She had a brother, nephew, and cousins all named George, so her husband acquired the nickname of Dutch, or Pop to me. Dutch joined the men of the family working at Bethlehem Steel in Baltimore. They lived in a small, narrow Baltimore city row house built around 1880, for which they paid cash, no mortgage. The 900 sq ft house was on a narrow one-way, very urban street. 510 N. Port St. had two rooms on the main floor, a long living room, and a large kitchen with a big table in the center of the room.

The small refrigerator had a freezer that could hold a gallon container of ice cream and nothing else. The freezer area regularly became encased in ice, so defrosting was a routine procedure. Pop carried home large blocks of ice, which were kept in the kitchen to help refrigerate perishable food. "Convenience" food didn't exist. I invested many hours in now unknown activities such as cracking, then picking walnuts with appropriate tools. Gran included the fresh walnuts in her Toll House cookies at Christmas time.

The Port St. house's second floor had three bedrooms, and one had to walk through the middle bedroom to get to the master room that overlooked the front street. The middle room where I often slept as a child had one small window, a skylight on the roof that captured every imaginable sound from rain and wind. To me, those sounds meant monsters stirring, especially during storms. My only option for using the bathroom at night was traveling down two quite steep flights of stairs to the cellar, where the bathroom was located. My Gran was thoughtful and always had a metal bucket near my bed, which was my nighttime toilet.

I ventured down the steep cellar stairs only in daylight hours when monsters slept. I knew if I wasn't quiet and careful, I might arouse them. A few times, I tumbled down the cellar stairs that were narrow and steep for little legs. One of those tumbles prompted Mildred to stand at the top of the stairs and say, "See, that is God punishing you." There was no coming down to comfort me or wipe my tears. She never explained what God's reasons were for punishing me or what I had done to deserve punishment.

Gran was superstitious and often spoke of how bad luck would come if a black cat crossed our path or if we walked underneath an open ladder. What prejudice against black kittens! Mildred forbade me to ever hang a wire coat hanger on a doorknob. Doing so would mean that someone in the family would die! How strange and silly a superstition can be. My girlhood years were spent being careful not to walk on the cracks in the sidewalks that were part of my urban daily life. I often used chalk to make outlines and play hopscotch on the sidewalks.

The cellar steps landed on a dirt floor that extended to the front end of the house. I dared not venture in that direction where zombies and vampires might be hiding. A small, partitioned area had a toilet, a claw foot bathtub, and a small sink.

There were wooden shelves and Gran's wringer washing machine, which rattled noisily when operating. Gran carefully fed each item through the wringer, which removed enough of the water to hang them for drying on the clotheslines extending the length of the cellar in the winter and the small urban backyard in the summer. Dripping wet clothes and sheets came from the other side of the wringer like damp cardboard that could stand on its own.

Gran's home had the historic Baltimore white marble front steps. Neighbors scrubbed steps with wooden scrub brushes and buckets to keep them clean and shiny.

It was a house of caution and unpredictability—a house where love and fear lived side by side.

And yet, in that narrow house full of superstition, silence, and watchfulness, there were days when the rooms broke open with color and warmth—when the world felt festive and full. Christmas at Mildred's was something entirely special.

8

Christmas at Mildred's House

> "Christmas is a necessity. There has to be at least one day of the year to remind us that we're here for something else besides ourselves."
>
> —ERIC SEVAREID

Christmas at Mildred's was a world entirely its own—bright, bustling, sugary, loud, and full of life.

Christmas at Gran's house was dazzling. It meant family, food, and gifts. For weeks ahead, Mildred baked, cut, and decorated sugar cookies with colored sugar. Gran stored old-fashioned Toll House cookies in her supply of tin boxes. Christmas Eve meant Gran's entire extended family came for the day. Every surface in her kitchen and parlor was covered with cookies, nuts to crack with nutcrackers, and sandwich items.

Growing up eating piles of sugary foods resulted in an addiction to sugar. Thankfully, I am a recovering sugar addict. No one had a clue that permitting a child to eat a diet of sweets could be harmful. No one took me to the dentist until I was a teenager with a mouthful of cavities. I wish sealants were available when I was a child.

The amazing part is I was always skinny—so skinny that everyone, and I do mean everyone, from kids in school to relatives made fun of me…like I could help it. This was before girls could wear pants to school, so I quietly endured the pain of almost daily comments about my skinny legs. I tried so many tactics for gaining weight, and nothing ever worked.

The German men in the family had a fondness for the holiday special—raw beef sandwiches. Yuck! They started with soft white bread slices spread with German mustard and pickles. Sliced raw onions and hefty raw beef were layered. I remember eating this holiday culinary specialty and thinking that I liked it. Nowadays, I can imagine how mortified guests would be if one served raw beef sandwiches on holiday trays. Back then, it was a special treat.

Presents were the culmination of the celebration, and I looked for the package with the big Santa on the front. Gran put that package in a prominent place because, after all, I was the only grandchild of her only child. I looked for that package every Christmas. My grandmother lived through the Depression and was a masterful recycler. Year after year, she carefully removed the wrapping paper from every gift, removed the tape, and carefully folded and stored each piece for next Christmas. The idea of throwing away anything was foreign. There was extraordinarily little trash since almost everything was reused.

I recall one afternoon when Gran was putting away the Christmas items and layering the used, folded wrapping paper inside a large rectangular box. There was clearly more wrapping paper than the box would hold, but she paid that no mind and was determined to make it all fit. Something would set her off, and she would pitch a real fit with thrashing arms, yelling at varying decibels. Usually, during these events, everyone around ran for quiet cover. When Gran behaved this way in the car, we were trapped and forced to listen as she vented herself to feel better.

This time, after numerous efforts to close the box and it popping back open again, Gran really lost it and started yelling and hitting the box as if she could beat it into submission. I stood by watching and working with everything in me to hold back the belly laughs. I failed to hold in my laughter, which incited Gran more in her comic rage against the recycling box.

Consumable items such as milk, soda, and even potato chips were delivered with a deposit for the containers that were returned to the deliveryman (always a man). Neighbors placed empty bottles outside their door for the milkman to pick up and replace with full bottles. The "Charlie Chip" man delivered potato chips. I recall a television jingle about having milk, butter, eggs, and cheese fresh from the farm to your door: "If you don't own a cow, call Cloverland Dairy now." That jingle still plays in my mind exactly as I heard it on the small television.

Have you known anyone who lived through the Great Depression? They viewed material possessions in ways that are difficult to comprehend today. Nothing was thrown away. Scarcity shaped them. It shaped our home. And though I did not understand it then, I see now that survival leaves its own kind of inheritance.

It marks you—quietly, daily, in ways you do not recognize until many years later.

I carry it still.

9

Eleanor and Her Mother

"No mother is formed in ideal conditions."

—ANONYMOUS

Every mother was once a daughter, shaped long before she ever held a child of her own.

When Eleanor was born on April 21, 1926, her biological father was there. She remembers seeing a photo of him holding her as a baby, yet the mystery of his disappearance would remain for many decades. His marriage to Mildred must have been so tumultuous that she erased his memory, and none of her relatives ever mentioned him. After going through a required waiting period and legal proceedings, including posting notice in newspapers concerning the whereabouts of Eleanor's biological father as a missing person, her mother, Mildred, married Dutch. He became the only father my mother ever knew.

Mildred was a mother who worked outside the home when most women were full-time homemakers. She could cook, sew, and create domestic tranquility and beauty amidst the dirt and clutter. Gran seemed to want to make up for the Great Depression by collecting doodads (my word for unnecessary clutter) and blessing me with toys, stuffed animals, and dolls.

Gran gave me my first doll that looked like a real baby. I named her Mary. I treasured Mary, carried her everywhere (until sexy Barbie and Ken came along when I was older). We sometimes took my dolls on Saturdays to the doll hospital, where a man made his living repairing dolls. As a professional seamstress, Gran taught me to crochet and sew doll clothes. I recall a warm, well-fitted, brown corduroy jacket that she helped me make when I was in high school.

Gran collected plants, and because she never threw away anything, I thought that when you acquire a house plant, it meant that you had a lifelong relationship with that plant. I had no clue that plants also have lifespans. Her front parlor displayed her plants. I eventually realized house plants need tossing. I felt guilty if I threw out a plant; I just couldn't, because it was a living thing. Now, when they start looking bad, they go into the trash with only a tinge of guilt.

Gran had well-to-do relatives, and one of them was a taxidermist. He gave Gran several large glass globes filled with branches and beautiful stuffed birds, which she kept amidst plants in her parlor. Surrounding the multi-colored birds was a beautiful jungle of plants.

African violets were everywhere, and there were always new violet leaves growing roots through aluminum foil over a glass with water. There was one prolific plant that fascinated me since Gran called it "Mother-in-Law's Tongue." I've never heard it called that by others, so I decided it was not the nicest name for an innocent plant.

Me in Mildred's Baltimore parlor with her plants and taxidermy birds under glass

Eleanor said her stepfather, whom she always introduced as her father, was not involved in her life. He was the sort of fellow who turned over his paycheck to Mildred, who paid the bills and made decisions about everything. I recall listening when they had to make decisions such as "Where do you want to go?" or "What do you want to do?" They'd go back and forth, asking each other. It would go the same way each time, a verbal game of tennis until my Gran finally decided, and Pop would follow her lead.

I think Gran would have liked Pop to make more of the decisions, or at least offer some assistance, but besides working at the steel mill and fishing, he left most of life to his wife. He was a passive, quiet, decidedly dependent man. Life was accepted as it came, and people usually did what they needed to do with the cards they were dealt.

Pop often went on deep-sea day-long fishing trips that meant going on a large boat with other men and returning home with fish he would clean and cook. Sometimes he would fish from the piers and would take me with him. He quietly taught me by demonstrating how to find things in his tackle box and bait the hook with bloody squid. I didn't mind and enjoyed catching a fish myself that Pop would later clean and fry for us to eat. There is nothing like eating the fish you caught earlier the same day.

Pop may have been a bit wimpy, but he was a diligent worker at Bethlehem Steel. Every workday, he packed a dark gray, rounded steel lunch box that clicked loudly when he closed it. He was harmless, and my memories of him are mostly him "being there," sitting in his recliner chair or driving…my grandmother had her license, but she rarely drove. When she occasionally did drive for a brief stint, the passengers were anxious and relieved when she turned the wheel back over to Pop.

I recall one time during my childhood when Gran got behind the wheel when I was on a summer road trip with the two of them. I yearned for the moment when she relinquished the wheel back to Pop, and I could breathe easily again. Something about her driving resembled her temperament, unpredictable and volatile. She was known at the bowling alley as one who tossed (not threw) the bowling ball while we all stood frozen watching it bounce its way down the wooden lane. I fought to hide my laughter at those times too.

Gran had her explosive moments, but never towards me. Whenever she had to tell me something, she spoke kindly because she adored me, her only grandchild. She sometimes told me not to tell Pop about whatever toy, jewelry, or game she bought for me.

Gran enjoyed buying things for me, and it was one of her most pleasurable endeavors. It was how she showed love to me, the best way she could. I do not recall hugs or kisses from Mom, Gran, or anyone except my other Gran, Anna. The closest thing to cuddling and affection I remember is riding on long car trips with Gran and Pop and leaning my head on Gran's very fat, soft, pillow arm. It felt good to be that close to someone and gave me times of pleasant naps. My relatives were not physically or verbally affectionate. It wasn't part of their culture or upbringing.

My mother received her share of Mildred's rage, and their relationship was on-and-off in Eleanor's early adulthood. My mom told me stories, such as one time when she came home to find that Mildred had, in anger, cut some of her clothes. My mom later eloped at age 16, partly to escape her tumultuous home life.

During later years when I was school age, I remember my mom adoring her mother and she would do anything for her. There was little mention of the tumultuous years when Eleanor felt criticized, misunderstood, and mistreated. The past was forgiven and forgotten. They did a beautiful job of loving each other with the time left in Mildred's life. Looking back, it was a vibrant illustration of how love is more powerful than all the hurt, resentment, or hate people can concoct. Love and forgiveness are possible. Love can and often does win out. This is beauty.

When my Gran suffered a heart attack, my mom tried to learn how to keep her alive and well, including having her and Pop come live with us in our Baltimore row house. Pop didn't like it and insisted they return to their house, which meant Gran did not have my mother and me to be there with her each day after school and work. My mother and I both thought it was selfish of Pop to focus on his self-interest rather than his wife's recovery and well-being. There's nothing like being with family, those loved ones, to aid in healing and health.

It wasn't long before Gran had a second heart attack, which proved fatal. At Gran's funeral, when I was sixteen, my mom threw herself at the casket and wailed uncontrollably, "Mom, Mom!!" I had already attended the funerals of her siblings, who also died of heart disease. I somehow learned how to be mostly numb to it all. I was usually like a piece of furniture, and no one inquired about how I was doing.

The day my mom and I returned from Mildred's funeral, my mother began yelling at me, telling me it was my fault that Gran had died. As usual, I was quiet with no response. I had no way to process what she was saying or meaning. I was 15 or 16 years old and bewildered. Gran was one person in my life who would have done anything for me if she knew of my needs. She bought me material things but had almost no knowledge of my isolated, lonely, inner world. I loved my Gran, and I know she loved me and expressed it however she could. My mom loved her mother and demonstrated it regardless of their struggles.

I loved my Gran, and I that know she loved me and expressed it however she could. My mom loved her mother, and she demonstrated it regardless of their struggles.

The lessons Eleanor absorbed loyalty, restraint, and survival—would later shape how she faced her own battles. In her world, love was not easily spoken, but its presence lingered in the quiet acts that bound generations together.

Some families shout their love. Ours lived it sideways—through gifts, effort, presence, and endurance. The tenderness was real, even when it was obscured. I did not understand any of this at the time. I only felt the confusion. Later, I would learn that love can be imperfect and still be true.

10

Men Lost to War

"They also serve who only stand and wait."
— JOHN MILTON

There are seasons in a young woman's life when decisions are made not out of certainty, but out of longing, fear, and the desire to belong to someone, or something larger than oneself. My mother came of age in such a season—when the world was still trembling from war and love often meant hoping someone would live long enough to return.

In the 1940s, Eleanor started college. The service members were not home yet, even though the war in Europe was officially over. They were still fighting Japan after Germany had surrendered. This was before America dropped bombs on Japan to force the beginning of the end of the war.

When Eleanor, at age sixteen, married Skeets, they ran away to another town where parental consent was not required. As she was a minor, Eleanor's marriage annulment was not difficult. There were times during the coming years when Eleanor wished she'd stayed married with Skeets. He loved her and he was a responsible man, capable of being a good husband and father. Who among us hasn't sometimes pondered how life might be in the present had our past choices been different?

Eleanor with Skeets

Right after her first boyfriend and brief husband, Skeets, went overseas as part of the forces in the occupied areas in Germany, Eleanor felt an increasing need to make a difference. Eleanor's strength and independence found another outlet—the United States Coast Guard.

When Eleanor enlisted, the Coast Guard was a branch that quietly carried an immense responsibility during World War II. Unlike the larger forces focused on combat abroad, the Coast Guard protected America's coasts, escorted convoys, enforced maritime law, and rescued sailors at sea. It was both a military and a humanitarian role, defending the homeland while saving lives.

For many women along the East Coast, including those from Baltimore, the Coast Guard offered something rare: meaningful service close to home, marked by skill, discipline, and purpose. It appealed to those who valued courage without aggression—the idea of protecting rather than destroying. It was, in every sense, a place for strong and capable women who wanted to serve their country with steadiness and heart.

Eleanor didn't see herself as adventurous or courageous, but she obviously was. She said there was a lot of cleaning up to do in the war-torn places after the German surrender.

Eleanor in a United States Coast Guard uniform

Although she already had a marriage annulment, Eleanor was worried about Skeets. She was still a young girl but wanted to help the war cause and make a positive difference. She longed to be involved since so many of our men were soldiers. The soldiers were far away, not on our own shores. Jobs and tasks that were usually under male authority were left for the women.

There was another reason Eleanor took the path of least resistance in having her marriage annulled with Skeets, and would not later go back with him, though he begged her. When he had to leave her shortly after their marriage, she didn't feel she could bear the potential heartbreak of losing him as a war victim. Too many men had already died in the same war.

Eleanor began working in a supply place, and because she wouldn't go out with the commanding officer, he started giving her a hard time in various ways, one of which was having her hair cut short. When Eleanor wanted out, he was willing to submit papers for her early release.

Eleanor's desires to influence her country and its freedom were interfered with by sexual harassment before it had a name. This is something Eleanor had to deal with throughout her life because men would hit on her; she was beautiful.

Eleanor had another boyfriend named Lou, who loved her and told her when he left for duty that as soon as he came back, he wanted her to marry him. They were unofficially engaged. She really thought he would be the one man of her dreams. When Eleanor asked Lou why he had chosen to become a paratrooper, he said it was because he could earn thirty dollars more per month.

Lou was killed on D Day in Normandy. His entire battalion died that day. Eleanor kept Lou's military pins all her life. Eleanor met another nice young man she liked at the Lutheran church; he also died in the war.

Just like Eleanor lost men to war, there are many single baby-boomer women in America because countless men of my generation were killed in the Vietnam War.

We rarely consider it, but there weren't enough baby boomer men to go around for the baby boomer women because many young men in the 1960s were lost in the war. Girl babies survive better than boy babies. When the toll of war further contributes to the disproportionate number of women to men, it destines some women to be alone, whether they want to be or not.

Lou before losing his life in Normandy

After losing boyfriends in the war, Eleanor was still the immature girl who had run away from her home. Skeets begged her to come back to him, but she couldn't handle the prospect of losing Skeets the same way, so though she would regret the decision in the years to come, she ran from him. She chose not to bear waiting to see whether Skeets would lose his life in the war too.

War did not just claim soldiers; it altered the shape of families, marriages, and women's hearts for generations. My mother learned early that love could be taken by war in an instant—and that knowledge shaped the choices she made for the rest of her life. There is no judgment in that. Only understanding.

Some stories are not about who we should have chosen, but about how the world we lived in shaped the choices that were possible.

11

Domestic Abuse

Control often masquerades as love.

Abuse almost never begins as violence. It begins as tenderness, admiration, and attention—and then slowly tightens into control.

No one enters a marriage expecting fear.

Love does not disappear in an instant. It is slowly suffocating.

Eleanor

How we relate to our creator is our number one life decision. Marriage is the second most important decision. One's marriage decision affects everything for the rest of one's life. The magnitude of this choice cannot be overestimated and should not be taken lightly. Some people remain single due to fear of making a bad or wrong decision, wanting to avoid their parents' failures.

After the annulment, Eleanor focused on working and her education. When she wasn't working her car-hop job she attended classes and studied. She studied bookkeeping and accounting, though she disliked math and thought she wasn't good at it. Whatever it was, she passed the narrative on to me. Often, I have endeavored things I had no natural interest or aptitude for to stretch and grow as a person. There is a risk in every decision we make, even getting out of bed in the morning.

Sam, a regular customer where Eleanor worked, asked her out repeatedly. She finally consented. They had a fun first date attending a football game with other young people. Sam continued asking her out, and it became a regular thing.

Sam was crazy about her, and Eleanor fell in love with him.

Less than a year later, Eleanor put her college courses on hold and left her car hop job to marry Sam. She worked as a bookkeeper for a man who owned several furniture stores. Eleanor and Sam lived in a basement apartment in the home of Sam's parents. Life was good except for Sam's incessant jealousy. Every day, Eleanor would endure Sam's interrogations about where she went and with whom.

When Eleanor was working in the furniture store office, she arrived at work one day to find her boss standing outside on the curb staring at the smoldering building. Somehow, the night before, the building had caught fire, and much of the furniture store's contents were lost.

When the fire was completely out, Eleanor helped her boss rummage through whatever business documents and records were salvageable from the ruins. She then accepted the task of helping re-establish all the business books and record-keeping systems. This was before computers or backup systems.

Similarly, I remember learning that the great American inventor Thomas Edison got his children out of bed late one night to see the fire that was burning down his research plant, where his experiments and manufacturing occurred. When Edison lost records for his experiments, the backup system was what he could locate in his cranial files. I sometimes think of Edison when I experience a setback or need to start something over because he didn't lie down and die but *"failed forward."*

"Although I am over 67 years old, I'll start over again tomorrow. I am well burned out tonight, but tomorrow there will be a mobilization here and the debris will be cleared away, if it is cooled sufficiently, and I will go right to work to reconstruct the plant, said Mr. Edison as he watched the flames destroy building after building."—New York Times, Dec 10, 1914

After the fire that burned one of the store buildings, Sam became very jealous of Eleanor's boss, the furniture store owner. Sam didn't think it was appropriate for his wife to have lunch with her boss.

This can still be a tough question for some couples today when finding themselves in work-related situations with the other gender.

We've all heard the stories of men leaving their wives for the secretary who always looks nice, is always supportive and helpful, compared to the wife whom he sees when she first awakens in the morning and listens to her concerns. Business is business, but on the other hand, one can never be too careful when guarding one's heart regarding the ease of marital faithfulness.

Eleanor had to spend a good deal of time with the furniture store owner since together they were trying to get the business re-established. Sometimes they discussed business issues and plans while having lunch together; it was a very busy time.

Sam began questioning Eleanor about the time she was spending during lunch with her boss. This shocked Eleanor, who dismissed his concerns as completely unnecessary. Not a light matter to Sam, a side of him began surfacing that would eventually prove fatal to the survival of their love. Once jealousy surfaced, Sam's obsession with it grew. Sam's verbal, emotional, and even physical control and abuse increased. When Eleanor married Sam, he tore up photos Eleanor had of any men in her past, old boyfriends, and especially photos of Skeets. The only surviving photos are the ones Mildred had at her house.

"Jealousy, that dragon which slays love under the pretense of keeping it alive."—Havelock Ellis *(British psychologist and author, 1859-1939)*

Whether Eleanor gave Sam legitimate fuel for the fire of his jealousy or not is unknown. Eleanor was a young, beautiful, impressionable woman. Whatever instigated it, Sam's jealousy worsened. Arguments between the two of them became part of a typical day. Eleanor started hating her life, and the genuine love she had for Sam grew colder as fear took over the happy feeling of love. There is never a legitimate excuse for any type of abuse.

Eleanor tried to get help from family members on both sides of their family. She tried talking to close friends about what was happening behind closed doors. Amazingly, no one believed her as Sam was a great guy and such a gentleman. No one could imagine him the way she was describing, and they thought for sure that Eleanor was exaggerating.

Research now shows that when a woman is physically, mentally, verbally, and financially controlled and abused, the norm is that few people, if anyone at all, believe her or take seriously what she says. Domestic abuse is usually hidden, overlooked, and denied by everyone, even the victims who rarely give up hoping and praying things will change for the better. For isolated victims, abuse is perceived as normal life.

A few facts about abuse:

- One in every four women will experience domestic violence in her lifetime.

- An estimated 1.3 million women are victims of physical assault by an intimate partner each year.

- 85% of domestic violence victims are women.

- Historically, females have been most often victimized by someone they knew.

- Females who are 20-24 years of age are at the greatest risk of nonfatal intimate partner violence.

- Most cases of domestic violence are never reported to the police.

(National Coalition Against Domestic Violence)

One evening, Sam's parents heard an inordinate amount of noise coming from their downstairs apartment, so they went down to see what was happening. They saw a very angry Sam with a knife in his hand, yelling at Eleanor. "What are you doing, Sam?" his mother cried out to him. "What's the matter with you? Have you lost your mind? Stop that right now." "Now you'll believe me!" cried Eleanor. After that night, his parents and some other relatives started believing that Sam got what he deserved when Eleanor finally left him.

One evening when Sam and Eleanor were home, the old-fashioned landline phone rang about eight o'clock. Eleanor answered and heard Skeet's voice from the other end. He began explaining that he had met a lady he thought that he might want to marry, but when he checked into getting a marriage license, he was told that there was no record of the annulment from his marriage to Eleanor. He didn't know what to do and wondered if Eleanor would help him with the necessary documentation that validated their legal annulment. Eleanor was glad to hear that Skeets was alive after all the war days and was happy to help him.

Sam overheard Eleanor on the phone and began questioning her about the caller. "Who is that on the phone?" Sam asked. "Is that a man? What does he want?" Eleanor was trying to listen to Skeets, and when she did not respond as Sam wanted, his anger escalated. Sam tried to grab the phone from Eleanor's hand, and a scuffle ensued. On the other end, the alarmed Skeets cried out to Eleanor, "What is happening there? Is he hurting you, Eleanor?"

The next day, Eleanor spoke privately with Skeets, and he told her to come to where he was staying in New York City to get away from Sam. She felt trapped with no place to go to feel safe, so this was her chance to find help from someone she knew she could trust. Eleanor quickly packed and was missing (on her way to New York) when Sam came home from work that day.

When Eleanor arrived in New York, she was so happy to see Skeets again. He did not marry the woman who was under consideration, and Eleanor would have stayed with Skeets from then on had it not been for one thing: he had to leave very soon after her arrival to go out to sea for a military assignment.

Skeets was a seaman, and the sea called him to duty. There she was again left alone. "Stay here and wait for me in New York until I can return", Skeets asked her, but she couldn't bear being alone or facing the possibility of losing Skeets to the war. Skeets gave her money to get her own place to live and get a new start in her life. When she arrived back in her Baltimore hometown, she stayed with her mother and stepfather until she could find her own place, get a new job, and resettle.

There was one more incident when Sam accosted her when she was out with some friends. He tried to grab her and interrogate her. He said, "We are not divorced, and you need to stay away from other men." Eleanor told him, "We are legally separated, and if you ever come near me again or lay a hand on me, I'll have you arrested." That was Sam's last attempt to control the woman who once loved him. Their marriage ended in divorce.

Eleanor survived not because she was unbroken, but because she refused to surrender the truth of her own reality—even when no one else could see it.

What is gaslighting? The 1944 film *Gaslight* offers a chilling illustration—just as unsettling today as it was then. The film helped give language to a pattern of psychological manipulation that would later be recognized in legal, clinical, and advocacy settings as a form of abuse and control.

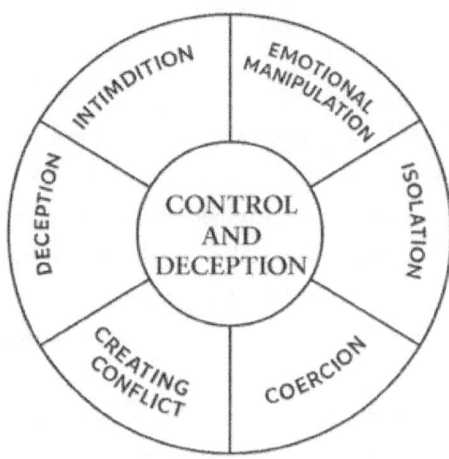

Control and Deception Wheel. Concept and illustration © Anne Odendhal. Represents six forms of manipulation that erode freedom through fear.

12

Annapolis and Marv

Marv-US Navy Midshipman

There is a kind of beauty that arrives quietly, when the heart is tired and not looking for it.

That is how Marv entered Eleanor's life.

Eleanor had endured two marriages that had collapsed beneath the weight of disappointment and hardship. Loneliness was her familiar companion. But one summer afternoon, when she and her friends stopped at a waterfront club after swimming, something different unfolded.

The upstairs dining room glowed with the well-dressed patrons, but the downstairs cabana level was casual enough for sun-warm skin and damp hair. Eleanor and her friends settled at a table, laughing softly among themselves. Across the room sat a cluster of young men in crisp white uniforms—unmistakable. Midshipmen from the United States Naval Academy.

One of them stood, crossed the room, and asked her to dance.

He was confident and warm, with the broad-shouldered ease of an athlete and a smile that could disarm a crowd. His name was Marv, he was a junior at the Academy whose family was from New York City. Eleanor's graceful presence and dark eyes captivated him. They danced, talked, and at the end of the evening, he asked for her phone number.

Weeks passed before he called. Not because he had forgotten—but because he had deliberated.

He wanted to be sure.

When he finally picked up the phone, Eleanor said yes.

That was the beginning.

Eleanor, the year she met Marv

Marv traveled to Baltimore on weekends when liberty allowed, and Eleanor traveled to Annapolis when she could—staying in small inns where families and sweethearts would wait for their midshipmen. The Naval Academy demanded discipline, endurance, and time, but Marv made room for her in his world.

They discovered they had much in common:

Athletics.

Adventure.

A shared delight in gymnastics, strength, and outdoor life.

Eleanor had served in the Coast Guard and had always found joy in physical activity. Marv was a gymnast—no, more than that—he was the Academy's champion rope climber. His classmates called him "Chimp" for his quick strength and fluid agility. A snippet from the Academy yearbook captured him perfectly:

"Marv kept trim in the gym, where he picked up the nickname Chimp, the finest set of muscles at the Academy, and, incidentally, the Eastern intercollegiate rope-climbing championship."

He was admired, magnetic, and vividly alive.

And with Eleanor, he was tender. Attentive.

He made her feel seen—and after what she had survived, that meant everything.

RED SHOES & CHRISTMAS BALL

One evening, he took her to see *The Red Shoes*, a ballet story of love, longing, and the tension between devotion and destiny. Eleanor loved it. She understood it. A woman torn between two loves—her gift and her heart.

Later that winter, Marv and his friends went Christmas shopping and stopped by the furniture store where Eleanor worked. They swept her into their holiday cheer, and Marv had purchased a deep navy-blue bathrobe—a soft, warm, and elegant gift for her. When she wore it, she felt wrapped in him.

Then came the Naval Academy Christmas Ball.

It was not merely a dance. It was a declaration. A midshipman did not take just any girl to the Ball. He took the girl who mattered.

Eleanor remembered every detail—the music, the lights, the winter air, the deep joy she could barely contain. She was not simply in love. She was safe in it.

CHIMP: CHAMPION GYMNAST

Marv had a future mapped out: graduation, commissioning, deployment, and eventually, command. The life of a Navy officer was demanding—months at sea, the loneliness of duty, and long separations from loved ones. Eleanor knew this. She had already loved men who served and had felt the sharp edge of loss. But love does not ask for guarantees. It only asks for trust.

By the spring of his final year, Eleanor believed—not foolishly—that she and Marv would marry. His friends believed it. Her friends believed it. Marv's intentions had appeared steady, true, and warm.

And then—something shifted.

There is no neat language for the moment when hope breaks. No date is stamped in memory. Only before and an after.

Whether fear spoke louder than love, whether duty overshadowed devotion, or whether Marv simply could not sustain the depth of connection he had begun, he withdrew.

The relationship ended.

Quickly.

Concisely.

Without an explanation she could hold.

The door closed abruptly with a finality that left deeper bruises than any storm.

Eleanor carried the weight of that ending alone. She never told him she was pregnant. She didn't tell anyone. The secrecy lived inside her like a locked room.

Some doors close once, but the sound of them echoes through generations.

13

Russian—German Wedding

*When you're dealt a crappy hand,
you play the best game you can.*

Eleanor had never felt more alone in the world than during the minutes and days after she left Marv for the last time. She had no one to turn to and no one to talk to. There was no listening ear that she could trust with the high degree of heartbreak that she carried. She felt humiliated and ashamed. Had she told her mother, she might have been rejected by her family. She just couldn't bear to risk exposing her shame, not to anyone. Eleanor never told a living soul the truth until she unexpectedly, unintentionally revealed it to me when I was about thirty-five of age. She carried and lived a web of deception for decades. Under Maryland law in 1950, a woman who intentionally induced an abortion could be guilty of a felony. In practice, it was usually the abortion providers who were prosecuted, not the women themselves.

Abortion was very illegal, a strong deterrent to seeking an abortion for her unborn child. She was also afraid to do something so medically and morally dangerous. At that time, for Eleanor, an American woman of decency, simply did not have a baby without being married. What she lived through was truly a "crisis pregnancy." She could not have a baby and not be married. She had to have someone to marry!

Soon after Marv left Eleanor, ran into an old friend named George. She and George were acquainted and had dated several times before he left with one of his buddies seeking adventure out west in places like Montana. After he served in the United States Army, he went after adventure and dreams rather than just talking about them, but never doing them, like so many of us. There are always good reasons why our dreams, especially the crazy ones, need to wait.

Both of George's parents were Russian. His mother's parents had brought her from Russia to America as a baby, while George's father arrived when he was sixteen. He had never finished school and always spoke "broken English" and Russian at home.

George, a first-generation American and an artist by gifting, had courageously ventured out west to see what he could see. That was more than most people have the courage to attempt. It just so happened that he had just recently got back from Montana when he and Eleanor ran into each other again.

Russian—German Wedding

George in the U.S. Army Air Corp

George was a handsome and kind man whose creative and artistic ways were winsome. Eleanor met George, of all places, in a bar where he was a bartender. George and Eleanor began dating early that spring. Around Easter time, although they had dated for a brief time, desperate Eleanor devised a plot, tricking George into going to bed with her. Not long afterwards, she unveiled her web of deceit by telling George the news that she was expecting a baby and that she was scared. Naturally, George believed her baby was also his.

Immediately, George wanted to marry Eleanor because it was what needed to happen. Eleanor was uncertain and hesitant, but George was insistent. He cried and cried that she had to marry him for the child's sake, so she agreed. They had a wedding with their families present, then found an apartment that they moved into. George worked at the Baltimore Bethlehem Steel mill, where the German men in her family and other immigrant men worked. Eleanor became a homemaker and soon announced to their relatives that she was expecting a baby. Everyone was thrilled for the happy couple.

I can barely fathom the emotional toll this had on my mom, carrying such a weight all alone for so long. Sometimes it helps me grasp why Mom had a longstanding love-hate relationship with me. Those who knew me while I was growing up were eyewitnesses to her unpredictable moods and shifting treatment toward me. I know she loved me the best she knew how, but I never ceased being a reminder of her past—and of the false reality she had constructed for the watching world.

I can't help but feel sorrow for her. The secrecy, the fear, and the effort to maintain a perfect image must have been exhausting. What she carried inside her was too heavy for one person to bear alone. Shame is a cruel master; it isolates, corrodes, and hardens what was once tender. Looking back, I see how her buried grief shaped both of us in ways neither of us could escape.

Mom had a habit throughout my life of reshaping truth. She often told stories that simply weren't accurate. She claimed we were descended from Cherokee Indians, though we knew that wasn't true. At other times, she said she was part Black, which was far-fetched when we knew she was German-Irish Caucasian. She twisted reality about all kinds of things, big and small. She even told people, with full conviction, that I attended Towson State College near where we lived in Baltimore. In truth, I never set foot on that campus. Yet Mom *believed* I went to Towson State!

The first time I saw *Gladiator* with Russell Crowe, I gasped at the scene where the emperor publicly embraced the gladiator before the watching crowd—appearing to honor him with brotherly love—when moments earlier he had literally stabbed him in the back. No one in the crowd could see the wound hidden beneath the robe.

That scene captured how life with my mother often seemed: the contradiction of being publicly embraced yet privately wounded.

She was a master of persuasion—able to convince others of her love and devotion even while quietly undermining me to them, most painfully to my own children.

It's hard to name that kind of duplicity for what it is. Gaslighting is a word I didn't learn until much later, but it fits. She controlled the narrative so well that, for years, I usually stayed silent and did not defend myself—believing that truth would eventually rise on its own, that people would someday see clearly. I've always believed that the truth prevails sooner or later. I had no idea how long untruths can prevail. When my mom was near death, she assured me she would speak to my children to explain some things that were inaccurate. She never got around to doing that.

I was often like a tower of Jello: Jello trembles, but it doesn't collapse. I didn't understand how long deception can stand before the truth steadies itself. I realize many realities will not be crystal clear in this life, but I believe in eternal life where all wrongs will be remedied.

For a moment in time at George and Eleanor's wedding, life looked safe again. The shame was hidden, the story rewritten. No one suspected the quiet storm beneath her new beginning. Yet the truth has its own heartbeat—it never stops echoing, even beneath layers of love and denial.

I often feel sad for George too. He was kind, steady, and deeply human, drawn into a story he didn't create and didn't deserve to bear. The deception that began as protection for my mother's shame quietly altered the course of his life as well. He spent his years loving a family built on a secret, unaware that he was living inside someone else's survival story. That realization, when it finally came to me, filled me not with anger but with grief for them both. George wasn't there in my life much, but he was the only "dad" I knew. I believe he also tried to love me the best he was able, but he was trapped on a very short chain to the bottle.

In marrying George, Eleanor found refuge but not redemption. The wedding ring became both her shield and her silence. What looked like safety was only a pause between storms.

Eleanor's marriage to George was the cover that allowed life to continue—but it was also a fragile bridge between what was lost and what was still to come.

What followed next was not a celebration, but the coldest season of all.

George and Eleanor on their wedding day

14

No Christmas Baby

"You're going to have a Christmas baby," the obstetrician told Eleanor.

"Oh, no I'm not," she responded.

Determination often overcomes obstacles, and Eleanor did not want her baby to be born on Christmas Day. She was adamant that her child would not have to share a birthday with holiday festivities or miss family gatherings because of hospital stays.

Christmas celebrated family, food, and tradition—and Eleanor intended to be *present* for all of it.

All through December, Eleanor and George attended every

holiday gathering. Each time Eleanor coughed, shifted, or sighed, her uncles hovered over her like anxious guardian angels:

"Are you alright?"

"Do you need to go to the hospital?"

"I'm fine," she repeated—firmly but lovingly.

After Christmas, Eleanor was ready. In her overnight bag she packed two outfits—one blue, and one pink—because they didn't know whether it would be a boy or a girl. Mildred had also spent December sewing and crocheting little jackets and hats in both colors.

This would be the first grandchild of Mildred's only child—and, as it turned out, the only surviving child Eleanor would bear. She had another pregnancy but lost the baby. People often assume that without contraception, everyone would multiply "like rabbits." Yet history shows otherwise. Human life is not something we manufacture. It is something we *receive*. Some couples never conceive. Many grieve miscarriages silently. Life is a gift—never guaranteed.

Complications developed during Eleanor's labor, and surgery became the only option if both Eleanor and the baby were to survive. After the long haze of anesthesia and pain, she awakened to the words:

"It's a girl."

Eleanor drifted in and out of sleep, flooded with relief and joy.

Her daughter had arrived—after Christmas, just as she intended.

15

Bring Me My Baby

Cesarean delivery in those days required a long stay in the hospital. Modern medicine now discharges mothers so quickly that it can feel like a drive-through experience by comparison, but then, childbirth recovery was slow, quiet, and carefully supervised.

Eleanor, still foggy from full anesthesia, kept repeating one urgent plea:

"Where is my baby? I want to see my baby."

She had an irrational but understandable fear that babies could be mixed up in the nursery. The nurses kept their daughter for nearly a full day. Eleanor wanted to breastfeed, but the nurses had already begun bottle-feeding—the standard practice then. Everything moved slowly, and mothers were expected to rest.

Hours passed. Eleanor grew frantic.

"If you don't bring my baby to me right now, I'm going to get up and go find her myself."

The nurse returned with a tiny, swaddled baby. Eleanor unwrapped the blanket and checked the identification bracelet.

A baby boy.

"Nurse—this is not my baby!"

After a small uproar, apologies, and hasty corrections, Eleanor finally held her daughter for the first time. Warmth, relief, and maternal certainty washed over her. She began nursing, and peace settled in.

A few days after returning home, Eleanor suddenly developed a high fever. Without a phone to call for help, George quickly gathered her and the baby and drove to his parents' house. His mother, Anna, took over newborn care while a doctor was called to the house.

The doctor urged hospitalization—Eleanor refused to leave her baby.

She was diagnosed with a severe kidney infection and required penicillin, which was still new and not readily available. It would take twenty-four hours to obtain. George stayed beside her, sleeping on the floor, while Anna cared for the infant. Slowly, Eleanor recovered.

Penicillin—new to civilian use after World War II—saved her life. And so, the Christmas baby who wasn't born on Christmas, and the mother who refused to be separated from her child, both survived.

Life had begun for the two of us together, mother and daughter, but shadows from earlier generations were already shaping what would come next.

16

Alcoholism: The Potential Robber

For the alcoholic, the possible outcomes are sobriety, jails and institutions, or death.

ALCOHOLICS ANONYMOUS

There are moments in life when brokenness is not dramatic or loud—it is slow, quiet, and creeping. The unraveling of a marriage, a home, and a future often begins almost imperceptibly, one disappointment and one drink at a time. Eleanor's story in this chapter unfolds in that slow descent.

ONE GIRL VS. A NATION ASLEEP

George, Eleanor, and me. Eleanor had been ill and was drained

I cannot recall who told me that my mom tried to commit suicide after my birth when she left the hospital. Maybe she told me. I am uncertain if it is true, but I know someone told me it was. It would be no astonishment since my mom had herself fully trapped in a web of deceit. Abandoned by the man she loved and hoped to marry, married to an alcoholic she had not wanted to marry, now with a new baby whose real father was unaware she existed, she had quite a drama to endure. Sadly, she wasn't a happy new bride or mother.

Eleanor was sick for months before she was able to care for her own baby. Her mother-in-law, Anna, was reluctant to bring the baby upstairs so Eleanor could even see her, as Anna feared exposing the baby to sickness. "I don't want the baby up there where she is sick," Anna would tell her son George, despite the doctor's confirmation that Eleanor's illness was not contagious.

One day, when the doctor came to see Eleanor (house visit), she begged him to let her move to their own apartment. He agreed, if she limited her activities, and George would be willing to take care of the housework.

When they left his mother's help, they were in a nice apartment. George was a good husband; he worked consistently at the steel mill and helped with the housework when home. He cared for Eleanor when he could be home, just as the doctor had advised.

It was not too long before they began going downhill financially and moving from one bad apartment to another. George kept changing his mind about his career and started spending his money in the beer saloons. Why George ever began drinking heavily is a mystery, but there is no doubt he fell into the abyss of alcoholism, which controlled him for the remainder of his life.

I do know that his mother left him and moved to New York. When Anna left, she took George's younger brother Bill with her, where she remarried and lived for years. Anna had left George motherless to live with his austere Russian father, who had immigrated at sixteen and spoke broken English.

Years later, Anna divorced the man from New York, and brought Bill back to Baltimore, then remarried George's father. By that time, George was a young man who had grown up without his mother. I suspect my dad felt abandoned when she left him for years, taking only his little brother with her.

Gran permitted my dad to live with her as an adult and supplied him with spending money for the bar. He was sometimes employed, sometimes not. Gran felt guilty for having abandoned her son long ago and tried making up for lost mothering time in the best way she could figure out. I knew her only as a lovely, hardworking, kind, loving Gran.

Anna, my Gran, loved me and cared for me when I visited. She never knew I was not her real granddaughter. No one knew the truth from that generation. They had all died before Mom revealed the truth. My mom intended to go to her grave with the secret, but God has His mysterious ways of bringing truth into the light.

George was a sensitive man and a gifted artist, happiest when he could draw or paint… but he was enduring grinding work at a steel mill. He began asking Eleanor when she would go back to work. Eleanor figured it would only make him worse, enabling him to have more money to spend at the bars.

George's main interest every day became getting out to the beer saloon. He would go straight from work with his paycheck and announce, "Drinks for everybody!" Classic. George often came home with very little money left. Tired of moving from place to place while trying to stay at home with her baby, Eleanor finally asked Aunt Annette (Mildred's younger sister) to watch the baby, and she took a job in the office at the steel mill.

George's drinking only worsened, so Eleanor eventually got an apartment for the baby and herself and continued working while her aunt watched her little daughter.

Alcoholism is not just a struggle for the individual. It is a thief of families, of security, of tenderness, and of stability. It robbed George of his potential and Eleanor of the husband she had hoped he could be.

But it did not rob Eleanor of her courage.

She walked away to save herself and her child. That, too, is a form of love.

Recovery begins the moment one refuses to be destroyed. Sadly, for my dad, George, that moment failed to arrive. He never became sober. It destroyed his health until he finally died.

17

My Parents

My first baptism in the Lutheran Church

Standing up in my carriage asserting myself early on. I wanted to stand up and be counted

When my mother Eleanor tried to make things work with George again, they returned to living with George's parents, Anna, and George Sr., so Eleanor could work during the day. Gran took care of me while tending to her household duties and helping my grandfather run the grocery store.

My mother tried to breastfeed me, but it did not last long when she became so ill. I commend her for trying and wish I had been able to continue with the more natural way of feeding. Years later,

I breastfed all my own children, with their lifelong health in mind. I wanted to do what was best for my children in every way I could.

Gran Anna took over much of my care as a baby and toddler during my early years. She was the best person to know how to care for me. She bathed, fed, and clothed me. She gave me the few hugs and kisses I remember. She was a cheerful woman, and I felt secure with her.

I remember her standing unclothed me on a tall stool next to the kitchen sink, so that she could sponge-bathe me. I also recall that whenever I had a fever or she thought I might be getting sick, she would have me lie down on the bathroom floor and administer a simple, homemade enema to "get me well." I was too little to question it and it always worked. This was one of many old home remedies widely used in America before the rise of big pharma.

George decided he wanted to return to school and study art, and Eleanor supported him in his ambition because he truly was a gifted artist. I remember being fascinated watching him draw and paint, mostly oil works. His paintings remained in my mom's home until her death.

When Eleanor discovered that George was not faithful in either his work or his studies at college, she became increasingly frustrated and moved out again—just her and me. George pleaded with Eleanor to get back together, and finally she told him that she would do so only if they bought a house of their own. She wanted no more moving from apartment to apartment or back with his parents. George agreed, and they bought a row house in the city outskirts.

Mom and Dad moved into a new Baltimore row house on MacBeth Drive. I stayed with Gran and Pop while they got the place mostly ready. They brought me home from staying with Gran on Christmas Eve, not long before my third birthday. It isn't easy to bring back memories from our earliest years, but I do recall being there in that house on that Christmas Eve. There were no curtains on the windows yet, and Mom had draped sheets on the front windows.

I was unaware of all the drama between Eleanor and George. But I remember that night. I felt happy with them both there—all of us together. I can still feel those indescribable sensations of security, stability, strength, belonging, and comfort. It was a happy time. I was a happy toddler. Life was good temporarily.

Much of a child's emotional formation happens in their first three years. I am thankful I have some good memories from early on.

Children benefit more than we can ever know from having both parents with them and *together*. The value of this should never be diminished. It cannot always be this way in our broken world, but it is certainly the ideal, for what the human heart is designed. There were photos and an old reel of film of that Christmas Eve together, I was a smiling and laughing child. That was a happy Christmas for me as a toddler.

That memory—just the three of us, together on Christmas Eve—remains one of the few unbroken places in my earliest childhood. A small but steady light carried forward.

18

Grandmother Mildred—
Love and Dedication

"Affection is responsible for nine-tenths of whatever solid and durable happiness there is in our lives."

—C.S. LEWIS

Mildred with her auto in the 1950s

Mildred

Both of my grandmothers were more than homemakers at the time when homemaking was the primary role for women, though some

Grandmother Mildred—Love and Dedication

were home-based businesswomen. They juggled both, as would my mother and I years later. Both grandmothers demonstrated genuine love for me, yet I often felt lonely and unconnected.

Gran Mildred adored me but found it hard to relate emotionally to me or be affectionate. She loved me by keeping me nicely dressed and curling my hair in rag curls. It was Gran Mildred who provided ballet and tap dance lessons, roller skating, and long road trips to other states in the summer.

She even took me on several trips to the Doll Hospital in Baltimore City, where the Doll Doctor repaired injured dolls. Gran put together the only album I have of family photos, and my baby pictures. She had the forethought to do that for me, a historical treasure I still have.

Gran bought me toys and games like Clue and Mr. Potato Head, which was played using real potatoes. I used to wear either a cross or a mustard-seed necklace, which she bought for me. The jewelry was reflective of American culture at that time. There was a Christian consensus where respect for Biblical principles was reflected in our laws and communities.

Mildred was a careerist. As an employee, she invested business hours sewing in a factory. Gran's Depression-era thrift meant she saved everything: jars, fabric scraps, buttons in a tin. There were no plastic containers or anything plastic. Throw away was very minimal. Milk and soda were bought in returnable glass bottles, which were commercially washed and reused. Life was much simpler.

Holidays brought hours of baking; I decorated her cookies with colored sugars until my fingers sparkled. I invested hours working to crack walnuts, then using a nut pick to remove every piece of nut inside the caverns. Nuts were never bought already shelled. I never saw already shelled nuts other than peanuts during my childhood. Nuts were found in bowls alongside nut crackers and picks. I never doubted Gran's devotion, even when her affection was quiet.

Mildred's example taught me that love can be sturdy and unsentimental, expressed in what we *do* more than what we say. During my teen years, she made me a homemade corduroy jacket. She began putting together blankets and other items in a cedar chest for me to have a hope chest. When she died, I was sixteen. I felt strangely numb—yet her steadiness had already become part of me.

She didn't speak her love; she *lived* it—in her work, her thrift, her constancy. Decades later, I still hear the soft echo of her presence whenever I sew a button, fold a blanket, or hold onto something that might one day be useful. That quiet faithfulness built the scaffolding of my life.

Her kind of love was not poetic or loud, but it lasted. It steadied me long after she was gone, teaching me that endurance, more than sentiment, is what keeps families from falling apart.

My Grandmother Mildred and me. She always dressed me in beautiful outfits.

19

Grandmother Anna—
Enterprising Role Model

"If we had no winter, the spring would not be so pleasant; if we did not sometimes taste of adversity, prosperity would not be so welcome."
—ANNE BRADSTREET

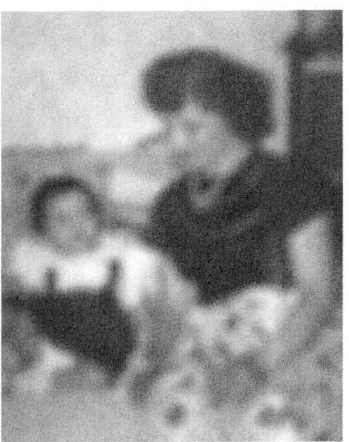

My Gran Anna and me

The mid-century Baltimore corner grocery store was part of the heartbeat of the neighborhood. Streetcars would rattle past on their way downtown, and coal smoke would drift through open windows in winter. Neighbors stopped by for bread, penny candy, or just to talk about the Orioles. It was in that little shop that I first sensed what community meant—how commerce and kindness could share the same counter.

Anna, my dad's mother, was a businesswoman before I even knew the word. She and my grandfather ran a corner grocery store built into their house. A bell buzzed whenever someone opened the door, summoning whoever was nearest to the counter. In summer, while Gran hung laundry in the backyard, she set me in a metal tub of water to keep cool—my own little swimming pool.

Her arms were noticeably strong, her voice calm, her kitchen spotless. She rose early to meet the bakery truck, filling the air with the smell of fresh pastries that could put any donut shop to shame. Workmen would stop daily for coffee, donuts, a sandwich, and conversation.

Gran treated everyone alike—Black or white, rich or poor— with the same steady respect and a smile that made people linger. One time I sat on the curb sharing half a peach with a Black girl my age. When Gran saw us, she smiled and kissed me later, proud that prejudice had never touched me.

Anna was my first role model in enterprise and kindness. She managed the store's accounts, sliced meats with precision, and knew her customers by name. Watching her taught me that freedom is not only political, but also the daily privilege of creating, serving, and living with integrity within your own sphere of influence in your own small corner of the world.

Between Mildred's devotion and Anna's enterprise, I absorbed two different blueprints for living—and spent years learning where my own balance lay.

20

Color Blind

Children are not born prejudiced; they absorb it.

While researching relatives who had suffered and been quarantined due to tuberculosis, I discovered the Henryton Tuberculosis Sanatorium in Marriottsville, Maryland. I was stunned to learn that it had been built specifically to treat Black patients. Later named Henryton State Hospital, it served as the tuberculosis facility for "colored people," the term used at the time.

The very idea unsettled me deeply. Categorizing human beings as worthy based on inherited physical traits has always struck me as irrational and morally hollow. It never made sense to me—not as a child, and not now.

Even growing up, when I heard people disparage others because of skin color or nationality, it clashed with everything in me. It felt wrong—intellectually, emotionally, and spiritually. I could never reconcile such thinking with the way the world is.

When I am asked to check a box for race on official forms, I am tempted to write in "human." I understand the sociological categories, but biologically and morally, they are thin substitutes for reality. Skin comes in a spectrum of hues. Culture is learned; pigmentation is not. God delights in diversity, and no shade carries moral weight.

I do not deny that people have different histories, experiences, or ethnic backgrounds. But so what? People of every race are capable of good and evil alike. To fixate on external traits as markers of worth is to miss the point entirely.

That is why I was profoundly moved by John Howard Griffin's 1961 book *Black Like Me*. Griffin, a journalist raised in Fort Worth, Texas, had been taught, as he later admitted, "the destructive illusion that Negroes were somehow different." Determined to confront that lie, he undertook a radical experiment. Under medical supervision, he used the drug Methoxsalen (Oxsoralen) to darken his skin so that he could travel through the Deep South as a Black man and document what he experienced.

Traveling through the segregated South in 1959, Griffin encountered rejection, hostility, and isolation. He faced "For Whites Only" signs at lunch counters, restrooms, and drinking fountains. White acquaintances who had once known him avoided him entirely.

Griffin later became a national voice in the civil rights movement. In 1964, he was brutally beaten by members of the Ku Klux Klan and left for dead on a rural road—punishment for daring to see clearly and speak honestly. To me, he remains a moral hero.

Every American who believes they are free from prejudice would benefit from walking alongside Griffin through his account. His courage exposed not only racial injustice, but the deeper human tendency to divide, rank, and dismiss.

Color Blind

A child, untouched by hate, sees the world as God made it—radiant, varied, and wondrous. But a nation that teaches its children to measure worth by color, convenience, or utility begins to unlearn love itself.

When human life can be graded in one category, it will eventually be diminished in every category. All prejudice—racial, generational, or otherwise—springs from the same blindness: the refusal to recognize the divine image in one another.

21

Art of Ironing & Where Are the Sidewalks?

"Order is not rigidity; it is a gift."
—G. K. CHESTERTON (paraphrased)

My dad, George, began as a good husband and father, but alcohol addiction slowly stunted both his personal and professional life. After a brief separation, my mother, Eleanor, agreed to reconcile, and they returned to live with George's parents, Anna and George Sr., Russian immigrants who owned a small neighborhood grocery store. The plan was to work, save, and rebuild. Had it not been for my father's drinking, things might have gone well. Both parents wanted to provide a stable future for their little daughter.

My grandparents lived in the city, where concrete sidewalks

connected homes and neighbors. People knew one another. During sweltering summers, families sat on their front steps in the evenings, escaping hot indoor air—there was no air conditioning, only fans—sharing iced tea and conversation. Presence was assumed.

Today, many suburbs have few sidewalks at all. Visiting neighbors has largely vanished. Obsessed with productivity, we move at the speed of light. There is little time to listen unless there is something to gain. The ministry of presence—simply being with one another—is an art badly in need of revival. As a child, I had no language for this loss; I only knew when it was absent.

During the day, my grandmother Anna cared for me while my mother worked. Gran Anna was one of the most industrious and ingenious women I have ever known—an astute businesswoman and an exacting homemaker. Growing up, I was fascinated by her methods for cleaning, ironing, cooking, and managing customers in the family grocery store that occupied the front of their corner house. There were no supermarkets then. The downtown market near Baltimore's Inner Harbor served as a hub for goods and commerce.

Gran Anna managed everything. Watching her negotiate with wholesalers, handle finances, and care for customers gave me an early education in responsibility. I spent countless hours in that store. I rarely remember her resting. She married young, worked relentlessly, and carried herself with purpose.

They often spoke Russian to each other. I remember words like the Russian command for "eat," which Gran repeated as she coaxed my finicky appetite. My grandfather, Pop George, worked hard too, though his broken English limited his communication. Gran was the life of both home and business.

I still iron clothes using Gran's method. She sprinkled garments with water by hand, rolled them tightly, and pressed them with military precision—zero wrinkles allowed. Shirts emerged transformed: crisp and disciplined. If ironing had been an Olympic sport, she would have taken gold.

While she worked, I sat near the ironing board, watching every movement. We talked. There is something deeply comforting about observing skilled work when you are a child and the worker is someone you trust. Those quiet hours were life-sustaining.

By watching her, I learned enough to earn money ironing for neighbors. They paid by the basket. Gran had no idea she was training me to be an entrepreneur.

Her house was always clean. People said you could eat off the floor. She taught me that if your kitchen and bed were in order—especially the kitchen floor—you were a good housekeeper. This contrasted sharply with my other grandmother's home, which was cluttered and often home to kitchen roaches. I wasn't afraid of the roaches; they were simply residents. I feared imaginary monsters instead.

I slept with a nightlight to keep vampires away, but the roaches? They just needed their own zip code.

My mother cleaned in bursts—big Saturday or holiday efforts—while Gran Anna cleaned continuously. She cleaned as she went, never letting disorder gain ground. I liked her approach, though you wouldn't have guessed it from the piles of clothes in my childhood bedroom. As an only child and only grandchild, I had plenty of possessions—too many, perhaps.

My mother later admitted she bought things for me out of guilt for being away so much. I was spoiled with stuff but starved for presence. Toys could not replace people.

As a child, I missed my mother intensely when I was not with her. Home, to me, was wherever she was. My fears lessened in her presence. I wanted her approval, her closeness, her love. That longing never left.

The generation that scrubbed its floors and ironed its linens also taught America to hold itself together—sometimes too tightly. Beneath their polished order, children quietly learned that a home could be spotless and still lonely. Out of that tension grew hunger—for love, meaning, and for something lasting.

The heartbeat of those old neighborhoods didn't stop at the front door. It spilled into places where people gathered, bartered, and belonged. For us, that place was Lexington Market.

22

Lexington Market

I enjoyed the trips that Gran and I took to the large Baltimore Harbor market on Lexington St. There were no super stores, so this market housed the largest display and selection of foods I had ever seen anywhere. Established in 1792, it remains the world's longest, continuously running marketplace.

Farmers and fishermen began selling their goods on Lexington Market's site after Colonel John Eager Howard, one of the heros of the American Revolution, gave permission for a market on a pasture in his family's estate. Named for the Revolutionary War's

Battle of Lexington, the Market burned to the ground in 1949. It was quickly rebuilt with the proceeds of a bond issue.

During my childhood visits to Lexington market, it bustled with the activity of the meat, produce, seafood, and bakery vendors, as well as the steady stream of customers. The aroma of baked items and fresh fish frying made the adventure uplifting and memorable. The market was centered inside a series of sidewalks and streets right in front of Baltimore city harbor.

The entire scene was gray and dingy. Outside the market doors, one could see the brown and gray ships anchored in the port harbor. I can still recall the fishy, salty air. There was nothing glitzy or tourist-worthy in the scene. Baltimore Harbor is now a tourist attraction featuring historic ships such as the USS Constellation. The city's harbor was an industrial pit during my childhood.

Occasionally, when on a market outing, Gran and I would attend a dance with her friends from a Russian Orthodox church. That's where I learned to dance the Polka. Large, rotund women would grab me and whirl me around the dance floor with or without my feet being on the floor. I loved it and never wanted to stop dancing.

Gran bought rye bread, Challah, and dark bread from the market. She let one of the loaves sit out to harden slightly, then rubbed fresh garlic cloves across the rough surface until the cloves disappeared into the bread. After adding butter and salt, she fed me to my heart's content with this vampire- and germ-chasing delight. I learned to love garlic from birth, thanks to Gran. Garlic bread was one of the few edibles—other than chocolate—that I willingly ate. I may enjoy longevity today simply because of the massive quantity of garlic that I consumed as a child.

As a child, I was what polite people call a "picky eater," and what many honest people call a girl who believed the major food groups were chocolate cupcakes, powdered donuts, and anything that melted into ice cream. If sugar had been a curriculum, I would have graduated early.

If given the choice, my daily menu would have been:

- breakfast: chocolate cupcake

- lunch: chocolate donut

- dinner: ice cream

- vegetables: absolutely not

Gran Anna was not going to let me avoid healthy foods. She'd set a plate of real food—things with actual nutrients—in front of me, plant her hands on her hips, and deliver the most Russian grandmother command ever spoken:

кушай, кушай

pronounced: KOO-shy, KOO-shy

meaning: "Eat, eat!" (Come on, eat!)

Russian grandmothers can turn even encouragement into an intervention. Gran affectionately coaxed and cajoled me every day. If I hesitated, she simply repeated it, louder, with hand motions worthy of air traffic control. You would think my refusal to eat peas was a national security threat.

Gran was convinced I might blow away in a strong wind if she didn't succeed in "putting some meat on my bones." Her mission in life—besides running the store, managing the house, and quietly holding the world together—was making sure I ingested something that grew out of the ground or came from an actual animal.

Looking back, I can still hear it: the soundtrack of my childhood meals, her loving exhortation echoing across the kitchen—

"KOO-shy, KOO-shy!"

And somehow, it always made me feel cared for—even if I still wished dinner was dessert. If I did manage to eat even a little "real food," Gran would sometimes put her arms around me and give me a big kiss on the cheek. She is the only adult I remember who gave me kisses, and it felt indescribably wonderful to be affectionately loved.

Gran also used old-world home remedies for anything she believed might be "brewing." I hesitate to admit this, but yes—these included enemas. Truth be told, enemas were a common remedy of the time, and they are still recommended in some naturopathic cancer protocols today for detoxification. If Gran thought I was sick—or might *become* sick—she lovingly took charge, laid me on the floor rug, and became my unofficial childhood "colon therapist."

Gran was, in many ways, my first teacher in natural therapies and age-old home remedies. I never stopped studying and searching for non-toxic ways to care for my own children—prevention when possible, gentler treatments when practical. I turned to modern medicine only when it was truly necessary.

When my youngest daughter developed pneumonia as a baby, I knew antibiotics were essential. At the earliest signs of illness, however, I focused on strengthening the body through increased nutrients, vitamins, and other natural supports.

When my children were small, I tried to recreate Gran Anna's "KOO-shy!" method, though they looked at me as if I were summoning woodland creatures. During winter sickness, I often made my own home-remedy soups—simple, comforting, and adapted each time to whatever ingredients were on hand.

Part III

Caught in the Cultural Crossfire

23

Brides of Dracula & Light

"Can you see God?"
"No, I cannot see God, but He always sees me."
"Does God know all things?"
"Yes. Nothing can be hid from God."
—Westminster Children's Catechism

Baby boomers were the first generation to grow up on a steady diet of television. This helps me understand how I became gripped by unnecessary fears and destructive fantasies. Had it not been for the influences of movies and television, my childhood and life might have been far healthier and happier.

My mother, Eleanor, took me to Gran's house every weekend when I was little. She thought I loved it—but I didn't. I loved my grandmother, but I longed to stay near my mom. Every separation, even for hours, hurt my heart. I didn't know how to express what I felt, and no one asked. I yearned for my mother's presence. Homesickness was my constant companion.

The weekends with Gran and Pop were emotionless. They took me wherever they went—bingo halls, Moose lodges, bowling alleys, racetracks, even casinos. I was usually bored and grindingly lonely. I remember little affection, only the sense of being a tag-along piece of furniture. One small joy was the jukebox at the lodges. I would select songs and dance by myself, oblivious to the adults around me. Those solitary dances planted a seed of freedom—learning not to care what others thought and discovering joy through movement.

Despite the mix of slot machines on Saturday and church pews on Sunday, Gran never neglected what she called "my religious education." She made sure I attended Sunday School every Sunday we were together. In Baltimore or on long road trips, she would always find a church and drop me off, often as the lone child visitor. She even asked for written verification of my attendance so it would count toward the perfect-attendance awards at her home church. I still have the long string of attendance pins she collected for me.

Well-dressed on a typical Easter Sunday with Gran, who always wore a corsage on holidays.

Though I remember little of what was taught, something from those Sunday mornings must have sunk deep into my soul. The popsicle-stick frame with Jesus' picture, which I glued together in a Sunday-school craft, somehow became a cherished image. The light that glowed in those simple moments stayed with me when darkness came.

One Saturday, Gran and Pop left me with Pat, the teenage girl next door, who took me to a movie despite clear instructions otherwise. The film was *The Brides of Dracula*. I was too young to separate fantasy from reality. The images branded themselves in my imagination. I believed vampires were real, waiting to claim me in my sleep. I spent years afraid of the dark, certain monsters would appear as soon as the lights went out.

I never told Gran or Mom what Pat had done. My fears grew—vampires, mummies, werewolves, the Pod People. I would stare into mirrors to see if my teeth were becoming fangs. It sounds humorous now, but as a little girl, it was torment. I slept under the covers, sweltering in Baltimore's summer heat, afraid to move. If I stayed still and hidden, vampires and monsters wouldn't find me. No one ever "tucked me in." Loneliness and terror kept me company.

Sometimes, when I visited my dad, I mentioned being afraid. He tried to comfort me, telling me that monsters weren't real. He was kind when sober—playful, gentle, making breakfast, or sharing oranges. Those rare moments were warm islands in a cold sea.

At Gran Mildred's house, bedtime meant climbing the dark stairs alone. I lay awake, studying wallpaper patterns by the night light's glow, listening to wind and thunder across the ceiling skylight window, imagining danger in every sound. It's no surprise I grew into a night owl who found it hard to rest.

The vampires faded, but the fear lingered—until faith began to speak louder than fiction.

Even in childhood, I wondered about God. I believed He existed—I had no doubt—but I couldn't stop asking, Who made

God? The question exhausted my little brain at night. Later, the question evolved: If God is good, why does He allow evil and suffering?

In time, I came to understand. God was not made; He always was. The eternal I AM. Father, Son, and Holy Spirit—one God in three persons, love existing before the world began. Creation wasn't to fill a need but to extend that love. Humanity, made in His image, was given freedom, and with it, the possibility of rebellion. Sin entered, and with it, fear and death.

It's a mystery scholars and saints have wrestled with for centuries—how divine sovereignty and human choice coexist. I didn't understand it as a girl, but I've come to see both as true. We are no longer truly "free" apart from Him, but He offers freedom still—the freedom of forgiveness and a changed heart.

As a child, I couldn't have understood this, yet even then, under the covers, trembling in the dark, He was there. Years later, I could picture Jesus sitting beside that bed, waiting for me to realize He had been there all along.

Light provides safety amid chaos. We all need the light that pierces darkness, becomes our guide, and helps us discern what's real and what's counterfeit.

My generation, the baby boomers, grew up between bright promises and moral decay—between televised dreams and spiritual drift. We were told we could achieve anything, even as truth was quietly removed from our classrooms and public life. God was pushed to the margins, and few noticed.

No one in my family prayed with me or explained the Bible to me, but a few people—teachers in my public school—would still read Scripture aloud each morning. From them I learned the 23rd Psalm and the Lord's Prayer. We recited them after pledging allegiance to the flag. I had no idea how privileged I was to grow up in a country that allowed both faith and freedom in the same breath.

Those moments of instruction—though I seemed to learn so little—kept a pilot light burning in my conscience. Later, I discovered that the only real light is the one that exposes the darkness within and shows us the way home.

Decades later, when I taught English to students from nations where such freedom does not exist, I was reminded how extraordinary that foundation was. Even a few words of truth, spoken into one's childhood, can shape a lifetime.

It was in those small exposures to light—Sunday School crafts and public school Bible readings—that I first met God, even before I knew His name.

God wastes nothing.

Even fragments of truth, scattered in childhood, can become the kindling of faith that burns forever.

24

Prejudices against Flowers and People

"The most persistent and urgent question is, 'What are you doing for others?'"

—MARTIN LUTHER KING JR.

Christmas, like all holidays, revolved around Mildred's family—her siblings and their children. Family was central and always meant buffet-style food, beer, and working-class prejudices. I was one of the few children at these gatherings and often hung around the adults. I gravitated toward settling somewhere by myself to play with my dolls or read. There was no emphasis on reading books, yet I loved them.

I listened as mostly the male relatives would drink beer and vent about why they didn't like people who were different from themselves. I marveled at the strange conversation that left me feeling sad and empty inside. I didn't like it but couldn't understand why. Most of the time I was alone in the crowd, incessantly unstimulated, and bored to tears. These were decent, caring, hardworking family people who were ignorant about important things.

America was ignorant. It seemed some people were viewed as if they had a contagious disease when they were just a bit different. Sure, there were social problems—and there always will be—but no one is ever innocent. Only a dishonest person denies ever noticing fears associated with prejudice; we are all prejudiced sometimes in our hearts.

I don't know how it happened, but I grew up largely color-blind. I could not understand the prejudice I heard from relatives. It made no sense and simply was not in my being. I always knew that all humans of all ages are people and thus worthwhile. Being different was okay—and even interesting—to me.

The Supreme Court of the United States has been wrong more than once. They were clearly wrong in their 1857 Dred Scott decision, ruling that dark-skinned people were not fully human and had no citizen rights—the obviously false narrative promoted by propaganda media and accepted by society.

It began when Harriet and Dred Scott sought to be free instead of being owned by the Emerson family in Missouri. Would anyone dispute today that the Supreme Court was wrong? When doing research for this book, I was aghast when I saw there was a separate tuberculosis hospital in Western Maryland for "Colored" People. I found it strange and appalling.

The Supreme Court was equally wrong in their 1973 *Roe v. Wade* decision, ruling that unborn people are not fully human yet. This battle still rages, even though the Court overturned that decision in June of 2022. Hitler once ruled that people with disabilities, the unborn, and eventually Jews and Gypsies were not fully human. It was a slippery slope of devaluing human lives.

Propaganda media too often promotes false narratives that devalue human life until those untruths are accepted as reality and become normal in our culture. Tragically, infanticide of handicapped newborns has been illegally occurring for a long time in the USA. As I write, there are now states promoting and passing new laws allowing "peri-natal" abortion. That means a baby can be left to die on a stainless-steel table or bassinet for up to twenty-eight days after birth—no handicap required as justification for the child's death.

Some states are passing laws permitting assisted suicide for terminally ill patients. Promoted as a compassionate option for those suffering, the slippery-slope logic is clear. There is an exceptionally fine line between voluntary and forced suicide, also called euthanasia.

What if a family member or judge decides a person is incapable of making a good decision on their own? Isn't it obvious that when we start down the road of playing God about the dignity and intrinsic value of all human life—at any stage or condition—we are devaluing *all* human life? All become vulnerable to subjective standards for who gets to live or die. God is clear that He alone decides who lives and when they die. His moral standards are eternal and valid for all people at all times of history, in all circumstances and life stages.

It's all irrational. Unless all human life is viewed—without exception or qualification—as intrinsically valuable and worthy of protection, there exists a slippery slope into the potential chaos of a dictator or a fifty-one-percent vote (the definition of a democracy—a fifty-one-percent mob rule). The USA has never been and is not now a democracy. We are a Constitutional Republic that utilizes democratic voting processes to elect representatives who are supposed to uphold the Constitution as the rule of law—the rule of our land. Even court-case examples are not sufficient to determine the law—only the Constitution. Most people unthinkingly follow like herding animals—more precisely, like dumb sheep. We can be smart yet astoundingly dumb.

The Sunday before Christmas, everyone spent the day at Uncle

Frank's house with his wife Ann and their only son, Irvin. Irvin later married Sandy, who was from another country and had an accent. They had two daughters before a drunk driver killed Irvin. When Frank died from a heart attack about a week later, the companionship of widowhood left Ann and Sandy looking sad together. The large floral arrangements that filled the funeral home later filled their houses so full that it was hard to find room to move in the house.

Christmas Eve was at Mildred's, and Christmas Day was at Mildred's sister Annette's house. The Sunday after Christmas was at Uncle Henry's, who married Libby but had no children. The family "watched their mouths" when at Henry's house because Henry and Libby did not swear or drink alcohol. I think they may have attended church regularly, but spiritual discussions were avoided.

I wish they had talked to me about spiritual matters—their beliefs and why they attended church. I sometimes wonder if they prayed for me, or if anyone in my ancestry prayed for me even before I was born. Did anyone in my ancestry know God or pray for the coming generations? I pray often for my children and grandchildren. I know God answers all prayers, whether we live to see the answers or not.

John Newton's father was a ship captain, and his mother was a devout Christian who prayed for John when he was a boy. John followed in his father's footsteps and eventually became a slave-ship captain—a cruel and heartless one at that. John's mother, Elizabeth Scatliff, was the daughter of Simon Scatliff, an instrument maker from London. Elizabeth died when John was around eight years old. John knew that his mom had prayed for him and that she provided what religious instruction she was able. She made John memorize the entire Westminster Confession of Faith, including the Scripture references. She drilled him as a young boy and his smart mind absorbed it all. Elizabeth never lived to see the astounding, world-changing answers to her prayers for her son. I hope this inspires many about the eternal value of prayer to a God who hears, listens, and answers. He is the God who is there!

John had a successful slave-trading business for nine years prior to a deeply genuine conversion to Christianity. In 1748, he lived through a severe storm and, although being non-religious, prayed to God for safety. His life radically changed. John became a pastor and joined a minority of citizens, including his young nephew William Wilberforce, a member of Parliament, to fight the inhumane slave trade. As a member of Parliament, Wilberforce battled tirelessly to abolish the slave trade. John lived to see the British Passage of the Slave Trade Act of 1807. The Act for the Abolition of the Slave Trade was a milestone, prohibiting slave trade in the British Empire.

Tragically, slavery in the USA lingered far too long until it was abolished in 1865 with the ratification of the 13th Amendment to the Constitution. This amendment prohibits slavery and involuntary servitude, except as punishment for a crime.

The German immigrant Lutherans I knew at church gathered for holidays, especially Easter Sunday and funerals. There were many funerals, with an average lifespan of sixty-three years. Social Security's full retirement age was sixty-five for everyone, but half had died before reaching that age.

Since Eleanor (my mom) was Mildred's only child and I became Eleanor's only child, our extended family died with my grandmother Mildred's generation, leaving us quite alone. Mildred's brothers gradually all died of heart attacks, her sister died of cancer, and Mildred (my Gran) died from a second heart attack when I was sixteen. She was in her fifties. When someone had a heart attack back then, it usually meant we then attended their funeral.

Funerals were a regular part of my childhood, and I grew to naturally dislike the sights and smells of certain flowers because they were always at funerals. Well into my adult years, I still associated the scent of most flowers with dying people because funeral homes during my childhood had many large and fragrant floral arrangements around the open casket. The flowers were bold varieties like gladiolus and lilies, such as the fragrant Stargazer. The beauty and fragrance nearly became a stench to me, and it took years to outgrow this floral prejudice.

Now, I love flowers and understand why they are part of everything important things, from holidays and birthday celebrations to hospital stays and funerals. Their sensory stimulation evokes joy when celebrating and comfort when ill or grieving. My poinsettias do this now at Christmas time—it is impossible to walk around my house without feeling uplifted by the poinsettias everywhere, and of course, the centralized Christmas tree. This is holiday cheer.

Holidays can be hard if one has suffered loss, is alone, or is estranged from family. It's interesting to ponder the history of flowers and how they affect our lives. Did God create the luxury of flowers just for our enjoyment? They are not a necessity—or are they? When I lived in a rural Swiss village, I learned that Swiss women used a portion of their food money (even if meager) to put flowers on their table. People are made in the image of God, and therefore, beauty is important.

What role do flowers play in your life? Even if you are a guy, you must notice them.

25

Great Gran

Great-grandma and me (really my step-Great-grandma, Pop's mother)

The final divorce between Eleanor and George took a while, but there were no further attempts at reconciliation. Eleanor would live in the same house until her own retirement decades later. The house had two apartments—upstairs and downstairs. I grew up living with my mom in the downstairs apartment, hearing renters moving about upstairs.

Mom began routinely taking me to stay with my grandmother,

Mildred, on weekends. I wish I could recall a weekend spent in the apartment with my mom. I sort of liked going to Gran's house, but usually I wanted to stay home with my mother. I kept such feelings to myself. I don't know if my mother ever knew how much I wanted to stay with her.

There were many times I went to stay with George, who ended up living most of his life with his parents, where his alcoholic lifestyle was accepted. Once I started school, I spent time with them since Anna was available to care for me during the day. This is where I gained so many lessons in housekeeping and business savvy. Staying with Anna did not mean I had much time with my dad, George, since he spent most daylight hours sleeping and evenings in a local bar.

Eighty-seven-year-old Great Gran came to live with us the summer before I entered first grade. Mom thought it best not to send me to kindergarten, so I stayed safely at home at age five when so many peers were herded, John Dewey–style, into early childhood education away from their parents. Age five just seemed too young for a little girl to be taken from her home and thrust into school. Mom had an inner sense that a child thrust away from home so early wasn't best. Bravo for her!

Snow-white-haired Great Gran needed somewhere to live and feel useful. My single-parent mom desperately needed help with her young daughter's care. The red-brick row house in Baltimore on which Mom paid her mortgage was two stories, with an apartment downstairs and another upstairs. The steady rental income from the upstairs apartment provided Mom with the funds sorely needed to keep us financially afloat.

Each apartment consisted of a living room, a small kitchen, one bathroom, and two bedrooms. I forfeited my bedroom so Great Gran could have her own room. That meant I kept my clothes in some of Mom's drawers and in some of Great Gran's drawers. I was happy to start sleeping in Mom's double bed—it meant I wouldn't be as lonely at night.

That arrangement led to Mom's unquestioning submission to the physician's determination that my tonsils and adenoids should be removed as I sometimes snored during the night. Can I get back my tonsils, please?!

Glassy-eyed, Mom fought tears on one of the few days she would ever be at my school. That 1957 Baltimore morning, we walked together into the first-grade classroom at Leith Walk Elementary. It was the first weekday after Labor Day weekend. School always started after Labor Day and ended before Memorial Day. Summers were deservedly long and family-oriented—a memory of when most of America's children were needed for work all summer on their family farms.

A college-age young woman, her light brown hair loosely drawn back in a bun, wearing a calf-length fitted calico dress over her shapely figure with flat pump shoes, came to the door where my mom stood.

"Hello, I'm Miss Mesbauer," she said as she held out her hand to Mom, then took mine. My new teacher led me into the room as I looked back at my mom leaving.

Miss Mesbauer took me to a wooden desk and chair near the line of windows on the left side of the rectangular classroom, not far from the teacher's large desk. Behind the teacher's desk, an American flag was mounted on the wall next to a large black chalkboard with long white chalk pieces and two black felt erasers on its ledge.

The surrounding walls held large, brightly printed cards with the alphabet, numerals, and pictures of animals, birds, and fish. The Pledge of Allegiance, the Lord's Prayer, and Psalm Twenty-Three were printed on large posters that were mounted to the wall between the flag and the blackboard.

Miss Mesbauer taught her class patriotic songs. *America* became my favorite. Love and respect for country went hand in hand with respect for a Creator who was infinite, personal, and outside of His creation. Freedom and liberty were dependent upon remembrance of such a divine intelligence.

Children were taught they lived in an open-system universe where

God could and did speak and act in history. The closed-system idea, placing humans as the center of the universe, with nothing bigger than themselves, was foreign. Even those without a desire to know such a God lived within a culture of overarching Christian consensus. There was widespread respect for things patriotic, biblical, and holy.

America
My country tis of thee,
Sweet land of liberty,
Of thee I sing.
Land where my fathers died!
Land of the Pilgrim's pride!
From every mountainside,
Let freedom ring!

Opposite the windows in Miss Mesbauer's classroom was a partial room divider separating the classroom desks from the coatroom. The dividing wall left plenty of room to enter on the left side and exit on the right. Each child had a place with a shelf and hooks on the inside wooden wall. During school days, it was easily stuffed with coats, hats, gloves, and boots on snowy or rainy days.

Just inside the entrance to the coatroom sat a metal bucket half-filled with water. Most days, the children and I did cut-and-paste activities—it was great fun. Miss Mesbauer handed out one paper with pictures to cut out with the small, blunt scissors each student had to bring to school.

I turned over each cutout and slid the white paste from my jar across the back, carefully getting it to the edges with my fingers. Then I placed it precisely in the right spot on another sheet where pictures and words needed to match. It was always easy—and such crafty fun.

After printing my name neatly in the lower corner, I carried the finished page to the windowsill, where completed projects lined up to dry. Then I headed for the coatroom bucket, where we children rinsed our hands. I stuck my hands in, rubbing them together until the paste was gone and the water turned cloudy. There was no sink in the classroom, so the bucket was rinsed and refilled each afternoon.

One school morning, there was heavy traffic entering the coat room. It was a cold winter day, and children had coats, hats, gloves, and scarves to carry. The tallest girl in the class, Becky, was ahead of me in line. She had short and curly reddish-brown hair and a face full of freckles. Suddenly, I saw Becky's right foot embedded in the cut-and-paste water bucket.

"Oh no!" Becky cried out.

Miss Mesbauer quickly appeared. "Becky, what happened?"

"I think she pushed me," Becky responded, pointing at me.

"What?!" yelled Miss Mesbauer. "How could you?"

I stood there, speechless, wondering how on earth Becky thought I was responsible. I was the teacher's pet—but not right now. Miss Mesbauer's face was red, and Becky's foot dripped as she unstuck it from the bucket. I'd never been in trouble at school and had no idea where this would end. Fortunately, by the next morning, Miss Mesbauer seemed to have forgotten both Becky's foot and her anger with me.

Still, I loved first grade. The days were filled with fun activities and learning. Worlds opened, especially when Miss Mesbauer read storybooks every afternoon near the end of the school day. No one had ever read a book to me before, and I loved it so much.

I quickly memorized the Lord's Prayer, the Pledge of Allegiance, Psalm Twenty-Three, alphabet letters, numerals, and words. Every morning, the class recited the Lord's Prayer, then the Pledge while holding our right hands over our hearts.

New songs were sung and learned—*My Country, 'Tis of Thee, America the Beautiful,* and *God Bless America.* The *Star-Spangled Banner* was always played at school assemblies in the auditorium.

Miss Mesbauer used homemade flashcards with vocabulary words to drill the class. She used a large book on an easel to teach from the *Dick and Jane* series—"See Spot run." Phonics had recently been replaced with this new "sight reading" method, where words were memorized rather than sounded out. Somehow, I came home from school touting the name of John Dewey to Mom and the neighbors, proud that Leith Walk was a "progressive" school, giving me the newest and best.

At the time, I did not understand that "progressive" was not simply a flattering adjective, but a specific educational philosophy gaining traction across the country. In schools like mine, phonics-based instruction—teaching children how to decode language by learning letter sounds—was quietly set aside in favor of "sight reading," a method that emphasized memorization of whole words and context clues. Children were expected to recognize words instantly, rather than learn how to sound them out.

For some students, this shift proved disastrous. When memorization failed, there was no fallback system—no tools for decoding unfamiliar words. I was fortunate. Through a combination of home reading, intuition, and sheer persistence, I managed to develop both skills: the ability to recognize words by sight and to sound them out when needed. Many of my classmates were not so lucky. What was introduced as educational progress would, over time, contribute to a quiet but profound decline in literacy—one whose consequences are still with us.

The change was ushered in not by parents or classroom teachers, but by educational theorists and administrators convinced they were modernizing American classrooms.

When the The New England Primer was first introduced into American public schools, the literacy rate was ninety-seven percent. Now, functional literacy is alarmingly low in America. It makes me want to cry.

Each morning after my first school day, Great Gran was there—up early to wake me, get me dressed, fed, and ready for the bus on the corner of MacBeth Drive. She was also there when I got home. This became a happy year: someone was home. I loved Mom and was homesick for her whenever we were apart, but she was usually asleep when I left and gone working most evenings. Great Gran was there. I felt secure. Sadly, that lasted just a year. By second grade, I was on my own thereafter.

I walked the cement sidewalk and up the steps to 6128 MacBeth Drive. I never had to fumble for keys, because Great Gran was there to open the doors and greet me when I got home from first grade.

One special day, she went into her bedroom and came out with a beautifully wrapped package. Handing it to me, she said, "This is something I got for you that I want you to have as my special gift. It's something I want you always to keep."

I liked presents. Sitting on the sofa with our dog, King, by my feet, I gently pulled the curled ribbons, untied and rolled them for safekeeping, then carefully unsealed the Scotch tape and unfolded the paper. I refolded it neatly to save, along with the ribbons.

Grandmother Mildred had modeled this throughout my entire childhood—everything was reused. I would see the same Christmas wrapping paper under Gran's tree year after year, the big smiling Santa face waiting there on every Christmas Eve. When people began crumpling and throwing away wrapping paper, I always cringed.

It just went against the grain of my being to throw away something reusable. Gran had modeled an ecological mindset long before that word existed. She had lived through the Great Depression, so resourcefulness came naturally.

Throwing away wasn't a lifestyle I ever saw as a child.

When the wrap and ribbon were safely stored, I opened the cardboard box and found a small white book inside. Reaching in, I lifted a 6½ by 4¼-inch book with mottled white leather binding. It was so white and beautiful. The words *Holy Bible* were engraved in gold across the top, and Anne appeared in gold cursive at the bottom.

The "Presented To" page inside read: "Presented to [your name] by Mary Davis, December 1957." Great Gran offered no explanation about the gift. Why she felt it was important for me, I never knew—

Great Gran

but I still have that small white King James Bible. Sometimes during years of loneliness, I'd open it and find something to read. It seemed like another language, but I absorbed it and learned that the Bible was something important—something to value and treasure.

Quiet though I was, I must have been difficult at times. Every morning before I left for school, Great Gran coaxed and pleaded with me to eat breakfast. She was the first among many who would take on the challenge of getting me to eat. Gran Anna would later do the same, telling me thousands of times—in both English and Russian—to eat. I rarely felt hungry. Given the choice, I'd take a chocolate donut instead of hot oatmeal.

Great Gran was kind enough to come live with us during the weekdays to take care of me. I rarely saw my mother before leaving for school. Thankfully, Great Gran was awake and would see me off every morning that first year of elementary school. She was also there in the evenings when Mom worked nights at the Bingo Hall or went out on dates.

When I started second grade, since Great Gran was gone, I went to school most days without any breakfast. It was too much for a seven-year-old to manage alone. I had my own bedroom back and was on my own each morning to get up, wash, dress, get myself breakfast—or not—and get out the door in time for the school bus.

Countless times, I missed school because I missed the bus. Sometimes, the next-door neighbor drove me if I knocked and pleaded for help, embarrassed. I'd make up excuses—saying Mom was sick. If the neighbor had already left for work, I stayed home that day. My resources were limited, and I did the best I could.

With Great Gran's absence, another thread in our family's fabric unraveled. Losing her was my first real brush with mortality—the moment I began to understand that people don't stay forever, no matter how much we love or need them. It was also when I started to sense how modern life was already breaking the generational bonds that once held families together.

26

Flower

> "The first grief is never forgotten."
>
> —C. S. LEWIS (paraphrased)

My baby box turtle, Flower, was one of the great joys of my childhood. One Maryland summer in 1960, while riding through the countryside with Gran and Pop, we stopped at a picnic table for lunch. I spotted a small brown box turtle crossing the road. I had always loved turtles, but I had never seen one so tiny. Flower was smaller than any I'd ever held—truly a baby—and I adored her instantly.

Her deep brown eyes told me she was a girl. Boy turtles had red or yellow eyes, but Flower's were soft and dark, watching me with quiet trust. I named her Flower. She was small enough to slip into the pockets of my shorts or blouse. She ate raw ground beef and crisp lettuce from my hand and drank gently from a little bowl I kept just for her.

Each night, Flower slept with me. We had our own ritual. I placed her under the covers at the foot of my bed, and she would crawl upward until she nestled into the warm spot beneath my arm. We slept that way for years.

On school days, Flower stayed in her cardboard box, but many mornings I smuggled her to Woodbourne Junior High in my shirt pocket. She stayed quietly in my desk during class, and I played with her between periods. She was so small the teachers never noticed. When I held her by her front legs, she swung herself back and forth playfully. At night, she lifted her head to help me peel away the dried skin she had, much like a dog turning its head to have its ears scratched.

Some children had dogs or cats who loved them back. I had Flower. She was my companion, my secret friend, and one of the few living beings I felt truly connected to in those early years.

One morning, I woke and Flower did not. Her eyes were sunken and closed. I screamed for my mother, "Flower is dead!"

My mother stood at the foot of my bed. "Well, it's your own fault she died," she said. "You didn't take care of her right."

I sobbed harder. I had not known she needed to hibernate. I had loved her as best I knew how.

In our clay backyard, I dug a small grave near the corner of the house. I placed her tiny brown shell carefully inside, covered it with dirt, and made a little cross from Popsicle sticks.

"I hope I'll see you in Heaven, Flower," I whispered. "I'm sorry I let you die. I love you so much."

Flower's life—and her loss—became one of the first quiet teachers shaping how I came to understand tenderness, responsibility, grief, and faith.

27

Cultural Taboo

"Death was once part of family life. Now it is something we try not to see."

—ANNE ODENDHAL

Just after my first year of school, Great-Gran became too ill to continue living with us or to help care for me. Other than the amusement of our silly arguments—during which I admittedly taunted the poor woman—she was kind to me. Most importantly, she was *there*, so I wasn't alone, especially in the mornings and after school.

I wish she had told me why giving me the Bible mattered so much to her. She never explained it in words, at least not that I remember. But when she presented it to me, she beamed with pride and quiet joy. I'm grateful that I still have her gift after all these years.

Cultural Taboo

The last time I saw Great-Gran was when my mother took me to visit her at one of her sons' homes. She was lying in a bed while relatives stood around the room. She kept repeating that she wanted to "jump in the river." I didn't understand what she meant. I imagined that cool water might soothe her suffering—or perhaps she was seeing some kind of river in her own mind's eye. It was the only time I ever witnessed something that was once common: a family member dying at home.

Historically, what we now call "sandwich generations" were the norm. For thousands of years, families cared for both the young and the old at the same time. Nearly everyone lived sandwiched between the oldest and the youngest at some point. Not living this way is what is truly unusual in human history. It is no surprise that life was—and remains—hard. What *is* new is the splintering of families. When generations are divided, everyone loses.

Children once grew up with death as a familiar presence. Animals and relatives died at home, on farms, and in communities where life and loss were visible. Today, death is largely hidden away in hospitals, nursing homes, or hospice facilities. Birth has followed a similar path. There was a time when people were born and died in the same house—sometimes even in the same room. Those days in America are long past.

While modern medicine has brought extraordinary, life-saving advances, something precious has been lost. Shielded from death and dying, our culture has turned mortality into a taboo—much as sex once was. When children once saw both birth and death as part of ordinary life, they were naturally confronted with the fragility and brevity of human existence. Mortality was not an abstract idea; it was an unavoidable reality.

The 1690 *New England Primer* used the Bible and theology to teach children how to read during colonial times. It conveyed simplified Calvinist doctrine, emphasizing the authority of God and of parents. It included martyr stories and poetry about death that would alarm most modern Sunday-school teachers. Colonial children were deeply familiar with loss; many families buried multiple children before adulthood.

My own children memorized one of the Primer poems in elementary school:

"I, in the burying place may see,
　　Graves shorter there than I;
From death's arrest no age is free,
　　Young children too must die.
My God, may such an awful sight
　　Awakening be to me!
Oh! that by early grace I might
　　For death prepared be."

And the prayer I learned as a child:

"Now I lay me down to take my sleep,
　　I pray the Lord my soul to keep;
If I should die before I wake,
　　I pray the Lord my soul to take."

Years later, while studying for my master's degree in religion and counseling at Covenant Theological Seminary in St. Louis, I read stacks of books on death and dying. Two remain vivid in my memory: Elisabeth Kübler-Ross's *On Death and Dying* and C. S. Lewis's *A Grief Observed*. Kübler-Ross articulated the stages of grief and the human confrontation with mortality. Lewis, however, spoke most powerfully to me. He captured the interior landscape of grief—the confusion, the ache, and the unsettling sense that God Himself had gone silent.

28

Waking Myself: School Buses and RX Drawers

"The family is the primary place where the value of the individual is learned."
—FRANCIS SCHAEFFER, *A Christian Manifesto* (1981)

Me in 2nd Grade

Although I stayed with my grandparents most weekends, my mother made every effort to keep me living with her during the week. This was no small task. Eleanor worked a full-time job during the day and often a part-time job several evenings a week. I remember her working nights at a large bingo hall. Occasionally, when Gran was there playing bingo, I tagged along and sat quietly beside her, trying to occupy myself as the evening dragged on. I was well-behaved, silent, and bored.

After my first-grade year, Great-Gran died at the home of another relative. There was no longer anyone to help my mother care for me. From first grade onward, a routine emerged that lasted for years. I woke up to a clock radio playing my favorite station. Music became my companion and anchor—especially later, during my teen years, when life without radio or records felt unimaginable.

My second-grade school photo tells a quiet story. My hair was uncombed and messy. I don't remember my mother brushing or fixing my hair before school. The only time I recall someone tending to it was when Gran Mildred put rag curls in my hair the night before Sunday school. I likely brought home the notice about school pictures, but Mom didn't remember. She still bought the photos. Looking at that picture now, I see neglect—not intentional, perhaps, but real.

It amazes me how often I managed to get myself ready for school and to the bus stop on time. I was six or seven and didn't really know how to prepare myself in the mornings. Somehow, I often left the house dressed and ready enough—though not always.

When I missed the bus, I usually stayed home. Eventually, my mother would get out of bed and leave for work, and I spent the day alone playing or watching television. It is surprising that no school authority ever questioned my frequent absences.

My favorite game was playing "school." A chalkboard hung on my bedroom wall, and I became a strict teacher to rows of imaginary students. I spent hours lecturing, writing assignments, and standing at the front of my pretend classroom. I even created handwritten worksheets and gave them to my girlfriends at school, instructing them to complete the assignments alongside their real homework. Remarkably, they complied—until one mother intervened after discovering her daughter was doing extra work assigned by me.

Preparing breakfast for myself was beyond my ability in those early years. Most mornings, I ran for the bus without eating. My mother was always asleep. She was never a morning person, and I later realized that her ability to keep her day jobs likely depended on the professional skill she brought once she arrived—often late, sometimes after missing a day or two.

There were many mornings when my mother insisted I call her office and tell her boss she was too sick to come to work. I hated making those calls. I was uncomfortable speaking to adults and uneasy with what I sensed was a lie—though I didn't have words for it then. I often knew she wasn't sick, just exhausted or hungover from being out late and drinking. I had no understanding at the time that she was also addicted to prescription drugs.

I remember hearing her in the bathroom at night or in the morning, sick from too much alcohol. Years later, I understood that she abandoned alcohol because it made her ill and turned instead to prescription medications to cope. Her dresser drawer was lined with rows of pill bottles—an entire drawer devoted to them. I didn't know what they were for. I only knew there were many.

In later years, doctors occasionally expressed concern to me about my mother's drug use. I learned she had been able to see multiple physicians and receive similar prescriptions from each other. There was no system then to track medications. I never discussed it with anyone. As usual, I observed quietly, like a piece of furniture.

I didn't know the word *lonely* then. But I knew the feeling—and I knew it was mine.

When home offers no stable place to land, the heart looks outward—for connection, for warmth, for proof that the world might hold something more. I formed good friendships with girls at school and treasured them. But I also longed to know the wider world beyond my neighborhood. So, I began writing letters to girls who lived far away. It was my first attempt to build a larger world than the one I returned to each day.

29

Latchkey

"Children need presence more than programs."
—DAVID ELKIND

"A society is judged by how it treats its children."
—FYODOR DOSTOEVSKY

My mother gave me a key to our front door so I could get into our house when the school bus dropped me off each afternoon. I can't remember where I kept it, but it hardly mattered—I was forever losing, misplacing, or forgetting it. That meant finding a neighbor with a spare key, waiting at someone else's apartment, or sitting on a hallway staircase until help arrived.

One day, my mom came up with a brilliant solution. She bought a long silver chain and hung the key on it. Each morning, I slipped the necklace inside my clothes, hiding it from view. It worked. No more lost keys. When I arrived home, I'd pull out the chain, stretch it toward the lock, and let myself into an empty apartment—except for the company of a dog, parakeets, turtles, fish, snails, and frogs.

Mom insisted that I call her office every afternoon when I got home, and I always did. She worked for a Baltimore steamship company, and that daily call became my fragile lifeline—my small connection to her voice. Hearing her say "hello" steadied me. I loved her voice after school, on road trips with Gran and Pop, and all the way until the end of her life decades later.

I give her credit for her ingenuity. She did the best she could with what she had. Still, I missed her constantly. I loved her painfully, carrying a persistent childhood fear that she might die—because she was often ill.

By later elementary school, I was more capable of feeding myself in the mornings. By fifth grade, a new product appeared on grocery shelves: Carnation Instant Breakfast. Each morning, I mixed the chocolate powder with milk, stirred out the lumps, and drank it down before school. It wasn't much, but it was something.

The word *latchkey* hadn't yet entered the American vocabulary, but I lived it before it had a name. Children like me represented something new—the first generation that came home to empty homes. The nation was shifting, quietly and profoundly. Mothers were leaving home in growing numbers, not only from necessity like my own, but increasingly in pursuit of independence and a modern identity.

Advertising and consumer culture made two incomes seem essential to the "good life." The result was the same: children returned to silent rooms where no adult waited. The price of progress was often paid in silence by the smallest voices.

This marked the beginning of a latchkey nation—a country learning to replace the presence of parents with programs, the warmth of family with institutions. Daycare and early childhood education rose as solutions, promising enrichment but often substituting for nurture. The assumption was that someone else could raise the children—and that the children would be fine.

But we weren't fine. We were lonely. We were children turning keys in locks and stepping into quiet apartments—safe, but unseen. The small rituals that once anchored family life—shared meals, morning prayers, someone waiting at the window—began to fade.

In earlier times, families lived contentedly on one income, not from lack of ambition but because simplicity was normal. People—especially children and the elderly—mattered more than possessions. Modest living allowed families to remain together. Mothers at home were not viewed as sacrifices but as a good and honored calling.

Family meant loyalty, forgiveness, and continuity. Care stretched from birth to old age. Most people died at home, surrounded by those who loved them. Children were protected and allowed time to simply be children. Home was not about appearance or affluence but belonging.

We were children turning keys in locks—and a nation turning away from its homes and neighborhoods. It marked a deep moral shift away from what had once been understood as true: that family is the foundation of a stable nation.

Extended families and close-knit neighborhoods once formed circles of belonging where people knew one another, watched each other's children, and forgave even serious faults. Life was lived in the present—not haunted by regret or driven by relentless striving. Home, faith, and community once defined success. When that foundation began to crumble, so did much of what made us whole.

30

Nature or Nurture?

"You can't go back and change the beginning, but you can start where you are and change the ending."

—C.S. LEWIS

How did I become the person I am? What portion of me is nature, and what portion is nurture? Genetics versus environment? There may be general patterns, but there are no neat formulas that fit every life.

When Eleanor Roosevelt championed the modern adoption movement, she promoted the belief that babies and children were essentially blank slates—fully moldable by their adoptive families. In doing so, she unknowingly praised Georgia Tann, founder of the Tennessee Children's Home Society, who aggressively advanced that same "blank slate" philosophy.

It was not discovered until Tann was near her death that she was a fraud who had built a lucrative network involving hospitals, law enforcement, and legal professionals to steal babies from poor families and sell them to wealthy ones. Many of the children died while awaiting adoption in her severely neglectful care. The web of deception—made more disturbing by Eleanor Roosevelt's unwitting endorsement—remains one of the darkest chapters in American social history.

My own life is a study in the mystery of nature and nurture. I unmistakably resemble my biological father, sharing not only his physical features but aspects of his temperament. I look more like him than my mother or anyone else in my lineage. As I entered my teenage years, my mother admitted that the resemblance was becoming stronger—something I now realize must have been painful, a daily reminder of the man she loved who abandoned her at the worst possible time.

I had no idea I was a walking reminder of her heartbreak. I didn't even know of his existence until adulthood. When I eventually sought him out, I met him only a handful of times—mostly sad, disappointing, and deeply unsettling encounters. How could I be so like a man whose presence I had never known?

I had no opportunity to imitate his mannerisms or behaviors. None.

Human individuality is a God-designed mystery. Each of us is made in His image—singular, unrepeatable, as distinct as fingerprints or snowflakes.

History, too, helps us understand ourselves and one another. It reveals human nature, exposes patterns of failure, and offers clues for building a wiser future. My past—the memories I retain, the ones I forgot, and even the history that predates my birth—shapes my present. My family's story and my nation's story are woven together in my life.

I carry historical suitcases—some filled with treasures, others weighted with burdens. Did my ancestors dream of me? Did any of them pray prayers that God, in His mysterious timing, is still answering?

Knowing the truth of my history—not the myths, spins, or omissions—helps me understand how my life and family came to be what they are. The history of my nation, with its structures, values, freedoms, and failures, shapes me as well. History shines light on the roots of present problems. The more truth we possess, the clearer the path forward becomes.

Each of us adds to history through our own successes and failures. By examining what has gone before, we learn about consequences and how to avoid repeating mistakes. This is true for families, governments, economies, and societies alike. I suspect I have accumulated an unusually high failure quota, and I hope the lessons have not been wasted.

History is essential for active citizenship. Understanding the story of my nation and its Constitution—the foundation of the Republic I love—clarifies my responsibilities and sharpens my awareness of the challenges facing my community and the world.

Reading the struggles and triumphs of others gives perspective, instruction, and hope. It roots us in identity and belonging. Connection to the past—personal and national—anchors us in ways nothing else can.

31

Towers of Jello

"I learned early how to bend without breaking."
— ANNE ODENDHAL

Have you ever felt as though you take one step forward and forty-two steps back? Growth—personal, emotional, even spiritual—rarely moves in straight lines. It happens only if we keep stepping, even when the ground shifts beneath us.

Resilience has been a defining feature of my life. People have often described me as confident, self-contained, a tower of strength. A kind friend once told me I light up a room when I enter. Another suggested my presence could provoke envy from other women. Those comments have always felt strange to me. External impressions can be wildly disconnected from the daily work of survival. If anyone knew the interior reality of my life, I doubt they would want it.

My mother and "dad" divorced when I was three. I have one early memory of him coming home from work at Bethlehem Steel, sitting on the sofa, and closing his eyes. Longing for his attention, I jumped onto his lap and pleaded, "Don't go to sleep!"

"I'm just resting my eyes," he said.

That memory includes my mother standing in the kitchen wearing an apron—an image unusual enough that it has stayed with me. There is something about both parents being present in a home that communicates safety to a child. I loved that moment.

But there were many others filled with shouting. My parents argued loudly, sometimes threatening physical violence. I remember standing quietly nearby, watching as though I were observing a movie. Unnoticed. Unacknowledged. Not comforted. This posture—being present but invisible—became a lifelong pattern.

My mother often released her anger by yelling. I don't believe she was angry at me, but I was there. One recurring drama involved her telling me to pack a suitcase because I was going to live with my father. I quietly obeyed, filling a large suitcase with as many belongings as I could manage and placing it by the front door.

She never took me there. Eventually, the suitcase would be emptied back into my drawers—until the next episode. Each time, I believed her. Children trust adults. They absorb whatever version of reality they are given.

That was when I became what I later called a Tower of Jello—quietly wobbling in whatever direction I thought might help me survive the moment.

When I was alone on school nights, I called my girlfriends on our landline phone and asked if their parents would let them stay up talking. I also knew the phone number of the bar where my "dad" spent many evenings. Usually, I was told he wasn't there.

Occasionally, he called back late and angrily scolded me for being "on the damn phone" when he tried to reach me. I listened silently. I never explained how lonely I was—how desperate I was to hear another human voice.

I don't know if anyone understood the depth of my isolation. Did it seem normal that a young girl spent most afternoons and evenings alone?

During elementary school, I contracted scarlet fever. One evening I lay weak on the sofa, feverish and exhausted. When my mother came home from work, I felt relief. I watched her reach for the front door handle. I held out my arm in a pleading gesture—no words, no tears. She looked at me, then opened the door and left. I stayed and sweated out the fever alone.

In high school, the threats changed shape but not substance. When my mother became angry, she told me to leave. Sometimes I stayed with girlfriends. Eventually, I ended up living across the street with a neighbor, Miss Louise. My mother did not speak to me for some time, though I lived only yards away. I missed her constantly.

Miss Louise, my mother, and I sometimes played canasta late into the night with another neighbor. We often played until two or three in the morning, despite school and work the next day. I didn't care. I was simply happy to be with people.

When I was sixteen, the man my mother had been dating died suddenly of a heart attack. She was inconsolable. One evening she told me she had swallowed many pills. I ran to Miss Louise, who came immediately. I overheard mom tell Louise that she did not have anything to live for. I felt numb. An ambulance took my mother to the hospital to have her stomach pumped. I sat quietly in the living room, once again like furniture.

At school, when other children mocked me—usually for being skinny—I absorbed it silently. I never defended myself. I became skilled at enduring rather than resisting. I soaked up cruelty like a sponge. The Tower of Jello metaphor fits perfectly: easily shaken, easily deformed, rarely allowed to stand firm.

Even as an adult, I could stand confidently outside my mother's home—only to revert to that same trembling Tower of Jello once inside. If only hindsight could time-travel.

Appeasing bullies does not work—personally or historically. Neville Chamberlain's appeasement of Nazi Germany is a lesson the world paid dearly to learn. Bullies interpret appeasement as permission.

I am not proud of how often I allowed mistreatment. Somewhere deep inside was a belief that I did not deserve to be defended. I recognize that flaw now and continue to work against it. The Tower of Jello is under demolition.

When teaching college psychology, I learned of cross-cultural studies showing a consistent pattern: when faced with problems, men tend to look outward for the cause, while women instinctively look inward, assuming fault. Draw your own conclusions.

Mine is simple: women must stop assuming everything is their fault. Sometimes a bully is just a bully. And a spade should be called a spade.

No more Jello Towers.

32

Penpals: The Outward Reach for Connection

"Loneliness is the space where imagination learns to breathe."
—ANNE ODENDHAL

I had little choice but to learn how to entertain myself as a young girl. Loneliness, paired with a deep desire to connect with others, became the unlikely soil in which my lifelong love of learning and growth took root. I created my own solution to isolation long before I had language for it—organizing what was, in hindsight, my first small business: a pen-pal network.

There was no internet then. No email, no texting. Even long-distance phone calls were rare and expensive. So, like many girls of my generation, I turned to paper, envelopes, and stamps to make the world feel larger and closer at the same time. Writing letters allowed me to explore life beyond my immediate surroundings.

Call it wanderlust. Call it curiosity. I wrote a simple template letter and sent it everywhere—addressed to *Any School, Any Fifth-Grade Girl* in cities and countries far from my own: El Paso, Texas; Detroit, Michigan; Ontario, Canada; Paris, France. I introduced myself, described where I lived and went to school, and explained that I wanted to be friends with girls my age from other places. I asked about their lives, their schools, their interests, and hoped for photographs.

To my delight, it worked.

Letters began arriving, and I kept a Rolodex-style file of penpal friends. Some of those friendships lasted for years. I wish I still had them—especially my pen pal in Guelph, Ontario. Her name was Carol Kane.

One summer, my grandparents took me on a road trip to visit Carol and her family. They welcomed us into their home, and the visit remains one of the most affirming experiences of my childhood. Carol often sent me things she loved, including cookie recipes she hoped I would try. Wanting to belong and to please, I sometimes stretched the truth, telling her I had baked them.

My mother noticed and corrected me. Baking, after all, was foreign territory in my world. Living with a single mother and spending much time alone, my culinary experience consisted mostly of opening cans or heating frozen dinners. I longed to be normal— to live like other girls with intact families and warm kitchens. I wanted Carol to like me, but honesty would have served us both better. I believe she would have liked me just the same.

I am grateful to my mother for giving me life and doing the best she could with what she had. Still, I often reshaped my reality in my letters, not by inventing stories, but by leaving out what was hard. It was just Mom and me—and at that time, that felt like an unusual family.

I also had a pen pal in France, Geneviève LeCalvez. She sent photographs—one of her playing the flute still stays with me. We wrote for years, and when I traveled to Paris with my high-school French class, we hoped to meet. It didn't work out, but I still wonder how she is today. She wrote to me in English; I answered as best I could in French, a language I loved and studied from an early age.

Those pen-pal friendships were a creative answer to isolation. Without realizing it, I had built my own small community—reaching outward instead of folding inward. It was an early expression of how I have always lived: thinking differently, acting independently, finding connection where no one seemed available.

That wiring never left me. My husband jokes that he wouldn't want to live inside my brain—it moves fast, expanding small ideas into big ones almost instantly. He's right. It's how God made me.

Those letters taught me patience, curiosity, and courage. Waiting for envelopes, recognizing familiar handwriting, discovering that people everywhere shared the same hopes and struggles—all of it shaped the writer and thinker I would become. I learned early that the world was both far bigger and far smaller than I had imagined.

What I couldn't have known then was that while I was reaching outward for connection, a cultural and spiritual earthquake was beginning beneath our feet—one that would reshape American childhood, family life, and belonging itself.

And none of us were prepared for what came next.

33

Possessions Can Own Us

"For where your treasure is, there will your heart be also."
— MATTHEW 6:21

I grew up noticing the contrast between my grandmother's homes. Mildred saved everything—each item a small safeguard against scarcity. Anna's house, by contrast, was immaculate, airy, and simple. I learned powerful lessons: thrift has its wisdom, but too much can weigh the spirit.

Even now, I feel uneasy in clutter. I love beauty, but too many things make me long to escape. Anything we own owns a piece of us—it must be dusted, maintained, or worried over. When our homes are clean and uncluttered, the mind breathes easier, and the soul is freer to love.

My mother, busy and unsure of homemaking, made our apartment functional and as homelike as she could. Mom wasn't into neatness or cleaning, but we did our best to maintain. I often ran a carpet sweeper when I got home from school. I don't recall learning other cleaning skills, but I observed Gran Anna, who kept everything clean and orderly.

I learned even more about cleaning during college, when I took jobs caring for professors' homes. I quickly discovered that regular cleaning products were toxic—they gave me headaches—and thus another door opened to the value of natural, non-toxic home-care products.

The true art of homemaking, and of living, lies not in abundance but in grace. Home becomes holy when what we keep serves what we love.

These lessons of home became the groundwork for how I later understood freedom itself—not just within four walls, but within a nation.

My grandmothers represented a generation that worked hard, prayed little, rarely participated in public worship, and often loved in silence. Yet even their quiet faithfulness formed a moral backbone for the nation they helped build.

From those marble steps and corner stores rose the children of America's postwar dream—a generation supremely blessed with comfort, unprecedented luxury, yet aching for connection.

From lessons about what we keep and what we discard in our homes, I began to see the same truth in how our nation treats people. It is moral stewardship—what we value and what we throw away says everything about our soul.

34

American Dark Dive Day

1963, Baltimore, Maryland

"Never give in. Never give in. Never, never, never, never—in nothing, great or small, large or petty—never give in except to convictions of honor and good sense. Never yield to force. Never yield to the apparently overwhelming might of the enemy."
— **WINSTON CHURCHILL**, Harrow School Address, 1941

"A gently burning wick he will not extinguish."
— ISAIAH 42:3

BEFORE THE BELL
The alarm buzzed, and the clock radio filled our small apartment with *He's So Fine* and *Surfin' U.S.A.* Music offered escape from what was ordinary—even lonely. My mother was still asleep as I hurried through the morning routine, drank my chocolate Instant Breakfast, and slung my schoolbag over my shoulder.

Our dog, King, waited by the sofa as always. I wore my key on a long chain around my neck—my silent badge of independence. No one used the phrase *latchkey child* then, but that's what I was. The apartment would be empty when I returned, except for King and the fish and turtles in the corner tank.

Outside, the autumn air bit through my wool skirt as I ran toward the city bus stop. Girls weren't allowed to wear trousers or slacks. Baltimore's row houses glowed faintly in the morning light. On the bus, I stared out the window, half awake, half praying—though I hardly knew how—to the God I was only starting to sense.

Thoughts of my mother's sickness haunted me. Was God warning me that she might die? Did He even hear me? I didn't know, but I kept asking. Something deeper than words had begun stirring—a child's untrained faith groping toward the light.

I didn't know it then, but that small stirring would soon be tested.

THE ANNOUNCEMENT

1963, my first year at Woodbourne Junior High in Baltimore.

When I reached Woodbourne, the children's chatter filled the hallway. Mrs. Decker, my homeroom teacher, stood at the front of the class with a solemn, uneasy expression—as if she were about to deliver a verdict that she didn't agree with.

"Boys and girls," she began softly, "although prayer and Bible reading have been part of schools since our nation's founding, the Supreme Court has decided we can no longer have them. We will still pledge allegiance to the flag, but we'll no longer recite the Lord's Prayer or read Scripture. The principal has chosen a new civic pledge to recite instead."

The room became silent. Chairs creaked and puzzled glances darted between classmates. Just like that, the next morning, something sacred was dismissed and replaced with a moral emptiness that felt cold and foreign.

Several years earlier, William Murray, a ninth grader at Woodbourne, refused to recite the Lord's Prayer, supported by his mother, Madalyn. I was twelve—quiet, shy, and nearly invisible—but that morning I felt a chill unrelated to the weather. Something vital had been erased by decree, and I could not go along with the replacement.

THE STAND

I still recited the Pledge of Allegiance every morning but replacing prayer with a patriotic substitute felt backward. Prayer to God as a citizen of His Kingdom—should come before pledging allegiance to any earthly nation. I sensed that truth long before I could articulate it.

No amount of coaxing made me budge. Something within me knew this was a hill worth standing on, even if I was only a child with a small, untrained sense of right and wrong. I didn't consider whether anyone else agreed. I didn't look around to see what others were doing. I simply stood in silence.

I wasn't trying to prove a point or draw attention to myself—especially not at that stage of my life. I just could not replace daily prayer with a government-approved recitation.

Eventually, the teacher sent me to the principal's office. She did try, privately, to persuade me to follow the new rules, but still I said nothing about why. I rarely spoke to adults, and I didn't explain myself. I simply could not do what they were asking.

Inside, the reason was simple: something very important had been removed, and I could not go along with the replacement. I spent a full week sitting on the principal's bench in her office before they finally stopped trying to make me comply.

My childish righteous indignation became ironclad, and I often felt hurt by classmates' teasing, but at that moment, none of their opinions mattered. My silent protest was not rebellion; it was conviction.

The principal coaxed me and tried to understand why I would not comply. At last, I spoke to her:

"I won't recite a pledge instead of a prayer to a nation that won't let us pray."

Students never talked back to teachers or administrators. Decency, civility, deference, and respect for authority were predominant aspects of manners and common sense. Little did I know that this one day in history would remove the foundations that supported all that and more.

Eventually, the staff gave up. I wasn't a troublemaker. I just simply would not participate in the new ritual.

I felt small and insignificant, but I know now that God saw my courage—before I even knew His name.

My mother was never contacted. And I never spoke to her about it.

THE MEANING

In the early 1960s, the Supreme Court removed state-sponsored prayer and mandatory Bible reading from American public schools. Children were suddenly deprived of a shared moral language that had framed daily life for generations. Is it any wonder that young people, raised amid relativism and secularism, began behaving in ways once considered unthinkable?

From what I witnessed in Baltimore, I came to see it as ground zero—a place where moral order gave way, unleashing a kind of moral anarchy that would profoundly shape America's children and spread far beyond the city itself.

When the Court considered school prayer and Bible reading, America was deeply divided. Some churches and state officials filed briefs urging the Court to retain the practices, but no unified national defense emerged. Silence had made its own argument.

I credit my Leith Walk elementary teachers for instilling in me a deep patriotic love for my country and early moral formation grounded in Scripture. When I reached seventh grade and the Supreme Court delivered its ruling, America changed in a single day. Baby Boomers know the difference—we lived it. We watched the light dim.

Removing prayer opened the door for much darker tides: rising violence, the sexual revolution, drugs, family breakdown, and a growing cynicism toward God and authority. Ten years later, in 1973, abortion became legal nationwide. What began with banning prayer had widened into banning our moral boundaries themselves.

It was the beginning of America's dark dive.

Freedom without truth becomes captivity. Nothing in life or law is morally neutral. As a nation, we either trust in God or drift into chaos.

THE CASES AND THE CONSTITUTION

The Baltimore case, *Murray v. Curlett*, brought by Madalyn Murray O'Hair on behalf of her son William, was combined with *Abington v. Schempp* before the Supreme Court.

In *Abington v. Schempp* (1963) and *Engel v. Vitale* (1962), the Court ruled that prayer and Scripture reading in public schools violated the First Amendment. Justice Clark argued that even voluntary prayer constituted an establishment of religion.

Thomas Jefferson's famous "wall of separation" phrase—written in a letter, not in the Constitution—was intended to reassure Americans that the state must never interfere with religion. The First Amendment protects religion from government, not government from religion. We desperately need a return to historical truth, not revisionism.

AFTERWORD: LIGHT THAT CANNOT BE EXTINGUISHED

Years later, I learned the deeper story. William Murray, the boy at the center of the Woodbourne case, renounced atheism, became a Christian, and dedicated his life to faith in public life. His conversion proved that the darkness of 1963 was not final. God rekindles light where the wick seems nearly spent.

I often think back to that seventh-grade girl standing alone in a Baltimore classroom. My defiance changed nothing outwardly—but perhaps it mattered to Heaven. The God who preserved my life before birth awakened courage in me long before I knew Him.

America's dark dive began quietly—in classrooms, in courtrooms, and in the hearts of people who stopped believing that their voices mattered. But even the smallest flame pierces the deepest shadow.

May prayer, Scripture, and truth again find welcome in our public life. And may the coming generations learn early what I discovered late: Standing for God, however small the stage, is never wasted.

35

The Murray Chronicles: The House That Took Prayer From America

"Right is right, even if no one is doing it; wrong is wrong, even if everyone is doing it."

—ST. AUGUSTINE

"All that is necessary for evil to triumph is for good men to do nothing."

—EDMUND BURKE

Before America's moral descent became visible on the national stage, its first tremors could already be felt in Baltimore. Behind the closed doors in one quiet neighborhood, a private rebellion against God was taking shape—one that would soon help reshape the conscience of the nation. What unfolded in that row house was more than domestic turmoil; it was the incubation of an ideology determined to erase God from America's heart. The storm began quietly, but its aftershocks would reach every classroom, including mine. This is that story.

ONE GIRL VS. A NATION ASLEEP

THE MURRAY HOUSE: THE BIRTHPLACE OF AMERICAN ATHEISM

The story of the Murray family unfolded like a historical thriller—only this one was heartbreakingly real. Before America's dark dive in 1963, that drama was already playing out in my own Baltimore neighborhood. Behind an ordinary brick row house, forces were gathering that would one day shake the conscience of a nation.

Baltimore in the early 1960s was a city of stoops, red brick, and close quarters. Neighbors shared clotheslines, row-house walls, and the sounds of radios that drifted through open windows on humid nights. The aroma of Sunday dinners—crab cakes, fried chicken, and Old Bay seasoning—was carried down the alleyways.

To the untrained eye, our neighborhood seemed ordinary, and even peaceful. Children walked to school, mothers chatted on porches, and fathers took the city bus to their jobs.

But one small row house just a few blocks from my own school, Woodbourne Junior High, hid a different world. Behind its closed door, a storm was blowing that would one day sweep across the conscience of America.

Madalyn Murray O'Hair filed a 1960 lawsuit against the Baltimore school system after her son William was required to participate in daily Bible readings and prayers at Woodbourne. She encouraged him to refuse, which became the basis of the case Murray v. Curlett.

I passed that house often without a clue of what raged inside. None of us children did. We walked by it on our way to class, swung our bookbags and talked about our teachers, music, and homework. But inside that house lived Madalyn Murray—a woman whose fury, ideology, and spiritual emptiness would ignite the crusade that changed American public life forever.

BILL'S CHILDHOOD: THE BOY BENEATH THE FLOORBOARDS

"Trouble is near and there is none to help."
—PSALM 22:11

Bill Murray's earliest memories were of the basement. Not a child's hideout or playroom, but a damp, musty underworld beneath their Baltimore row house. The smell of mildew seeped through the cracked concrete. A single dangling lightbulb buzzed, its glow was dim and uncertain. It was here that his mother, Madalyn, sent him after an explosion of rage one morning when he didn't move fast enough.

"Since it takes you so long to get your lazy body out of bed," she screamed, "you might as well move your bed down there and live where you belong."

Bill's grandfather tried to soften the blow, helping carry the twin mattress down the narrow stairs, setting it on the rug near the washer and the shelves of Marxist books. "C'mon, boy," he said quietly, "let's get this over with before she kills us both."

Against the wall, Bill carefully stacked his few treasures: a row of comic books—*The Amazing Spider-Man, My Favorite Martian, The Flash*—and the science fiction novels of Robert Heinlein, whose stories of space travel and courage became the boy's only escape. He lined up the small wooden airplanes he built from model kits, their wings smooth and symmetrical, each one a symbol of fragile order in a collapsing home.

Madalyn's voice would crash through the air above, the shriek of a woman possessed by rage and ideology. Her arguments with her father shook the house. Sometimes plates flew, sometimes knives. Her father, a weary man who still clung to belief in God, called her "Spider"—a nickname from her youth that now seemed prophetic. She spun webs of anger that trapped everyone in her orbit.

On one of her worst days, she stormed down the basement stairs to inspect her son's cleaning. "Can't you ever do anything right, you worthless brat?" Bill tried to explain, pointing to the freshly swept floor and neat stacks of his toys.

She grabbed one of his model airplanes and crushed it in her fist. The fragile balsa wings splintered. Then another, and another. She tore his comic books in half and stomped them into the concrete. When Bill tried to save his last model—his favorite silver jet—she grabbed his arm and bit it hard enough to draw blood.

Bill screamed. His grandfather heard the cries, rushed down the stairs, and pulled him free. "You stay out of this, old man!" Madalyn spat. But the old man scooped the boy up and drove straight to Johns Hopkins Hospital.

As doctors cleaned and bandaged the wound, Bill was silent. His grandfather explained that his daughter had "lost her temper again." No one called the police. No one questioned it further. It was just another night in the Murray house.

Later, Bill would write that his mother's violence was relentless, her cruelty purposeful. In her eyes, he was "the mistake that had ruined her life."

Once, she tried to persuade Bill to poison his grandfather. "He's a burden," she told Bill. "If you had any guts, you'd help me get rid of him." Bill refused. The idea horrified him. But within months, his grandfather was dead. Whether from natural causes or something darker, Bill was never sure. He only knew the house felt emptier—and colder—afterward.

In the stillness of that basement, he whispered into the dark, "God, if You exist, where are You? There must be good somewhere… because this is evil."

THE UNDERGROUND CELLAR MEETINGS:
IDEOLOGY IN THE SHADOWS

"Religion is the opium of the masses."

—KARL MARX, 1843

The Murray basement became more than a living space. It became a cell.

Each week, Madalyn hosted her "study meetings"—communist gatherings meant to be discreet, though the neighbors were aware of what was going on. They saw strangers slipping through the alley door at night, briefcases in hand, eyes darting. The men wore wrinkled jackets, and the women long, shapeless skirts. They preferred the side entrance, not the front stoop—secrecy mattered.

The air downstairs was thick with cigarette smoke and the sour odor of beer. Folding chairs circled a threadbare rug. On the shelves were stacks of *Das Kapital*, *The Communist Manifesto*, pamphlets in red ink, and cheap statues of naked animals copulating.

Bill's job was to make the place ready. He swept, polished, lined up the chairs, and filled the refrigerator with bottles of Coke and beer. The more meticulous he was, the more likely he was to avoid his mother's wrath.

When the guests had arrived, Madalyn would stand near the old Frigidaire, her eyes blazing as she opened each meeting.

Her voice echoed down the concrete walls: "Comrades! Religion is the opium of the masses!" she would shout, quoting Marx with an almost evangelical fervor. "The production of too many useful things results in too many useless people," another favorite line from Marx, came next.

She would then turn to readings from her heroine, Margaret Sanger. Sanger's words were venomous, yet Madalyn recited them with near-religious devotion: "Colored people are like weeds and need to be exterminated." "We don't want the word to go out that we want to exterminate the Negro population." "More children from the fit, less from the unfit—that is the chief issue of birth control."

The group would nod, mutter agreement, and sometimes clink beer bottles in applause.

Sanger's writings, especially from *Woman and the New Race* (1920), *The Woman Rebel*, and her infamous "Negro Project," filled the Murrays' conversations.

Madalyn admired her as "the great liberator of women," ignoring that Sanger's liberation was soaked in racism and eugenics.

Bill's mother's basement wasn't just a club—it was an underground cell of early American communism. Even then, at the height of the Cold War, Madalyn's faith was not in God but in the dialectic of Marx and Engels.

Neighbors whispered about the shouting that went on late into the night—the pounding of fists on tables, the clatter of bottles, and the bursts of profanity that could be heard even from the street.

Most of those neighbors were immigrants from Poland, Hungary, and East Germany—people who had *fled* Marxism's real tyranny. To them, Madalyn was deluded, even dangerous. "She doesn't know what she's inviting," one Polish man muttered on his stoop. "We've seen this before. It destroys everything."

Yet Madalyn didn't care a bit. She laughed at their fears. "They're slaves to superstition," she told Bill. "We're the enlightened ones."

When she wasn't hosting meetings, she sent her son out to hand-distribute communist pamphlets along the sidewalks between their house and the school. He hated it. Mothers would pull their children indoors, muttering, "That's the Murray boy—stay away." Sometimes older boys would throw rocks, calling him "Commie pinko" and "traitor." He came home bruised and empty-handed, to face more yelling.

One day, an exhausted Bill asked, "Why do you make me do this?"

"Because" Madalyn snapped, "we are changing the world—and no one changes it by being liked."

To her, ideology was family, and propaganda was parenting.

MADALYN & THE SOVIETS: A WOULD-BE DEFECTOR

> "Communism begins from the outset with atheism; but atheism is at first far from being communism; indeed, that atheism is still mostly an abstraction."
> —**KARL MARX**, *Private Property and Communism*

By 1959, Madalyn had grown restless. The row house in Baltimore wasn't enough. She wanted the revolution—the *real* one.

In her mind, Moscow was the promised land. The Soviet Union was, she believed, where "true equality" reigned—a society without religion, without God, without the "chains of morality."

She wrote repeatedly to the Soviet Embassy in Washington, D.C., demanding to be allowed to defect. Her letters declared her lifelong loyalty to communism and hatred for American hypocrisy.

When that failed, she took it further. She forced young Bill to compile an elaborate scrapbook filled with clippings and photographs from *Life* and *Look* magazines: the Soviet space program, Yuri Gagarin's flight, and Soviet parades filled with red banners. When the scrapbook was complete, she drove him to Washington and made him carry it into the embassy as a "gift to the comrades."

A polite receptionist accepted it, praising his effort, but that was all. There was no invitation, no approval, no call.

Madalyn was furious. "These fools don't know how committed I am!" she shouted. She then hatched a new plan: to go to Paris and make her case directly at the Soviet Embassy there. She raised money through "study donations," Tarot card readings by her mother, and whatever else she could find.

Eventually, she made it to Paris—but even there, the Soviet

officials were unimpressed. They refused her request to defect. Their written reply said, politely but firmly, that "the Soviet collective has no need for further assistance."

She returned to Baltimore angrier than ever. "If they won't take me," she fumed, "I'll bring Moscow here."

That vow soon found it's outlet—not through guns or banners, but through the courts.

In 1960, she enrolled her son at Woodbourne Junior High—my school.

In 1963, her case, *Murray v. Curlett*, merged with *Abington v. Schempp* before the Supreme Court. And when prayer and Bible reading were outlawed in public schools, Madalyn Murray O'Hair proclaimed herself "the most hated woman in America."

Years later, her son William Murray would write in his memoir *My Life Without God*:

"Those years were the birthplace of organized American atheism."

He also revealed that during her crusade, his mother was "employed by the Communist Party," a claim reported in a 1983 United Press International (UPI) article.

No verified record has proven that the Soviets had formally commissioned her, but the timing and ideology raise haunting questions. The exact source of her financial means has never been fully explained.

Madalyn didn't need Moscow's permission to do Moscow's work.

What began in one Baltimore row house did not remain private. The conflict that had been seeded in a troubled home, shaped in a basement of ideology and rage, now rose to the national stage. In 1963, the case born out of that household was carried all the way to the steps of the United States Supreme Court. What had once been a family struggle would soon alter the moral direction of every classroom in America.

FALLOUT AND THE BALTIMORE CONNECTION: DARKNESS IN BROAD DAYLIGHT

> "The light shines in the darkness, and the darkness has not overcome it."
>
> — JOHN 1:5

The Murray house at 1526 Wingate Road was a few blocks from my school, Woodbourne Junior High.

While I was taking the city bus, clutching my books, and beginning to awaken to faith in a classroom stripped of prayer, Bill Murray was trudging home to a basement cell filled with Marxist pamphlets, rage, and despair.

We were both Baltimore children of broken homes, each raised by a single mother in a world that still called that abnormal, in a culture that still expected intact families. One of us was quietly reaching toward God; the other was being pushed away from Him.

It chills me even now to realize that the two stories—mine and his—ran parallel in time and space, only streets apart. His mother's fury, my confusion, and our nation's moral drift were all part of one unraveling tapestry.

The forces incubated in that dim basement—the ideology of Marx, the racial elitism of Sanger, and the militant atheism of Madalyn Murray—would spill out to stain the conscience of the nation.

What began as shouted creeds in a Baltimore cellar became the ruling decree of the United States Supreme Court.

When the Court's decision was handed down in 1963, removing prayer and Bible reading from public schools, it was as if a switch had been thrown. The daily acknowledgment of God that once steadied America's children vanished overnight.

Within a few short years, moral certainties began to dissolve. The generation that had started each day with "Our Father who art in heaven" now marched to the chant of "Do your own thing."

Drugs, the sexual revolution, family collapse, and spiritual cynicism swept through the nation.

I often think of how much it began in that little Baltimore house—a place that I could have passed on any given school day. None of us imagined that such darkness could spread from one family's rebellion against God to an entire nation's cultural rebellion.

Madalyn's personal crusade against faith became a public crusade against our conscience. Her hatred of authority, born from personal brokenness and ideological blindness, translated into a judicial precedent that still echoes today.

Her son, William, lived long enough to tell the truth. He wrote that he had been "the unwilling symbol of atheism," forced into a spotlight he never sought. "Years later, he would open the very Bible his mother had banished from the nation's schools—and there he met the Savior she had despised."

He became a Christian, a pastor, and a man who spent his later years warning others about the cost of living without God.

"When prayer was removed from the schools," he wrote, "the presence of evil rushed in to fill the vacuum."

That was not hyperbole—it was history. We saw it unfold in real time. The Murray family's story was not merely the drama of a mother and son—it was the prelude to America's dark dive.

AUTHOR'S NOTE

The story of the Murray family is not written to sensationalize but merely to illuminate. It reveals how personal rebellion against God can become a cultural revolution, and how ideology divorced from truth can wound generations. I walked the same streets and passed the same schoolhouse that played host to this history. What began in one Baltimore basement grew into a nationwide movement—and the consequences are still with us today

36

Assassinations and Aftershocks of 1963

"The malice of the wicked was reinforced by the weakness of the virtuous."

—WINSTON CHURCHILL

"It is impossible to rightly govern the world without God and the Bible."

—GEORGE WASHINGTON

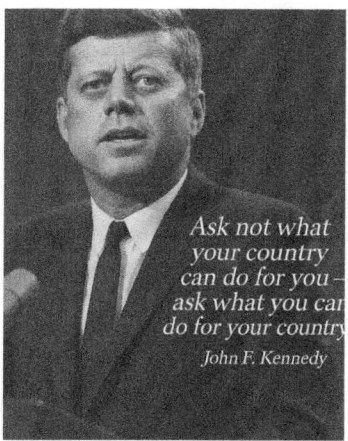

John F. Kennedy during his 1961 Inaugural Address, where he spoke the famous "Ask not" line.

ONE GIRL VS. A NATION ASLEEP

When World War II ended, Europe lay in ruins. In 1948, the United States launched the Marshall Plan, a thirteen-billion-dollar effort led by General George C. Marshall to clear rubble, rebuild cities, and stabilize shattered nations. Peace—not revenge—was the goal.

The Soviet Union, having helped defeat Hitler, demanded influence in postwar settlements. Germany was divided overnight. East Germany fell under Soviet control; the West was administered by the United States, Britain, and France. For millions, liberation from Nazi tyranny gave way immediately to communist rule.

Repressive regimes build walls—ideological and physical—to keep people trapped. In 1961, the USSR erected the Berlin Wall, severing families and communities overnight. Watchtowers, barbed wire, and armed guards ensured escape meant death.

President John F. Kennedy chose not to interfere. The world was still reeling from global war. "A wall is a hell of a lot better than a war," he said. He remembered Soviet Premier Nikita Khrushchev's chilling warning from 1956:

"Whether you like it or not, history is on our side. We will bury you."

The threat was real.

In October 1962, Kennedy addressed the nation after U.S. reconnaissance revealed Soviet nuclear missiles in Cuba, ninety miles from Florida. This time, restraint was impossible. After days of tension that brought the world to the brink of nuclear war, Khrushchev backed down—but hostility deepened.

Yet no tanks were needed to weaken America from within.

Comfort, prosperity, and complacency had already begun eroding vigilance. Many Americans grew more attached to personal peace than to civic responsibility. Others became willing ideological tools—voices that undermined moral and spiritual foundations from inside the culture itself.

President Kennedy—the first Catholic president—opposed abortion, calling it "repugnant to all Americans." He supported civil rights, challenging entrenched political machines and racial hierarchies, including those within his own party. He underestimated the resistance he faced.

Jesus' parable in Luke 12 warns of those who trust in their own strength, unaware of judgment approaching quietly in the night. Dale Ralph Davis captures Kennedy's tragic confidence:

> "I'm forty-three years old. I'm not going to die in office."
> — **JOHN F. KENNEDY**, *My Exceeding Joy*

History answered otherwise.

Presidents who have been assassinated—Lincoln, McKinley, Kennedy—or nearly so—Washington, Reagan—share a common trait: they disrupted entrenched systems. Resistance followed.

Long before America existed, Providence preserved another leader. During the French and Indian War, George Washington survived extraordinary odds. Horses were shot from beneath him; musket balls pierced his coat; yet he remained unwounded.

> "By the all-powerful dispensations of Providence, I have been protected beyond all human probability or expectation."
> — **GEORGE WASHINGTON**

History is not simple. It is morally intertwined. But truth matters—because forgetting it is how nations lose their way.

The Cold War was fought with missiles and ideology, but the deeper conflict unfolded quietly—in classrooms, living rooms, radios, and school halls. While walls rose abroad, America's moral foundations were weakening at home.

And then came the Beatles.

Four young men arrived just as the ground beneath America's feet began to shift. Their music would become the soundtrack of a generation stepping into cultural upheaval, moral confusion, and the long shadow of Vietnam.

37

The Beatles—When the Ground First Shifted

"The feeling that something is happening, but you don't know what it is…"

—BOB DYLAN (1965)

Mom worked part-time evenings at a large Baltimore bingo hall, usually after sleeping during the day. She and her mother, Mildred, both loved bingo, so the hall provided extra income. Whatever Mom earned, she poured into me—clothes, toys, Barbie dolls, and the crown jewels of my adolescence: Beatles and Rolling Stones vinyl albums.

One evening she returned from her bookkeeping job carrying a wrapped package.

When I opened it, I gasped.

The Beatles—When the Ground First Shifted

"Oh, Mom!"

Four faces stared out from the glossy *Meet the Beatles* album cover. Mom's smile said everything—my delight was the only payment she needed.

Everything about the Beatles felt like sunlight breaking through a familiar sky—new, thrilling, and just a little dangerous.

Girls everywhere fell in love with Paul McCartney. John was "okay." Ringo had his loyal admirers. But for me, it was George Harrison. Paul seemed too pretty; George felt mysterious.

Owning *Meet the Beatles* before my friends made me a neighborhood celebrity—at least for a week. After school, girlfriends crowded into our living room, playing the songs on repeat until our ears rang. *I Wanna Hold Your Hand* and *She Loves You* became instant anthems. We memorized every track before bedtime.

We didn't know it then, but we were rehearsing for a cultural earthquake.

THE NIGHT THE BEATLES TOOK BALTIMORE

My closest girlfriend and I somehow secured tickets to see the Beatles at the Baltimore Civic Center during their first American tour in 1964—their only Baltimore performance.

When tickets went on sale, we bought them immediately.

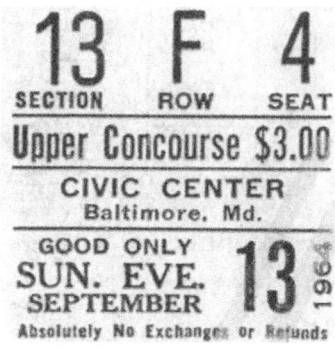

The real ticket stub from the 1964 Baltimore Beatles concert

On the long-awaited night, I dressed carefully and walked to my friend's house. We boarded the public bus bubbling with anticipation. As soon as we reached 1 West Pratt Street, the shock hit us: a wall of noise and movement—hundreds of teenagers already in a frenzy.

Girls shrieked. Boys elbowed through the crowd. Police tried to maintain order but looked as bewildered as we were.

We had never seen anything like it.

Inside the arena, the air crackled. When the lights dimmed, a shrill roar surged like a tidal wave. The Beatles appeared—silhouetted, iconic, barely visible through the hysteria.

Then the music started.

And the crowd detonated.

Girls leapt onto their seats, waved their arms, shook their hair, and collapsed into sobs. Some screamed so loudly they drowned out the very band they came to hear. At first, I hesitated—chairs were for sitting, not standing on like daredevils. But the energy pulled us in like a riptide. Soon my friend and I climbed onto the chair arms too.

Balancing there felt strange, but exhilarating. Under the spell of the music and the electricity of thousands of young voices, the stadium seemed to shake.

It was chaos—wild, joyful, unchecked.

We were witnessing something more than a concert.

We were witnessing the birth of a new youth identity.

A CULTURAL TIDE RISING

Looking back, that night feels like standing on a shoreline moments before a storm. None of us—dancing on chair arms and screaming lyrics—understood the magnitude of what we were living through.

The Beatles weren't just a band.

They were a signal flare.

American culture was loosening its collar. Generational norms were beginning to shift. The music that thrilled us was also tugging at the threads of a tightly woven society—threads that would unravel in ways we could not yet imagine.

Beatlemania wasn't an isolated craze.

It was the first tremor before the national quake.

THE TURNING OF THE TIDE

The energy that electrified us that night also marked the beginning of a cultural current that would soon carry us into deeper waters—unrest, upheaval, and the heartbreak of the Vietnam era.

The Beatles had arrived.

And with them, the ground beneath us quietly began to shift.

The music promised freedom, joy, and belonging—but it did not tell us where that freedom would lead. While we were learning the words to new songs, a far older language of duty, sacrifice, and consequence was quietly set aside. Within a few short years, the same generation that screamed for the Beatles would be handed draft notices, body counts, and a war they did not understand—or trust. The soundtrack changed first. The cost came later.

Original photograph of George Harrison and John Lennon, taken by the author at the 1964 Baltimore Beatles concert.

38

The Teachers Who Shape Us

The Beatles had ushered in something electric, something new—an energy that swept through the young and left the old uneasy. Their sound danced through the airwaves and into our imaginations, promising freedom, rebellion, and a world unfurling at a dizzying pace. But beneath the excitement, another truth was quietly forming. The people who shape us most are not celebrities or cultural waves, but the adults who stand near us every day.

After the noise of concerts and the shimmer of pop idols faded, the steady voices of teachers rose to the forefront. Some lifted us, some wounded us, and all of them left marks that lasted far longer than any hit song. Fame flares and fades, but the imprint of a teacher—kind or cruel—etches itself into the deepest layers of a child's identity.

With that cultural roar still echoing in my ears, I stepped back into the classroom, not knowing how profoundly the teachers of my youth would shape the girl I was becoming.

My ninth-grade courses at Woodbourne Junior High included required Algebra. I had always been a good student and truly loved school. Learning was a joy, and school was where I felt alive and connected. My best memories from childhood, the times when I felt happiest, came from those school years. They were my refuge, the place where life made sense and where I could breathe.

But everything shifted with Algebra. And with Mr. Pyle.

MR. PYLE—THE TEACHER WHO WOUNDED CONFIDENCE

Mr. Pyle was young, tall, and acne-faced. His voice filled the room—too loudly, too often. His teaching style was uniquely negative. He would walk up and down the rows, ruler in hand, suddenly slamming it down on my desk and shouting, "What's the answer to number 7?"

Whether I knew the answer or not, it didn't matter. The shock and aggression froze me.

I became silent. Paralyzed. Bullies always turned me into a tower of Jello.

I struggled to grasp algebra. My mom tried helping by paying for a tutor—my Girl Scout leader's husband, Mr. Jim, who came to our apartment two days a week. I also attended Mr. Pyle's after-school coaching class every day. But fear had taken over. I froze on tests. I froze when questioned. And eventually, I failed.

Mr. Pyle gave me an F for the year.

That failure was etched into my identity. I must not be any good at math.

It was the first academic failure of my life, so I believed it meant something true about me. I carried "I am bad at math" for many years. The human mind is so impressionable at that age; one adult's hostility can drown out all the years of success before it.

Because of that F, I had to attend summer school. I rode the city bus both directions every weekday to a downtown high school. I expected humiliation. Instead, I found a gentle, kind, patient summer schoolteacher who made algebra make sense. I understood it. I liked it. I excelled. I earned an A.

One day, the male teacher looked at me, confused, and with some passion in his voice, asked:

"What are you doing here?"

"You don't belong here."

I couldn't answer. It took years to realize that the summer schoolteacher was trying to inform me that my algebra capability was top-notch, and he was baffled at how I'd ended up failing it during the school year. There was no way to explain that I fully believed the way Mr. Pyle treated me was the real me—a dumb girl incapable of understanding mathematics. This carried into my belief that I was not intellectually capable of handling college.

I didn't yet understand how deeply Mr. Pyle's fear-based intimidation had shut down my mind. Even as I succeeded in summer school, the idea that I was "math dumb" traveled forward with me into high school. It wasn't until my time living at L'Abri that I began recognizing that I wasn't dumb but smart and capable. It took way too long for my self-confidence to match the reality of who I was and am.

Fast forward many years to when a medical doctor did a thorough cognitive testing process on me. She told me the results showed me as "one smart lady, smarter than any of her patients ever." I asked where she'd been my whole life. No one had ever told me I was smart, other than a male student friend in college who told me I had a high IQ.

Sometimes our gifts lie dormant simply because no one ever reflected them back to us.

MR. PENNIMAN—THE TEACHER WHO OPENED A DOOR

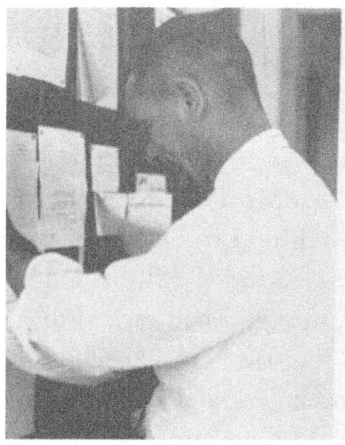

Mr. Penniman, Industrial Arts Teacher

At Northern High School the following year, I noticed what the boys were doing in Industrial Arts: woodwork, leatherwork, and metal enameling. I wanted to learn those crafts, not because I had something to prove, but because they sparked interest and joy. I loved doing anything creative with my hands. I wanted to make leather wallets, bookmarks, wooden frames for my paintings from art class, and metal jewelry.

The message to me was clear. Girls didn't take "Shop." But I enrolled anyway.

The instructor, Mr. Penniman, made a big deal out of it and took the problem to the school administration. He had never had and did not want a girl in his class. But he was forced to allow it, and I did not care that I was the only girl there. I didn't even notice the boys in the shop as I was so intensely interested in the crafts.

Once class began, I thrived. Working with my hands felt natural and deeply satisfying. I often stayed after school to do extra projects. I even brought an oil painting from art class, and Mr. Penniman helped me build my wooden frame for it.

My interest, not any rebellion, softened him. His resistance slowly dissolved. And without intending to, I became his favorite student.

I know he was sad when the year was over, and I don't know if any other girls followed my lead. Interest and curiosity have the power to break barriers. Mr. Penniman opened doors for me to see that I could learn anything I truly wanted to learn.

During this same period, I still held the belief that I was terrible at math—even though I had earned that A in summer school. I didn't understand that the summer schoolteacher had seen what was true: I was an intelligent and capable person. What we believe about ourselves is often determined by the voices we encounter at vulnerable ages.

And tenth grade meant Geometry, on the heels of algebra.

MR. STACK—THE TEACHER WHO RESTORED CONFIDENCE

Northern High, school photo

At Northern High, I signed up for daily geometry coaching before school even began, because I was afraid that I would fail again. But when school started, I walked into the classroom of Mr. J. Richard Stack, and everything changed.

Mr. Stack was different. He was a great teacher and a good man. He explained things clearly. He encouraged us. He treated every student with dignity. The logic of geometry made perfect sense under his guidance. I found myself excited to solve problems. Geometry became enjoyable—stretching, strengthening and expanding my thinking.

Mr. J. Richard Stack, Geometry teacher

I stayed after school most days in the geometry room—helping other students with geometry! Other students came to his classroom after school. That classroom became a place of community, learning, and belonging. I earned As. I fell in love with geometry! Solving problems was a pleasure. I felt proud of my work. I felt less alone.

During that time, I worked evenings at one of my first jobs ever—behind the candy counter at a movie theater. Silver coins were still in circulation then, though fading. I noticed their value and quietly collected them. I filled an entire bag with silver coins. Later, on a trip, I asked my mother to keep them safe. When I returned, she told me simply, "I had to use them."

No apology. The coins were gone.

Yet some bright memories stand untouched.

I was thrilled when I could offer a gift of two free movie tickets to Mr. Stack. One school night, he and his wife made a point of coming to the theatre while I was working. That meant the world to me. They greeted me kindly and with warmth. His wife thanked me for the movie tickets. I beamed so fully that I could hardly stop smiling. I know now why that meant so much: He valued me and he saw me. He was steady, strong, and good.

Mr. Stack was one of the few father-like figures in my entire life. He remains a treasure to me. Kindness and respect awaken confidence. Loving guidance shapes identity.

Years later, before cell phones and internet, I tried hard to find him and thank him for his impact on my life. I contacted Northern High. I searched phone books and directory assistance. I didn't know he had moved to North Carolina—the very place that I had lived for twenty-eight years. We were practically neighbors, and I was completely unaware.

Only while writing this chapter did my stepdaughter, Emily, finally locate him. He had passed away in 2013, the same year my mother died. He was buried in Apex, North Carolina—near where I lived. If only I had known.

If one of his daughters or grandsons ever reads this, I hope they know:

I have never forgotten him. His kindness shaped my life. Helped me become myself. I hope to thank him in heaven one day. And I would love to connect with any of his relatives.

These experiences revealed something profound:

Not all parenting happens inside the home. Children are shaped by the adults who teach, challenge, humiliate, encourage, or simply believe in them.

Teachers can harm. Teachers can open doors. Teachers can save something precious in a child.

And sometimes, one good teacher is enough to light the way back.

As the culture shifted, so did the classrooms. Authority was questioned, trust was uneven, and young minds learned early that adults could either steady them or unsettle them. I was learning, quietly, which voices to trust—and which ones could wound.

Beyond the school walls, the nation itself was moving toward a reckoning. The children shaped by these classrooms would soon be asked to carry consequences far heavier than grades or reputations. And for my generation, that reckoning had a name: Vietnam.

39

Vietnam

"No one hates war more than the soldier who has seen it."
—Anonymous Vietnam Veteran

Brewing since 1950, the Vietnam War erupted in earnest in 1965 when American forces entered heavy ground combat. Young men were deployed. Bombs fell for a decade, until the fall of Saigon in 1975.

Draft notices arrived like unwanted verdicts. And when President Lyndon Johnson escalated the war—after Kennedy, who was no war hawk, was gone—the draft became a specter in nearly every American home.

More than 2.7 million Americans served. Sixty-one percent of those killed were younger than twenty-one. The average age was twenty-three. Nearly ten percent of an entire generation went.

I was in high school and college through most of it, watching violence unfold nightly on television in a way no previous generation ever had. The war entered our living rooms, narrated by sober newscasters. The draft made everything personal. Immediate. Terrifying.

Some boys I knew talked about leaving the country. Some whispered about Canada. Others enlisted strategically, hoping to steer their fate away from the jungle. But if your number was drawn, you went—regardless of dreams, fears, or future.

I had a friend several years older—not a boyfriend, but someone I cared about—who was drafted while I was still in high school. He didn't want to go but had no choice. He asked me to write, so I did—often. My letters were probably naïve, but I knew enough to send kindness. Soldiers far from home need reminders that someone remembers them. He wrote back with stories and photographs—glimpses of a world no young man should ever have to see.

Years later, my daughter's fiancé was deployed to the Middle East. She said, "You don't know, Mom." She was right. I began writing him nearly every day while traveling for work—postcards, short letters, and notes from every town I passed through. A small act, perhaps, but sometimes proof that someone sees you can soften a brutal day far from home.

The necessity of the Vietnam War was deeply questioned by Baby Boomers. Many believed it was senseless—and wars often are. Vietnam itself, I've been told, is breathtakingly beautiful: a country older than its conflicts, desiring peace, not occupation. "Freedom from communism" was the slogan. Control of resources was the reality.

The war was not the military's fault. It was their leaders'.

Vietnam's soldiers were thrust into a nightmare—dense jungles, constant danger, nowhere truly safe. Unlike open terrain, the jungle feels alive with threat. That kind of stress grinds down the soul.

Then came the heartbreak of coming home.

Instead of being welcomed, many Vietnam veterans were met with hostility—mocked, spit on, treated as villains in a war they did not choose. Many still carry that wound. PTSD, isolation, silence—these are scars left by a nation that turned its back on those it sent to fight.

It is a tragic legacy.

And many still long to be understood.

Yet even as soldiers bled in distant jungles, another movement was rising at home—a cultural rebellion fueled by music, protest, drugs, and the promise of freedom without obligation. America was splitting at the seams. A generation disillusioned by Vietnam began searching for meaning elsewhere.

Music became its banner. Rebellion its identity. "Do your own thing" its creed. By 1969, that restless spirit converged on a muddy New York farm, giving birth to a counterculture that promised love without limits, peace without principle, and freedom without restraint.

It was Woodstock.

The nation was changing.

And so were we.

40

Woodstock Nation

Max Yasgur's Farm, Upstate New York, 1969

"You write the laws, let me write the music, and I will rule your country."
— Scottish patriot **ANDREW FLETCHER**, 1703

THE COST OF REMOVING RESTRAINT

When prayer and Scripture were removed from America's public schools in 1963, a vital moral restraint disappeared. What followed was not neutrality, but vacuum. And vacuums are never empty for long.

Woodstock was not merely a music festival. It was a prophecy—a nation attempting to live on the fumes of freedom after its moral foundations had been quietly removed. We have been living with the consequences ever since.

Music steers culture: it shapes imagination and gives language to longing. Woodstock did not erupt suddenly in August of 1969. It was the visible fruit of a cultural drift already years in motion.

ONE GIRL VS. A NATION ASLEEP

THE FUSE WAS LIT BEFORE THE FESTIVAL

Long before young people danced barefoot in the mud, America was already tilting. In the late 1950s, the Beat movement—figures like Jack Kerouac and Allen Ginsberg—began dismantling inherited moral boundaries. Restraint was mocked. Authority was rejected. "Free love," drug exploration, and radical individualism were celebrated as virtues.

When I was young, I didn't hear about a "Beat movement." I heard about beatniks—a media-coined term adults repeated with a mix of worry and dismissal.

History is not only what happened, but what people were taught to notice and fear.

Their rebellion became the seedbed of the counterculture.

Then came 1963.

When the Supreme Court removed prayer and Scripture reading from public schools, the last shared moral framework that had shaped generations of American conscience was erased. The space left behind was not morally neutral. Into it flowed the philosophies already waiting—unchecked and unchallenged.

The 1960s did not explode overnight. They simmered, cracked, and then split wide open. By the time Woodstock arrived, the nation was already reeling from assassinations, Vietnam, civil unrest, and the collapse of moral consensus.

THE SETTING THAT BECAME A SYMBOL

The Woodstock Music & Art Fair—ironically not held in Woodstock—was relocated to Max Yasgur's dairy farm in Bethel, New York. Yasgur, a conservative farmer, believed young people had a right to gather. He could not have imagined what followed.

Nearly half a million people arrived—far beyond what organizers had planned. Roads collapsed into gridlock. Food ran out. Sanitation failed. Helicopters ferried supplies. And still the masses came, seeking meaning, rebellion, escape, or belonging.

A GENERATION UNLEASHED

To its admirers, Woodstock symbolized peace and love. Beneath the slogans lay something deeper: a generation newly severed from moral restraint, experimenting with freedom without guardrails.

Drug use was open and celebrated. Sexual boundaries dissolved. Music—powerful, brilliant, unforgettable—became the emotional and spiritual soundtrack of a worldview forming in real time:

- liberation without responsibility

- pleasure without restraint

- emotion without wisdom

None of this happened in isolation.

America had already removed biblical instruction and moral formation from its classrooms. When a culture discards its compass, the next generation builds on sand.

To some, Woodstock was utopia. To others, it was a warning flare.

Real freedom requires truth.

Moral freedom requires boundaries.

National freedom requires virtue.

A society cannot abandon restraint and expect peace.

A NATION ALREADY TILTING

Long before Jimi Hendrix played the national anthem, the philosophical roots of Woodstock had been planted.

When prayer left the classroom…

When biblical literacy disappeared…

When discipline yielded to permissiveness…

America had loosened its grip on the foundations that had steadied earlier generations.

By 1969, the shift was complete. Woodstock merely revealed the fruit.

Into that wide-open moral vacuum stepped the loudest voices of cultural rebellion—among them Abbie Hoffman, Berkeley graduate, agitator, and co-founder of the Youth International Party.

Hoffman attended Woodstock and shortly afterward wrote *Woodstock Nation (1969),* a manifesto celebrating:

- sex without boundaries

- drugs without shame

- rebellion without responsibility

His book gave ideological shape to what had unfolded at Yasgur's farm. The counterculture didn't stay contained to just one festival. It traveled home with millions, altering classrooms, campuses, living rooms, and eventually the educational and political institutions.

And just four years later, the cultural logic of Woodstock reached its most devastating expression yet. In 1973, the Supreme Court legalized abortion nationwide—the next American unthinkable, after slavery, when Negroes were deemed less than human and unworthy of constitutional rights. This time the highest court in our nation decided that pre-born human beings are not fully human and thus unworthy of any constitutional or civil rights, including the right to life, simply having their life protected. A moral framework built on limitless sexual freedom inevitably demands a way to erase its natural consequences.

Eight justices validated a worldview Margaret Sanger had advocated decades earlier: sexual autonomy without responsibility, reinforced by the elimination of inconvenient life.

By 1992, the free-love, drug-steeped ethos of Woodstock had seeped into the highest halls of power.

- In Unlimited Access (1996), FBI agent Gary Aldrich detailed the unprecedented number of White House staff who could not pass the security clearance due to drug use and other disqualifying issues—yet they were still granted access.

- In Crisis of Character (2015), the Secret Service officer Gary Byrne described the moral chaos and disregard for security standards that characterized the Clinton White House.

What began in fields and festivals eventually shaped federal culture.

WHEN MUSIC BECOMES A MORAL FORCE
Civil arenas merely reflect what music and art already preach.

Beautifully arranged songs like *Crystal Blue Persuasion* floated through the air, promoting peace and love, while under them surged a movement of:

- unrestrained "free love"

- drug-fueled escapism

- authority rebellion

- the glamorization of sexual exploitation

- the objectification of women and even children

The music was intoxicating; the moral cost was catastrophic.

A culture that discards biblical restraint quickly descends from disrespect to hostility toward authority, then into moral anarchy.

Never mind that Abbie Hoffman died by suicide following years of turmoil and drug use. Never mind that countless young people shaped by this ideology now live out their worldview through virtual violence, despair, and very tragic decisions.

When the last guitar chord faded at Yasgur's farm and the crowds returned home, America did not return to what it had been. The counterculture's message—freedom without boundaries, autonomy without accountability, and desire without consequence—did not die in the mud of 1969. It matured.

Just four years later, in 1973, the cultural logic of Woodstock reached its most devastating expression yet: the nationwide legalization of abortion.

A moral framework built on unlimited sexual autonomy inevitably demands a mechanism to erase its consequences.

What began as "free love" required something darker to sustain it.

The ideology matured.

It entered universities.

It entered policy.

It entered courts.

It entered medicine.

It entered the family itself.

Once a generation accepted desire as sovereign, responsibility became optional—and life itself became negotiable.

Woodstock loosened the soil.

The courts cleared the way.

And the seeds that were planted would grow into something far more lethal than any music festival.

41

Planned Barrenhood and Slippery Slopes

"Even the smallest person can change the course of the future."
—J.R.R. TOLKIEN

"The greatest danger to truth is not hatred of it, but indifference."
—T.S. ELIOT

"No civilization can survive for long without a moral foundation."
—WILL DURANT

Prejudices are heavy-duty preconceptions—about people, life, or reality itself. They shape cultures long before anyone recognizes their presence. Some announce themselves loudly; others settle in quietly, spreading through assumptions, academic theories, economic fears, and shifting social norms until they appear respectable.

Preferences are different. They are benign and human. I enjoy people who adore their cats, though I do not share the affection. My calico was sweet, but allergies shortened our relationship. Preferences are harmless. Prejudices—especially cultural ones—are powerful.

As an only child of an only child, loneliness threaded its way through my early years. I envied families filled with laughter, cousins piled into living rooms, and generations anchored in shared ritual and memory. Such abundance is a gift.

Many only children never feel alone because they are surrounded by engaged parents or extended families who weave a fabric of belonging. For me, that fabric thinned when my grandparents died, taking with them the lineage for which I longed.

We imagine we control fertility—but do we? God is the author of life. I have known many who longed for children but were granted none, or only one. I advocate early marriage and large families when God allows. Scripture's call to "take dominion" is not a mandate for exploitation but for stewardship—cultivating the world like a gardener who replenishes the soil rather than stripping it bare.

Wherever I live, I try to leave the land better than I found it. Exploiting the earth for profit while ignoring replenishment is the opposite of biblical dominion. My love of bulbs came from my friend Chris Wiesinger, "The Bulb Hunter," who taught me how they carry beauty across centuries. Planting bulbs are planting memory. Long after the original planter is gone, the bulbs multiply and bloom, quietly testifying that someone once believed in the future.

The modern fear of "too many people" rings hollow. The overpopulation crisis, promoted as scientific certainty, collapses under scrutiny. Fertility rates worldwide are shrinking. Agricultural and technological advances have expanded resources. The world is not collapsing under human weight. What is collapsing is our valuation of human life. We face population implosion, not explosion.

Cultures rarely collapse all at once. They erode—one concession, one silence, one "necessary compromise" at a time. The myth of overpopulation softened our conscience.

Materialism numbed our instincts. Fear replaced faith. Autonomy replaced obedience. Desire replaced duty. Once a society treats children—the smallest image-bearers of God—as burdens, the ground beneath it begins to tilt.

What began as discomfort with fertility hardened into resentment, then into the belief that human life itself is negotiable. That belief did not remain private. It became ideology. Then policy. Then law. Planned barrenhood—first in the mind, then the heart, then the culture—prepared the way for something far darker. The next step was not surprising. But it was devastating. And that is where the story now leads.

Anthony Comstock was born in 1844, in an era shaped by the Second Great Awakening—a time that forged men with iron spines and tender consciences. At eighteen, Comstock surrendered his life to God and soon found himself engaged in one of the most turbulent moral battles in American history.

His 1913 autobiography, reprinted a century later, reads like a dispatch from a forgotten war. As a United States Postal Inspector during the Industrial Revolution, Comstock confronted an exploding and highly profitable pornography trade—fueled not only by businessmen and publishers, but at times even by clergy. Working closely with the YMCA, he raided dens, seized obscene materials, and made citizen arrests with fearless regularity. He believed moral corruption was not merely a private vice, but a civic danger capable of hollowing out a nation.

In 1873, after years of relentless pressure, Congress passed the Comstock Act, outlawing the mailing of pornography, contraceptives, abortifacients, and other "instruments of immorality." Modern commentators deride it as a "zombie law," yet legally it remains on the books unless repealed. Comstock, for all his imperfections, understood something few others did: when contraception and abortion rise together, they feed the same appetite—the belief that desire is sovereign and life disposable.

What Comstock could never have imagined is what now passes for "education" in some public-school libraries. What once required secrecy and coded mailing lists now sits openly on taxpayer-funded shelves.

THE SECOND FRONT: BIRTH CONTROL AND THE WOMAN WHO CHANGED THE WORLD

Until the mid-twentieth century, it was illegal to import or sell contraception in the United States. Not only Catholics, but virtually every major Protestant denomination—Lutherans, Presbyterians, Methodists—opposed it.

They understood contraception to be morally dangerous because it separates sexuality from responsibility, pleasure from covenant, and intimacy from accountability. Early Protestant thinkers warned that once contraception was normalized, abortion would inevitably follow.

They were not wrong.

Into that world stepped Margaret Sanger.

In 1921, she founded the American Birth Control League, later renamed Planned Parenthood. Sanger was not secretive about her beliefs. She openly championed eugenics, supported forced sterilization, and advocated preventing the birth of the "unfit." Her writings confirm this in her own words.

To this day, a disproportionate number of Planned Parenthood clinics operate in minority neighborhoods. This is not coincidence. History has a long memory.

For an unfiltered view of the movement Sanger began, the film *Unplanned* is essential. Abby Johnson—once a rising star within Planned Parenthood—tells the story the organization works tirelessly to suppress.

As Sanger's influence expanded, Protestant denominations quietly abandoned their historic opposition to contraception. Not because of new theological clarity. Not because of rigorous moral debate. But because the culture changed—and the Church followed.

By the 1960s, contraception was mainstream. Few understood that common methods, including the Pill and IUDs, could function as abortifacients. Fewer still cared.

Comstock had warned that contraception would become the

hinge on which pornography and abortion would swing. History proved him right.

FROM MYTH TO MACHINERY: OVERPOPULATION PANIC
In college, I was immersed in Malthusian fear—population pyramids predicting catastrophe, professors warning that having more than one child was selfish and environmentally dangerous. Questioning the narrative was treated as ignorance.

Yet the "population bomb" was propaganda.

R. J. Rushdoony's *The Myth of Overpopulation* exposes how population panic has repeatedly been used to justify control—most often aimed at the poor, minorities, and the politically inconvenient. Stephen Mosher's *A Mother's Ordeal* reveals how that panic hardened into machinery in China's one-child policy, with forced abortions, forced sterilizations, and unspeakable suffering. The book reads like dystopian fiction—except that every detail is true.

This worldview reshaped how Americans came to see children: not as blessings, but as burdens; not as image-bearers, but as consumers of finite resources. It was a mindset rooted not in love, but in fear.

THE REAL COST OF THE ANTI-CHILD MENTALITY
By the time I was expecting my fifth child, I had grown accustomed to disapproving glances and unsolicited lectures about "overpopulation." There were no congratulations—only judgment.

Yet I have known families with many children whose homes radiate joy, order, maturity, and depth. Children flourish when they grow within multi-generational relationships, not isolated in age-segregated peer dependence.

The modern prejudice against large families is one of the last socially acceptable discriminations. People rarely hear themselves:

"How irresponsible."

"Why so many?"

"Aren't you done yet?"

Children have been reclassified from human beings to lifestyle choices.

Even many Christians rarely pray about family size. They seek God's will for jobs, houses, schools, and relocations—but quietly reserve fertility decisions for themselves. Faith yields to comfort. Children are postponed until an "ideal season" that often never arrives. I have watched couples grow profoundly grateful for the children they did have—and quietly haunted by the children they prevented.

LOVE AND ITS COUNTERFEITS

I remember the sympathy expressed when my daughter got married at nineteen. To others, it was a tragedy. To me, it was beautiful.

Our culture preaches sexual purity while simultaneously postponing marriage indefinitely—making purity nearly impossible. "Wait but stay pure" has become an unwinnable command.

Dr. Albert Mohler's *The Case for Early Marriage* and Mark Gungor's *Singles and Stinking Thinking* dismantle this contradiction. For centuries, earlier marriage was normal—and it worked. Children raised by young, energetic parents often receive gifts no amount of money can replace.

Kevin DeYoung observes with painful clarity:

"At no time in history have people been having fewer children. The human race seems to have grown tired of itself."

A culture that fears babies is a culture in decline.

WHEN SLOPES BECOME CLIFFS

1. Normalize contraception.

2. Normalize abortion.

3. Redefine personhood.

4. Devalue the disabled, the sick, and the elderly.

5. Introduce assisted suicide.

6. Normalize the disposal of the inconvenient.

This progression is not theoretical. Nazi Germany followed it step by step—beginning with abortion for the "unfit," then infanticide, then children, then adults, and finally entire populations.

Today, in parts of America, abortion is permitted up to the moment before birth. Babies born alive after failed abortions have been left to die on metal tables.

I know this reality personally.

I once stood beside Gianna Jessen at the North Carolina legislature—a survivor of a saline abortion who lived because one nurse defied orders. Her twin brother did not survive. Gianna pleaded with lawmakers to protect babies born alive. They refused.

The slope is no longer slippery.

It is vertical.

A society that forgets the worth of its smallest members will soon forget the worth of any of them. And when human beings are starved of meaning, love, and belonging, they will seek substitutes wherever they can find them.

Before long, the emptiness created by this unraveling demanded to be filled.

42

Love Hunger

"You know my foolishness; my wrongdoings aren't hidden from you."

—PSALM 69:5

Love hunger is not about romance. It is about absence.

It begins early, when a child grows up without secure attachment—without the steady presence of a father, without emotional safety, without the quiet assurance that someone will stay. When that hunger goes unmet, it does not disappear. It waits. And it looks for substitutes.

When my grandparents died, the fragile fabric of belonging dissolved with them.

Into that vacuum stepped culture.

We baby-boomers were the first television generation. Television, movies and music do not create the hunger, but they give it a language. Romantic love was presented as rescue. This wasn't a malicious lie; it was a faulty promise.

I did not know the word *lonely* then. I only knew the ache—the constant low-grade yearning to be seen, chosen, secured. Like many girls of my generation, I yearned for and imagined imagine connection The culture offered stories where love fixed everything. I eagerly absorbed them.

Love hunger does not always look reckless. Sometimes it looks industrious.

I learned early how to entertain myself. Out of loneliness came curiosity, initiative, and imagination. I built a pen-pal network long before such language existed—writing template letters and mailing them to "Any Fifth-Grade Girl" in towns across America and even overseas. The system worked. Letters came back. Real friendships formed. I built a community on paper because I needed one in life.

That same hunger fueled learning, achievement, work. I earned Girl Scout badges, organized projects, and pursued excellence. These were good things. But even good things can be recruited to fill a deeper ache they were never meant to satisfy.

Love hunger also makes people vulnerable to shame.

I wanted to appear normal.

As I grew older, love hunger matured into something more dangerous.

Romantic attachment or attention felt like oxygen. Disapproval felt catastrophic. I became adept at absorbing mistreatment, appeasing bullies, and blaming myself. Somewhere early, a taproot formed: *I am not worth being loved or treated well.* That belief did not arrive suddenly; it accumulated quietly.

Culture reinforced it.

When a society detaches from moral foundations it trains people—especially women—to confuse love with all kinds of counterfeits, especially modern views of love marriage.

Love hunger flourishes where truth is postponed.

When children grow up without secure attachment, and adults are trained to pursue desire without restraint, the result is not freedom but fragmentation. Broken families produce broken expectations, which produce broken promises, which require broken logic to sustain.

And still, God wastes nothing.

The ache that once drove me toward needy love hunger eventually drove me toward truth. The hunger itself became a signpost—not of deficiency, but of design. We were made for attachment, covenant, and faithfulness. When those are missing, the soul protests.

Love hunger is not healed by indulgence. It is healed by restoration.

A culture that forgets the worth of its smallest members soon forgets the worth of every member. And when meaning collapses, people search desperately for substitutes—power, pleasure, control.

That search does not end well.

What began as discomfort with children hardened into resentment toward fertility. What hardened into ideology became law. What became law reshaped medicine, education, and the family itself.

We did not reach this moment suddenly. Cultures rarely fall all at once. They erode—one concession, one silence, one "necessary compromise" at a time. The slope beneath us has been tilting for decades. And now, it has become steep.

Loss, however, is never the final word.

What has been fractured can be repaired. What has been forgotten can be remembered. And what has been buried beneath layers of fear, propaganda, and distraction can be uncovered again—if we are willing to look honestly and act courageously.

Restoration does not begin with institutions or policies, but with truth. With the refusal to numb ourselves. With the humility to ask not only *what happened to us*, but *what kind of people must we become now.* When truth is recovered—about history, about human nature, about love and responsibility—the path forward becomes visible again.

The next step is not despair, nor nostalgia, nor rage. It is recovery. It is re-anchoring us in reality. It is the slow, demanding work of restoring what was lost—in homes, in consciences, and in the soul of a nation.

And that work begins with seeking truth.

Part IV

Restoring What Was Lost

43

Truth Seeking

"Woe to those who call evil good and good evil."
—ISAIAH 5:20 NIV

Being on the receiving end of one of God's "woes" is terrible. God is love, but He is also just. It is far better to fall at His feet now, pleading for mercy, than to face Him later still unrepentant.

If we dislike how God ordered the universe, railing against Him is futile. He is the Creator; we are His creation. We can either seek and trust the living God and His wise providence—or rebel, spiraling into deeper confusion of heart, mind, and soul. Each night, He reminds us who is in charge: He makes us sleep. When He spoke the universe into being, He did not ask our opinion. Turning our back on Him is always a step from light into darkness.

EARLY SIGNALS

During my later elementary years, there were occasional weekends when I was allowed to stay with my mother instead of going to my grandparents' house. I don't know why, but on some of those Sundays, I would quietly get dressed in the morning and walk nearly a mile to Reformation Lutheran Church on Loch Raven Boulevard.

I slipped into the sanctuary alone, found a seat, and stayed through the service. When it ended, I left with the other worshippers. No one ever spoke to me. No one offered me a ride home. I simply walked back to our apartment and found my mother still asleep in bed. I doubt she ever knew I had gone to church.

Books were already working on me. I had heard about On the Road (1957) and later devoured A Walk Across America (1979) by Peter Jenkins. Jenkins had set out to discover what America, and its people were really like. His adventures—especially his conversion to Christ while living with a Black family in their trailer—moved me deeply. His story stirred the same hunger growing inside me: a longing for truth, for people, and for the real America.

The day after my high school graduation in 1969, I moved to Ocean City, Maryland. I rented a house with three other girls and landed what felt like the dream job—waitressing at Phillips Crab House. My mother came to stay with us for a vacation, and I loved having her there.

Life felt almost perfect. I made good money at Phillips and spent my days at the beach until it was time to work in the late afternoon. On days off, I stayed by the water until evening, when families packed up for baths and dinner and the surfers finally took over the waves. Those quiet hours—watching surfers glide across the crystal-blue Atlantic—were serene and almost holy.

The beach culture and the emerging hippie movement promised meaning through freedom—freedom of dress, freedom of thought, freedom from rules and expectations. But the promise never quite satisfied.

Truth Seeking

One snowy winter day while living in Annapolis, Maryland, restless for something more, I decided I needed to get on the road myself. I wanted to see the country, to test ideas, to expand my search for truth.

Hitchhiking was as common then as breathing. It was far safer than it is now—though still foolish. I was fearless and hungry for adventure. I stuck out my thumb and began traveling.

I found rides up and down the East Coast, then across the country, and finally straight into California. I fell in love with Southern California—the weather, the people, the beauty. I had always wanted to be a "surfer girl," or at least a "California girl," and now I was there.

Along the way, I met all kinds of people—including Christians in a park handing out sandwiches and gospel tracts to hippies. One tract, which included the passage on love from 1 Corinthians, captured me completely. I read it, reread it, and kept it. I had never seen love defined that way before, and it stirred something deep inside me.

ON THE ROAD

My search for truth led me to enroll in a World Religions course at Anne Arundel Community College in Annapolis. I read every sacred text assigned—and many beyond the syllabus—related to the major world religions. I was on a mission to think my way through the question that would not leave me alone: Was there one True Truth for all people, or was Hinduism correct in its claim that there are many gods, many paths to god, and that we are all part of the divine?

As I studied, I began praying with increasing urgency—asking that God, whoever He was and wherever He might be, would reveal Himself to me. I prayed that He would be real, and that He would let me know He was there.

One day, while hitchhiking to class, a woman driving with her young daughter stopped and offered me a ride. She later told me she never stopped for hitchhikers—but that day, she did. Before dropping me off, she invited me to a Bible study her husband led on Friday evenings for college students. He was a physics professor at the Naval Academy.

I'm not sure how it happened, but I went. That decision changed my life.

That family became one of God's great gifts to me. They loved me, helped me, and remained part of my life for years. That Christmas, they took me with them to hear Handel's *Messiah* at the Naval Academy chapel. I felt as though I had stepped halfway into heaven. My dear mother later bought me the vinyl record set, and I memorized nearly all the lyrics—everyone drawn directly from Scripture. Handel has remained a sacred thread of Christmas joy for me ever since.

Still, I continued my study of world religions, determined to test each one for truth. I read the Hindu *Bhagavad Gita*, Taoism's *Tao Te Ching*, Islam's *Quran*, the *Book of Mormon*, and the Baha'i sacred text *Kitab-i-Aqdas*. I studied Buddha's Noble Eightfold Path. I read deeply in both the Old and New Testaments of the Bible. I later came to recommend a firsthand account titled *Seeking Allah, Finding Jesus*, which chronicles a devout Muslim's journey to Christianity.

During this time, I devoured *The Best of C. S. Lewis*, loaned to me by a kind student from St. John's College. Lewis's clear thinking arrived like oxygen in a suffocating fog. His voice was sanity. His reasoning reshaped my mind and changed my life.

Music also exerted its philosophical pull. Bob Dylan, George Harrison's fascination with Eastern spirituality, and many others competed for space in my imagination. The soundtrack of the era was not morally neutral—it carried ideas, assumptions, and invitations.

Jefferson Airplane chillingly captured the spirit of the age when they declared, "We are forces of chaos and anarchy." The line was celebrated as liberation. But chaos dressed up as virtue always ends the same way.

What such declarations never acknowledge is their inevitable outcome: when people refuse to govern themselves morally, someone else will do it for them. Anarchy never leads to freedom. It leads to control—often enforced by the very powers it once claimed to oppose.

I began to recognize the pattern repeating throughout history. Nero blamed Christians for Rome's fires. The Nazis blamed Jews for Germany's collapse. Deception always shifts blame onto the innocent and the vulnerable.

I witnessed the same pattern again on January 6, 2021.

Countless ordinary, law-abiding American citizens traveled to Washington, D.C., to attend a rally and pray for the nation on the Capitol lawn. Riotous behavior was orchestrated and then blamed on the peaceful crowd. In the aftermath, homes of innocent citizens were raided by the FBI.

Many lost everything—jobs, livelihoods, property, reputations, voting rights, and freedom itself. Grandparents, young mothers, and military veterans were imprisoned without trial or denied basic constitutional protections. Others were funneled into D.C. courts where fairness was impossible. All were convicted on inflated or fabricated charges and sentenced to prison or house arrest.

Some were subjected to treatment that mirrored Soviet-style gulags: denied medical care, adequate food, religious services, clothing, and even blankets. Others were pepper-sprayed or beaten while held in solitary confinement—not for violence, but for attending a rally that questioned government authority.

In my lifetime, I have seen countless marches, protests, and demonstrations in Washington, D.C. Never had I witnessed my beloved Republic treat its own citizens this way.

For those who doubt that such things happen in supposedly "free" societies, Aleksandr Solzhenitsyn's *The Gulag Archipelago* stands as a permanent warning—a firsthand account of what occurs when the state decides truth is optional and power is supreme.

SEARCH FOR MEANING

The Search for meaning was a large part of the Hippie culture. I followed George Harrison into the Eastern thinking. I taught yoga and tried meditating, though I never did it well at it. The sought-after state was becoming one with everything because everything was a part of God. God was impersonal; nothing personal about the pantheistic god/s. I later called this form of pantheism "pan-everythingism", a Schaefferian term.

I came to realize that my resistance to the desired Nirvana state was because it is the opposite of what God calls us to do. He says, "Come, let us reason together!" Which means thinking, intellectual endeavor, communication, and interchange. with the infinite-personal God who is there, not far off, impossible to reach.

I am designed by God to think rationally and reason with Him which is amazing. He says this reasoning will lead us to "Though your sins be as scarlet they shall be as white as snow; though they be red like crimson, they shall be as wool." God also clearly says that we must seek to "Renew our Minds." Eastern philosophy, to me, is anti-intellectual. Christianity is the opposite: renewal of our mind, rationality, and thinking clearly.

I began a habit of regularly going into the historic St. Anne's Episcopal church in Annapolis during the daytime when it was empty. Occasionally, I was a one-person audience when an organist would be practicing. I would walk around the sanctuary studying the stories on the stained-glass windows, or sit in a pew, listen to the quiet, and pray. One day, desperate and sincere, I whispered aloud:

"Jesus, others are telling me that You are God, and the only God. If this is all true and you are the living God, I want to know it and want to know You. If you are there, would you reveal and make Yourself real to me? Help me to know."

He did.

Almost immediately, He began doing countless things to my life. He was, in fact, very much there. One day, I suddenly felt overcome with the reality of how much sin and badness was in me, how much I had hurt others and done wrong throughout my life. I was so overcome with consuming grief, even despair, that I wanted to roll into a ball and die. Right on the heels of that came a flood of light. I was completely overcome with the reality that I had been forgiven for everything. I knew I was free. People noticed the change. There would be setbacks ahead, but never a turning back.

One window in St. Anne's intrigued me as I pondered its meaning. "The fear of the Lord is the beginning of wisdom, and knowledge of the Holy One is understanding." (Proverbs 9:10 NIV). I still think about the depths of meaning surrounding fear of the Lord. Jesus did say, "Do not be afraid of those who kill the body but cannot kill the soul. Rather, be afraid of the One who can destroy both soul and body in hell." (Matthew 10:28 NIV). Fearing the Lord, for me, means maintaining awe and reverence. The King of Kings was, is, and always will remain on His throne.

SHELTER AND FORMATION

A few months after I gave my life in totality to become a resolute follower of Jesus—not merely a believer, but a disciple—I boarded a plane bound for Geneva, Switzerland.

I was rendered speechless by my first sight of the French Swiss Alps. As with God Himself, one can only stand in awe. From Geneva, I traveled by train to Lausanne, then by bus up into the Alps toward the small village of Huémoz.

With every turn along the narrow mountain road, I wondered if this might be my last day on earth. When the bus finally stopped, it left me and my luggage on the side of a breathtaking mountain road, facing the Dent du Midi range, framed by endless snow-covered pastures. As spring arrived, I marveled at the wildflowers carpeting the mountainsides—a vast, living tapestry of color and life.

The village itself was simple and beautiful: one small store, a chapel, and a post office, accompanied by the distant clanging of cowbells. Wooden chalets were nestled into the mountainside, each one carefully designed to preserve the natural terrain and wildlife. The chalet where I lived, Les Sapins—*The Pines*—welcomed me with a bed of lily-of-the-valley blossoms by the front door.

On my first walk up the mountain to find my lodging, I encountered a man wearing knickers and hiking boots. He stopped and introduced himself as Dr. Schaeffer. We walked together for a time, talking easily. He radiated a warmth I had rarely encountered. When our paths parted, he paused, smiling broadly, and said words I can still hear clearly:

"I am so glad you are here!"

Thus began one of the most meaningful seasons of my life—studying and working at L'Abri, "The Shelter," the study community founded by Francis and Edith Schaeffer.

Each weekday, I studied at Farel House, a small chalet beneath the L'Abri chapel. I sat at my desk with books, notebooks, a dictionary, and reel-to-reel recordings of lectures that opened an entirely new world. Bible studies and lecture series covered philosophy, art, science, history, music, culture, logic, and theology. I began with Dr. Schaeffer's study of Romans, then devoured everything I could.

Afternoons were spent working in the garden or helping Edith Schaeffer prepare meals in the kitchen. Evenings often brought lectures in the chapel, where scholars such as Os Guinness and Hans Rookmaaker spoke. I began learning about the Reformation and its enduring significance. Jane Stuart Smith, a former world-renowned opera singer, lived at L'Abri at the time. She lectured on music and sometimes sang during Sunday worship. I can still hear her voice—especially when she sang *"Balm in Gilead."* It shook me to my core in a way no voice ever has before or since.

On days off, I hiked alone or with friends. One day, I discovered a small flowing pond surrounded by wildflowers. Sitting there to eat my lunch, surrounded by pristine beauty, remains one of the most serene moments of my life.

"He leads me beside still waters and restores my soul."

Never had those words felt so literal.

One day during my study of Romans, something extraordinary happened. As I listened to the lecture, gazing out the window at the Dent du Midi, it felt as though lightning struck my soul. I must have spoken aloud:

"This really is the Truth."

I knew with absolute certainty that my search was over. Jesus is who He said He is. The gospel is true. Everything I had been seeking had finally found me. I was never the same. There was no turning back.

At L'Abri, I attended lectures, studied diligently, and listened quietly during meals. Often, I barely understood what was being discussed. The vocabulary was foreign; the ideas were new and complex. I was bombarded with words I had never heard before. Afraid of revealing how uneducated I felt, I stayed silent and took notes.

I began writing down long lists of unfamiliar words. During study time, I poured over the dictionary, carefully copying definitions into my notebooks. I learned about philosophical presuppositions—how they shape worldviews and determine how people interpret reality.

Slowly, something remarkable happened. As my understanding grew, I realized I *was* following. I *was* grasping the ideas. I was understanding—and loving—the pursuit of truth. My mind opened to an entirely new world of intellectual and spiritual clarity, including what it means to live out a Biblical worldview where humanity, as God's image-bearers, is called to take dominion by creating beauty, order, and goodness.

Mealtimes were unlike anything I had ever experienced. Tables were adorned with flowers and candles, even in their simplicity. Edith taught that people—made in the image of God—are worthy of beauty, care, and attention. Beauty was not an indulgence; it was essential to daily life.

My eyes were opening in more ways than one. I realized I had been deceived into believing a false narrative about myself. I was not unintelligent or incapable. I was, in fact, a very intelligent person—and I was finally beginning to recognize it.

Later, I would write a seminary paper on what the Bible teaches about ecology. I learned that God's command to take dominion over the earth was never a license for exploitation, but a call to cultivate and steward creation as a faithful gardener tends a beloved garden. There was no room for greed or cruelty—including toward animals.

From the Schaeffers' lives, I learned how to live the Christian faith fully—intellectually, spiritually, and practically. I learned hospitality, generosity, sincerity, and genuine love. My entire world was transformed.

I have regarded Francis Schaeffer as my spiritual father ever since.

Dr. Francis Schaeffer, Farel House Chapel, Huemoz, Switzerland, 1972

I learned that the finished work of Christ is enough and all we need. Nothing needs to be added nor can be added to His work. I was delivered out of a horrible pit of destruction and set free from bondage to sin, darkness, and fear. I could see reality, with an unprecedented ability to discern and distinguish between right and wrong. I was *"Born Again."* I have confidence in where I am going in this life and for all eternity because I know He is and will always be with me. Never alone.

THE WIDER WORLD

Leaving Huémoz, I joined Youth With A Mission (YWAM) in Lausanne. I never made it to Venice as planned; instead, I traveled across Europe with the YWAM, heard Corrie ten Boom speak in Amsterdam (saw the book and film The Hiding Place), and visited Anne Frank's house.

We stopped in Dachau to tour the concentration camp that had been operated there. Few things could be more difficult to see. One time was enough, but it was necessary for true understanding.

We stayed with the Sisters of Darmstadt, a remarkable Protestant Evangelical group of nuns founded in 1947 by Basilea Schlink. They formed their sisterhood after WWII and built their beautiful community out of the war-torn rubble. I'd never seen happier people than these gracious, hospitable women.

> "When the city was destroyed by an air raid in 1944 the group of young women under their leadership faced the reality of death and eternity. In view of God's holiness, unconfessed sins were brought to light and repented of and gratitude for His forgiveness made way for hearts filled with love for Jesus and a desire to live in community to serve Him. The Evangelical Sisterhood began a few years later."
>
> —(https://kanaan.org/en/)

We traveled to Hurlach, Germany, staying in a castle donated to YWAM. One early morning, while in my room, I beheld Jesus exactly as He is described in the first chapter of Revelation.

Let me explain that I was never a person given to seeking or experiencing supernatural or otherworldly experiences. I am characterized by a deep desire for facts, evidence, and concrete clarity. Each experience must be supported and substantiated by evidence, and by one's reasoning capacity. I was not looking for any type of experience, yet suddenly there He was in front of me, looking at and through me.

> "And when I turned, I saw someone like a son of man, dressed in a robe reaching down to his feet and with a golden sash around his chest. The hair on his head was white like wool, as white as snow, and his eyes were like a blazing fire. His feet were like bronze glowing in a furnace, and his voice was like the sound of rushing waters. In his right hand he held seven stars, and coming out of his mouth was a sharp, double-edged sword. His face was like the sun shining in all its brilliance."
> —REVELATION 1:12-16 NIV

At the time, I was especially drawn to focus on his eyes of fire and his mouth with the double-edged sword. One edge is to protect his people behind Him: the other edge to attack enemies on the way ahead.

I was speechless and frozen but felt no fear, only awe. I did not know and still do not know why He showed Himself to me in this way. I was just a baby Christian. I've noticed countless times in the Bible how God does completely unpredictable, out-of-the-ordinary things. He seeks out one very unimportant person or event, not just crowds clamoring to see or hear Him.

One example is the Samaritan woman who was alone at the well. (John 4:5-52). Conversing with a woman, and a Samaritan one at that, was completely unacceptable in the time and culture. Another time, Jesus went out of his way to visit the Gadarenes. There, he met just one man who was suffering from horrible demonic oppression and possession.

This man suffered day and night and lived in obscurity in a graveyard. (Mark 5:1-20). Jesus focused on this one man in great need and healed him. The next time he visited the Gadarenes, the entire village thronged to him seeking healing and help. The healed man had spoken and had demonstrated the evidence of a completely changed life. Same with the Samaritan woman.

I still do not know why He showed Himself to me. Perhaps simply to say, I see you. I love you. Tell others.

My Graduation from Covenant Seminary with an M.A. in Religion & Counseling

I later attended Covenant Seminary in St. Louis, Missouri because Dr. Schaeffer encouraged me to do so before I left L'abri. My respect for him was enormous so I proceeded with my life as he recommended. Years later numerous people strongly admonished me to attend law school at night or part time. I wish I had listened to those words of advice from those who cared about me and recognized my abilities.

44

Robbing God

> "Bring the full tithe into the storehouse, that there may be food in my house. Test me in this," says the Lord Almighty, "and see if I will not open the floodgates of heaven and pour out so much blessing that there will not be room enough to store it."
> —MALACHI 3:10 ESV

When I became a Christian at age twenty, I was like a sponge—hungry to learn, eager to obey. One of the first lessons I learned was about tithing: giving the first fruits of one's harvest or income—ten percent—back to God. It can only be done by faith. Without faith, we will never feel we have "enough" to give.

How easy it is to rationalize; to say we give our time or talents instead. But tithing is not about God needing our money; it's about freeing our hearts from fear. Nothing reveals our trust—or our unbelief—more clearly than how we handle what we call "ours."

When I first learned this principle, I obeyed immediately and never stopped. As a college student, when I earned ten dollars, I rejoiced that one dollar would go to God. When I earned a hundred, ten went to Him right away.

Through decades of lean and abundant seasons, I have never failed to give at least ten percent—and always strive to give more. The freedom from fear and want is real. True freedom lives inside generosity.

God loves cheerful givers. He gives joy along with more blessings when we give more. I know it as a fact from my life experience. There have been times of severe loss, setbacks, and uncertainty. I knew that giving was even more vital for me during the most financially difficult times of life. God gets his ten percent of *all* incoming money first, before anything else, bills, debts, necessities, or even basic needs. He won't fail on His part.

TESTING GOD'S FAITHFULNESS

God invites us to test Him. Not in defiance—but in trust. He says, *"Test Me in this."* How astonishing that the Creator gives us the opportunities to prove His faithfulness.

"Whosoever sows sparingly will also reap sparingly, and whosoever sows generously will also reap generously." (*2 Corinthians 9:6 NIV*).

The less we think we can afford to give, the more we must give.

The tighter our grip, the emptier our hands. The more we open them, the more He fills them.

We don't give to get more. But receiving more is the natural consequence of giving to God.

THE WIDOW'S EXAMPLE

In *1 Kings 17*, the widow of Zarephath faced starvation during a severe famine. When Elijah asked her to share her last bit of flour and oil with him before she nourished her son and herself, she did, and as a result, he promised that her food supplies would not run out. This act of faithfulness and obedience resulted in a miraculous provision of food for her and her son throughout the famine. That story isn't myth—it's recorded history. God honors trust, and He provides.

Jesus taught, "Where your treasure is, there your heart will be also." He wants our whole heart, not a partial offering. It grieves me how fear—or selfishness—keeps so many from discovering the abundance that begins with open hands.

"It is more blessed to give than to receive."
—ACTS 20:35 NIV

The route to a blessed life is found in radical generosity.

"A generous person will prosper; whoever refreshes others will be refreshed."
—PROVERBS 11:25 NIV

Generosity results in personal benefit and blessing. Is God unreliable or a liar? Or is He one hundred percent trustworthy? Does He say things He doesn't mean? Or is he always faithful to His promises?

THE HEART OF THE MATTER
Everything we own already belongs to God. We are stewards, not owners. When we tithe, we simply return to Him a small portion of His own gift.

Throughout the Old Testament, the Israelites were told to give a minimum of ten percent of their resources (income or money) to God. That tithe or "tenth part" was a requirement of the law.

The New Testament emphasizes giving from a willing and cheerful heart rather than obligation.

Tithing our money should remain a priority, even while paying down debt, as it demonstrates faith and obedience to God.

- "Give, and it will be given to you. A good measure, pressed down, shaken together and running over, will be poured into your lap. For with the measure you use, it will be measured to you."—(Luke 6:38 NIV). Giving will be rewarded.

- "Whoever is kind to the poor lends to the LORD, and he will reward them for what they have done."—(Proverbs 19:17 NIV). Giving to those in need is a loan to God, who promises to repay.

- "Give what you have decided in your heart to give, not reluctantly or under compulsion, for God loves a cheerful giver."—(2 Corinthians 9:7 NIV). The key to giving is a willing, joyful heart.

- "For where your treasure is, there your heart will be also"—(Matthew 6:21 NIV). Giving is connected to one's priorities and affections.

FAITH IN ACTION
Is stepping out in faith easy? Even Jesus, the perfect, sinless, Godman incarnate, prayed to His Father that, if possible, the cup of the cross ahead of Him would be removed. Could there be another way to erase the sins of His rebellious image-bearers? Jesus clung to faith in His Father, believing His promise of His resurrection after three days. He went forward in faith, no matter what.

So don't wait another day.

Test Him.

Take God at His word.

You will find, as I have, that the windows of heaven are still open.

45

Cannot Have Children?

"A mother's grief and a mother's joy come from the same place."
— MADELEINE L'ENGLE

Having children was both a physical and spiritual battle for me. Few women could have longed more intensely for the blessing of motherhood. During my college years, I chose to believe God when He said that children are a gift from Him—without qualification or redaction.

In my twenties, two physicians told me I would never be able to have children because of health complications. My response was immediate and instinctive:

"Just tell me I can't—so I can prove you wrong."

Both doctors urged surgery and heavy medication. I declined. Instead, I began researching natural fertility approaches with determination and prayer.

At twenty-eight, I gave birth to my first child. That labor lasted thirty-six hours and ended with forceps delivery. Though I admired home births, I never quite managed one myself. Still, when my daughter arrived, I felt as though I had invented motherhood. I nursed her—as I did all my babies—until around age two, except for my one living son, who happily weaned himself early because solid food held greater appeal.

In the early 1980s, Franklin Square Hospital was among the busiest maternity hospitals in Baltimore. My second baby was born there. My third was born at the Baltimore Birthing Center with midwives—the closest I came to a home birth. My fourth and fifth pregnancies were both boys. Both ended before birth.

They were beautiful, perfectly formed, miniature sons whom I held in my hands.

JONATHAN AND JACOB

Jonathan, my only true home birth, arrived too early to breathe on his own. Alone, with only my doctor on the phone, I followed her instructions: cut the umbilical cord, wrap him in a towel, and get to the hospital immediately. Friends arrived in time—one to drive me, another to stay with my toddler.

At the hospital, I learned that when a baby dies before or during birth, the remains are routinely disposed of by incineration. I could not bear that. I asked that Jonathan's small body be placed in a plastic container so I could bury him properly.

Some found this strange. I did not. Scripture consistently treats the human body with reverence, even in death. God's people carried Joseph's bones from Egypt. Names in biblical genealogies are not abstractions; they are lives known to God.

That reverence shaped my decision.

We later buried Jonathan and his brother Jacob together in a church cemetery in Howard County, Maryland. A friend sang from Job:

"Naked came I from my mother's womb,
And naked shall I return.
The Lord gives, and the Lord takes away;
Blessed be the name of the Lord."

Medical explanations for the deaths never came.
Then something wholly unexpected occurred.
I am not a person who seeks experiences. I am emotional, yes—but deeply fact-oriented and skeptical by nature. One ordinary day, while fully awake in my home, I turned—and there stood my two sons, Jonathan and Jacob.

They were radiant with joy. Between them stood Jesus.
No words were spoken, yet everything was communicated—mind to mind, heart to heart. My sons appeared as strong, grown young men. Their faces shone with peace. They wanted me to know that they were whole, happy, and grateful—grateful for life, and for having been loved. They were waiting for me.

I have never doubted that encounter. My sons are real. They were taken home early, spared this world's sorrows. I miss them, but I rejoice that they are safe with Him.

THE MIRACLE BABY

> "Miracles do not cluster, and what has happened once may never happen again. But the age of miracles is not past."
> —DANIEL WEBSTER

When I became pregnant again, fear accompanied every step. My church prayed continually for this child's survival. Around that time, a friend mailed me a torn magazine article about Dr. Jerome Check, a fertility specialist in Philadelphia researching pregnancy hormones.

I contacted his office immediately.

Dr. Check was compassionate and precise. He explained that during early pregnancy, progesterone produced by the corpus luteum sustains life until the placenta takes over. In my case, that transition failed—causing repeated losses.

Treatment began immediately: progesterone injections, suppositories, and oral supplements, monitored weekly. A nurse from church administered my injections. We prayed constantly.

Near the same gestational point when my sons had died, I felt compelled to stop by my obstetrician's office simply to hear the heartbeat. The nurse searched with the Doppler. Nothing. An ultrasound followed. The baby lay motionless. No heartbeat.

The medical team confirmed the death. I was scheduled for induction the next morning.

That night, grief and disbelief wrestled inside me. My pastor, Rev. George Taylor, asked if he could bring friends to pray. When someone suggested praying for the baby's life, I protested: "My baby is dead. I need prayer for the delivery."

Pastor Taylor replied gently, "We don't picket funerals—but let it not be said we didn't ask for miracles."

All night, one verse echoed within me: "I am the resurrection and the life."

Morning came. At the hospital, one final ultrasound was performed. The moment the probe touched my belly, the screen lit up. The baby was alive—moving, kicking.

The room fell silent.

The hospital later called it a mistake. Those who knew the facts did not. That child was later born by emergency C-section and grew into adulthood, becoming a mother herself.

Dr. Check still practices through the Cooper Institute for

Reproductive Hormonal Disorders. I remain deeply grateful for his care.

A FAMILY IN HEAVEN AND ON EARTH

In total, I bore five daughters and one son who lived, along with four children who await me in heaven: Jonathan, Jacob, Taylor, and Susannah.

I watched Susannah's heart weaken on ultrasound despite every medical effort. When she died, I grieved—but I knew she was safe with her brothers.

Each of their names is written in my heart—and in His.

When people once remarked that six children were "too many," I would ask, "Which ones should we get rid of?"

Our culture increasingly views children as burdens rather than blessings. Too often, finances replace faith, and convenience replaces trust. Yet Scripture reminds us to ask daily for our bread—not to hoard security at the expense of life.

Things wear out. People endure.

When we trust God with our families—whether He gives many children, few, or none—we learn that His purposes are always good.

46

Teaching Freedom: A Journey Through Fear, Family, and Home

"Children are not a distraction from more important work. They are the most important work."

—C.S. LEWIS

FEAR'S ANTIDOTES

When I was a little girl, I often felt like a little doll with a blank expression on its face, sitting alone amidst the furniture. That was my childhood world.

The fears that became a backdrop for my childhood robbed me of fun times. This makes me want to do something to rescue other children from unnecessary childhood fears. My own children were permitted to sleep with the light on or whatever made them feel more comfortable and secure. When they expressed any fear or uncertainty about the difference between reality and unreality, I wanted to listen.

I tried to demonstrate care and do everything possible to soothe their questions, fears, and concerns. I was super attentive and affectionate when they were babies and toddlers, but regretfully, I don't think that I carried it on long enough. I do know that I invested hours reading to my children, right next to them on the sofa. Sometimes, I started falling asleep, and they would beg me to read just one more chapter. We read many books together. We listened to *Peter and the Wolf* with a library record and acted out the story together.

When my children grew older, we often all sat together and told a story. One of us would start the story, then stop, and the next person would add to the tale, then stop, and on it went. Each of us could take the story in whatever direction we chose. We all did our best to add drama. I recall one time when it was my turn to spin the tale, I was so dramatic with the story that my third daughter shuddered like she was watching an action movie.

My children and I did many fun things. We picked berries. We regularly went to the library and brought home a shopping cart of books for everyone's age. I'd been so scared of too many things and decided I would do all I could to prevent my children from falling into similar pits.

I never really learned to swim other than doggie paddling, as I was afraid of putting my head under water. I had too many fears that robbed me of childhood fun. I think this began when I was an older toddler and at the Atlantic Ocean with Gran and her extended family. I remember falling under the water and being unable to get out. My head was underneath, and I managed to hold up one arm for help.

A relative came after what seemed like a very long time, grabbed my hand, and pulled me out. Then she just left me without any words or touch of comfort for my little trauma. I didn't hear "Are you okay, honey?" or anything. I was so fearful of someone throwing me into a pool that, as a teenager, I missed out on going with friends to local swimming clubs on hot summer days.

My fears prevented me from following in my parents' footsteps as gymnasts and swimmers, but I made up for it with roller skating and dancing. I went skating every week for years. Dancing began with tap and ballet thanks to Gran Mildred paying for it and taking me. I liked tap dancing the best. When my school started having dances, I was always there. On summer nights, there was dancing every week at local swimming clubs.

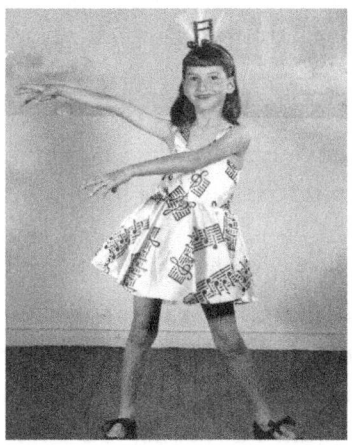

I was born to love dancing!

As an adult, several times weekly, I attended the East and West Coast swing dances. Those were my athletic endeavors in addition to regular times at the gym doing aerobics and weightlifting. I never sat and watched. I danced every dance. Real dancers are serious athletes, and it can get competitive. Some good dancers dislike dancing with beginners, while others will do so to help develop a dance community.

For several years, I was part of a worship dance ensemble at my church, and we often included dance performances as part of worship services. My favorite was when we danced to Rich Mullins' song, *Ready for the Storm*.

I started swimming lessons early with my oldest children and made sure they all learned to swim and enjoy it. A victory in my mothering efforts! I wanted to expose my children to as many opportunities as possible so they could decide what they liked best.

I feared many things in gym classes. Scared to roll over, tumble with my head, scared on the balance beam, scared I might get hit with a ball. My parents were both gymnasts! Interestingly, I loved the rings and was decent at rope climbing.

My father was a champion rope climber while a Plebe at the Naval Academy.

I got my children involved in their interests the best I could afford and did not incite their father too much. He was generally opposed to fun activities or events. He even became angry with me for taking them to the library, stating that I would do an inadequate job of screening them from bad books. This was hilarious, as no one was more of a protective mother bear than I was.

My children attended lessons and participated in gymnastics, ballet, hip-hop, dance, modeling, soccer, roller skating, lacrosse, swimming, sewing, quilting, music, and more. They were on the gymnastics and swimming teams. If they asked to try something, I did all I could to say yes and give them a chance.

The older children studied the Suzuki violin. One of my quieter daughters asked if she could learn violin. She usually didn't make requests, so I knew I had to listen to her and let her try. As usual, I was strongly opposed by their father. I used my earnings to rent a violin and hired another mother in the homeschool group who had graduated from the renowned Eastman School of Music in Rochester, NY.

The music teacher told me after the second lesson that my daughter was highly gifted and, though brand new, didn't squeak on the violin! I continued her lessons, despite home opposition, and she later performed in her university orchestra. I loved hearing her play so much.

My daughter during her early violin lessons

One of many homeschool field trips, photographed during a family visit to the zoo.

I used the money that I earned from my home businesses to pay for lessons and equipment, travel costs with a travel team, and to attend athletic games, whether at home or on the road. I especially fell in love with lacrosse too. The players are so well padded and protected that you cannot see who it is underneath all the uniform protection.

One night, I hosted dinner at our house for the team. When I saw the players without their uniforms, I realized I didn't know who they were. I'd never seen their faces before that night.

The only genuinely American sport, lacrosse, was invented by the Native Americans and was originally how they fought and settled disputes. Lacrosse is so exciting that if you talk to someone for a minute, you've missed the non-stop action. Some think baseball is slow and boring if they don't understand it. I like baseball, but no one could think lacrosse is boring.

My second daughter became very involved in my home nutrition and health business, selling Shaklee products and doing nutrition workshops. She liked getting on the phone with customers and the home office, placing orders, and developing good relational skills. I did very well for years with Shaklee at home while being with my children and homeschooling the best I knew how.

I believed in the products and helped moms and their kids with their health. I earned enough for me and the children's clothes, school supplies, haircuts, and extracurricular activities. I maintained an earned Shaklee bonus car for years and got a new one every two years.

My oldest daughter didn't prefer the Shaklee business, but she and I enjoyed another business together, selling mother-daughter dresses with a company that was called Bonny Lass. This company made the sweetest mother-daughter outfits and had bow ties and vests for boys that matched their sisters. My daughter and I had no difficulty scheduling home parties where we wore and displayed clothes and took orders that were shipped to the customers.

We had fun working together. I think it was great that some of my children learned business skills at home as part of their "schooling." Sales is mastering the art of persuasion and being a caring servant of others. Years later, I ran my own insurance business and hired the youngest children to put together client folders and other odd jobs. My son was masterful at negotiating things like a rate increase per folder he prepared.

The older children and I did plenty of cooking and baking. We bought 50 lb. bags of wheat berries, ground them in our flour mill, then used our Bosch bread machine to make fresh bread several times per week. We made our own yogurt, soups, pasta sauce, and more. Everyone learned to fold laundry.

The three oldest girls and I took sewing and quilting lessons. We shared many craft projects together, including machine quilting with our Bernina. I saved from my earnings for the Bernina, a serger, and a sewing table that held both. I enjoyed smocking dresses and bonnets.

I could have done better at all good things, like affection, praying with them, and laughing with them more. I was there most of the time. My presence could be seen and heard, even if I was sometimes busy on the phone with a customer, conducting my business. I recall when the older ones were young teens, asking the children who was "cuddly-wuddly." My oldest daughter announced that she was. We had fun together.

I homeschooled my children as long as I could until our family was blown apart. I know they think I did an inadequate job, but I tried so much. One of my daughters complained that it was my teaching inadequacy when she had difficulty with college math. Keeping with my habit of not taking up for myself, I was quiet. I wish I'd said, "I went to school all the time but had struggles with math." And I wish I'd said, "Welcome to reality, where everyone has difficulties."

As the family grew, the older children helped immensely with the things like cooking, fixing the younger ones' hair, and much more. We became a unit, all pitching in to the tasks at hand. I wanted them to learn to work as well as pursue their academic studies.

My perspective and observations are that whatever didn't go well for my children as they grew into adults, was my own fault. I was responsible for the difficulties of the universe or certainly anything in their own lives. I became the family scapegoat who could do nothing right or well; I'd only failed as a mother and was never there for my children.

I wonder sometimes who they think carried them, gave birth to them, fed them, changed their diapers, potty trained them, cared for them, and helped them learn so many skills. I was there when they were sick, upset, and had to undergo necessary surgery. I studied and fought hard for their health and sought natural, non-invasive alternatives whenever possible.

Sometimes a child or even an adult can be stricken with fear over something trivial and insignificant. At times, the fears of another can be laughable to us. We can help others to see through fear fog. With a bit of help, any fearful person can recognize that entertaining unwarranted fearful thoughts is ludicrous.

This is one reason children need parents, and people need each other. We can help reality-test one another's fears and provide rational feedback and guidance. It amazes me now that I lived so many years in isolation with my fears. No one knew how scared I was or of the monsters and vampires that roamed about my thoughts, plaguing me—especially when the sun went down.

I wonder why the adults in my world didn't question why I had tried any maneuver I could come up with to avoid bedtime. The aversion triggered habits that to this day regulate my biological clock. I doubt that I'll ever achieve being a morning person, though perhaps it is more virtuous and healthier. Hooting with the owls seems less than ideal.

My recommendation to parents is to try your best to keep asking your children questions—not just factual ones that can be answered in a sentence, but open-ended questions such as "What was it like today at school?", "What helps you feel happy?", "What was the best part of your day?" or "What worries you?" We can learn to ask open-ended questions and teach children how to elaborate by asking follow-up questions such as "How so?" or "What do you mean?"

The art of asking open-ended questions and then being a good listener makes one a good conversationalist and it can help others, especially kids, feel much less isolated. Reflecting is another superb skill—saying back what we heard: "So, you felt hurt when they called you names?" Reflecting helps others feel heard, valued, important, and understood. It's a golden skill.

I wish I'd heard someone take an interest and ask me, "What did you do all day with the babysitter?" or "What is that book about?" A simple question such as "What are you feeling?" was not something I learned to ask until adulthood. I'm glad I learned such skills later. A good place to start is the classic *How to Win Friends and Influence People* by Dale Carnegie.

Now I think, "If only." If only someone had asked me questions when I was a child, I would have felt much less alone.

TEACHING LIBERTY

> "The philosophy of the school room in one generation will be the philosophy of government in the next."
>
> —ABRAHAM LINCOLN

The modern homeschool movement emerged as parents from many different backgrounds—some inspired by John Holt's progressive "unschooling" ideas, others by Dr. Raymond and Dorothy Moore's faith-based research—challenged the growing uniformity of public education. Both streams shared a conviction that children thrive when they are taught with patience, purpose, and respect for their individuality.

By the early 1980s, the movement had gained national momentum, and in 1983, attorneys Michael Farris and J. Michael Smith founded the Home School Legal Defense Association (HSLDA) to defend the rights of families to teach their children at home. Through their work, homeschooling eventually became legal in all fifty states.

Home education is not a modern experiment. For centuries, it was the natural way that children were taught—long before formal schools became the norm.

The tutorial method, used by royalty and scholars, offered a tailored education that shaped thinkers, inventors, and leaders.

Princes were tutored by philosophers; artists were apprenticed by masters; and in the ordinary homes, parents instructed their children in faith, virtue, and practical skill. Nothing has surpassed this personal form of instruction where lessons follow a child's unique gifts, interests, and pace. Homeschooling, in its truest sense, restores that timeless art of individualized learning.

As a pioneer in the American homeschool movement, I first learned about home education from Dr. James Dobson when he had hosted Raymond and Dorothy Moore to discuss their book *Better Late Than Early*. I was immediately challenged and intrigued. My first thought was, *I could never do that*. Yet something in me knew it was right.

I began learning all I could about how to educate my own children. When I later began our school at home in earnest, there were few curricula or examples that I could follow other than the classical approach of the Calvert School, which missionaries often used. There were no national laws that governed homeschool families; each county, city, and school superintendent developed their own view.

While learning about the benefits of home education, I was confronted by members of the community who thought that I was venturing into something questionable—perhaps even illegal. In those early days, homeschooling was still viewed with suspicion.

Most people I met who were teaching their children at home were themselves public-school teachers. They had seen, from the inside, what was happening in the system and did not want their own children subjected to what they had observed and lived daily as educators. Their example strengthened my resolve that parents, not institutions, are best equipped to recognize and meet the needs of their own children.

Educators such as Charlotte Mason in Britain and Raymond and Dorothy Moore in America shared a belief that true education respects the child's individuality and natural pace. Mason and the Moores alike viewed the home as the best learning environment, encouraging parents to be patient and responsive teachers who nurture curiosity and character rather than pressuring their children for early academic achievement.

Mason used the term "living books" to describe works by authors who loved their subject and conveyed truth with warmth and vitality. These books engage both heart and mind, awakening imagination and moral insight. They stand in sharp contrast to lifeless textbooks that merely recite facts.

Engagement with great books is essential to any culture that hopes to remain free. In early America, high literacy was the norm—ordinary citizens could read complex documents like the *Federalist Papers*, the Bible, and the classical works. Today, even functional literacy has become a national concern.

To recover the moral and intellectual strength of our republic, we must once again value reading and restore the love of books in our homes and schools.

Prior to that era of vast educational freedom, I decided early on that no one else would give their life for my children, however much they cared. No one else would know each child's uniqueness better than I would.

Thinking as a visionary, I realized that the world was our school—anything and everything could be an educational field trip, experience, or lesson.

I often thought that if homeschooling ever became illegal in America, we would buy a small boat and somehow live in international waters so that I could remain free to tutor my own children. That was a serious intention—especially considering that I routinely suffer from seasickness whenever I am on a floating vessel.

Many parents who believe they cannot handle homeschooling are often surprised to discover how realistic it can be. Education at home can take many creative forms. Online curricula, homeschool co-ops, and shared instruction among families make it possible for nearly anyone to participate.

A few other mothers and I once hired a chemistry teacher to come one night each week to teach our high-school students—a reminder that homeschooling can be both flexible and communal. Even parents who must work outside the home can often find ways to make it fit. Home education rarely requires the long hours of institutional schooling, where much time is lost to bureaucracy and distraction. When learning is focused and personal, far more is accomplished in far less time.

Homeschooling was never simply about reading, writing, and arithmetic. It was about freedom—the freedom to think, to believe, and to raise children who could discern truth for themselves. Looking back, I realize that those early days around our kitchen table were more than just lessons; they were a declaration of independence. Families like ours quietly reclaimed what had been surrendered to institutions: the sacred duty of forming the hearts, minds, and souls of the next generation.

In teaching my children at home, I was, in a sense, teaching America how to be free again.

CLOSING REFLECTION

Looking back, I see that every fear I faced as a child, every choice I made as a mother, and every book stacked on our kitchen table became threads in a larger tapestry—one woven with hope, perseverance, and a longing to pass on what truly matters. Teaching my children at home was never about perfection; it was about presence. About forming lives shaped by curiosity, beauty, responsibility, and love.

Freedom is first learned in the home—grounded in truth, nurtured through relationship, and strengthened by the courage to live differently. If my journey proves anything, it is this: ordinary parents, in ordinary homes, can accomplish extraordinary things when they choose to invest their whole hearts in the next generation.

47

Multigenerational Divorce

America's divorce rate remains among the highest in the world. While statistics are often cited, the true cost is rarely measured. Divorce does not simply dissolve a marriage; it fractures a web of relationships that stretches backward and forward through generations. It wounds spouses, disorients children, burdens extended family, weakens communities, and strains churches. What is lost is not only stability, but continuity—the passing on of love, identity, and moral formation.

Divorce magnifies existing fractures. Though sometimes necessary for safety or survival, it is never neutral. It leaves scars even when it is the least harmful option. Children do not experience divorce as an abstract event; they experience it as a rupture in the world they trusted. Grandparents lose the joy and duty of shepherding the young. Family narratives splinter. What should have been a place of refuge becomes a site of grief.

THE COST YOU DON'T SEE

Those outside a troubled home often see very little and judge far too much. Abuse—especially nonphysical abuse—is frequently invisible. Words are twisted. Memory is distorted. Gaslighting clouds reality. Embarrassment and fear seal lips.

Many well-meaning people hold rigid views about divorce without understanding the lived reality of coercion, control, and psychological harm. Others offer quick judgments or "hot takes" that compound the damage. In such environments, victims often remain silent, hoping against hope that change will come. Despite years of effort, prayer, and endurance, real change rarely follows.

When truth is finally spoken, it is often met with disbelief. The abused are told to try harder, forgive more, submit longer. Children learn early that honesty carries consequences, and silence becomes a survival skill.

CHILDREN CARRY WHAT ADULTS LEAVE BEHIND

Children do not need to be told everything, but they sense everything. They absorb tension, fear, and unspoken conflict. They learn what love looks like—or does not look like—by watching. When deception and domination replace trust, children internalize confusion about authority, worth, and truth.

In homes shaped by fear, children learn to read moods, anticipate danger, and adapt themselves to preserve peace. They grow adept at emotional management long before they should. What looks like maturity is often trauma in disguise.

WHEN THE CHURCH MISUNDERSTANDS

Church communities often struggle to respond well. Some, to uphold moral standards, minimize suffering. Others avoid involvement altogether. Both responses leave victims isolated.

Scripture calls for truth, protection of the vulnerable, and justice tempered with mercy. When institutions prioritize appearances over safety, they unintentionally reinforce abuse. Silence, once again, becomes the rule.

THE COURAGE TO BREAK THE PATTERN

Leaving a destructive marriage is not an act of rebellion; it is often an act of survival. It requires courage to step into uncertainty, financial risk, and social judgment. For many, it also means confronting the weight of generational patterns—recognizing that what has been tolerated, excused, or hidden must end.

Breaking such cycles is costly. But refusing to break them is costlier still.

WHAT CHILDREN REMEMBER

In the aftermath of the police removing the abuser from our home, one of my children handed me a small note. It read simply, "Thank you for protecting us."

That sentence did not erase the losses. But it named a truth that mattered: safety had been restored. The cycle had been interrupted.

THE LONG WORK OF HEALING

Divorce does not end pain; it changes its shape. Healing is slow and uneven. It requires truth-telling, forgiveness where possible, and boundaries where necessary. It requires humility, wisdom, and time.

Yet healing is possible. Families can be rebuilt—not always in the form once imagined, but in ways marked by honesty, stability, and renewed hope.

A PRAYER

Lord of truth and mercy,
You see what is hidden and hear what is unspoken.
You know the full weight of what has been endured—by women, by children, by families fractured by fear and control.
Protect the vulnerable.
Heal the wounded.
Give courage to those who must choose between endurance and safety, and wisdom to those called to help them.
Where truth has been named and harm confronted, we ask You now for the deeper work of healing. Teach us forgiveness that does not deny reality, mercy that does not excuse injustice, and boundaries that protect life while leaving room for redemption
Restore what has been broken across generations.
Soften hardened hearts.
Mend relationships where repentance and humility make reconciliation possible.
Bring comfort where restoration is delayed, incomplete, or not yet within reach.
We entrust to You estranged children and grandchildren—those separated by wounds, distance, or misunderstanding. Hold them in Your care. Keep them from bitterness. Let love outlast silence, and truth outlast fear.
Teach us to walk faithfully, to love wisely, and to guard the hearts of the children entrusted to us.
Redeem what has been lost.
Bring light where there has been shadow.
And make all things new, in Your time and by Your grace.
Amen.

48

A New Name

"I will give you a new name that the mouth of the Lord will bestow."

—ISAIAH 62:2

God often changed a person's name when He changed their life.

Abram became Abraham. Sarai became Sarah. Cephas became Peter. Saul became Paul.

A new name marked a new identity—a transformation of heart, destiny, and purpose.

A trusted medical professional, who knew me for many years, strongly supported the decision. A dear friend went with me to the courthouse the day I submitted the papers.

The name I had carried since birth was freighted with sorrow—

years of low self-esteem, devaluation, and mistreatment. Each time I heard it, memories surfaced that I no longer wanted to live under. My new name brought a deep sense of freedom, a symbolic and spiritual break from the shadows of my past.

FACING THE REALITY OF ABUSE

For most women who have endured mistreatment, facing family reality requires monumental courage and risk. Simply admitting that "all is not well" feels impossible. Speaking it aloud—to anyone—can feel more terrifying than the abuse itself.

Many who finally reach for help encounter disbelief or judgment. Because they've spent years hiding pain, their composure convinces others "things can't be that bad." Abused women become experts at concealment. Abnormal life becomes normal for adults and children living in such situations.

Meanwhile, abusers are equally masterful at publicly presenting an entirely different picture of family life before the watching world. Behind closed doors is a different matter. Abused women and children are trained and conditioned to believe the abuser. Well trained to view themselves according to what is conveyed in a myriad of distortions, those abused are trapped, no longer able to see themselves or reality appropriately. Behaviors are learned that enable the abused to, if possible, avoid mistreatment. Survival in small and large ways is the game.

THE DUAL LIFE: *DR. JEKYLL AND MR. HYDE*

Robert Louis Stevenson's *Dr. Jekyll and Mr. Hyde* struck me as an eerily accurate portrait of dual existence—the outwardly respectable person and the hidden monster within. Every human heart carries the capacity for both good and evil.

Without God's transforming grace, the darkness prevails.

COURAGE TO TELL THE TRUTH

For someone trapped in abuse, telling the truth is like jumping off a cliff without wings. It means risking disbelief, rejection, poverty, and even physical danger. It means stepping out of the familiar prison into a blinding unknown. That is why so many return to the cycle—because at least they know the rules inside the cage.

Friends and family who suspect mistreatment must ask, gently but persistently. The first answer will likely be denial. Don't stop asking and speaking about true observations. Don't stop caring.

There are clues: unexplained injuries, chronic stress, constant fear of making mistakes, physical illness, or a partner who monitors, dominates, and isolates. The signs are often subtle—but real.

HIDDEN PRISONERS

I once knew a woman whose wealthy husband never let her go anywhere without someone following her, so he always knew her whereabouts. Outwardly, he was charming, generous, and "successful." Inside their locked home, he unleashed verbal and physical abuse at will. Imprisoned in the locked walls, even when she was alone, there was no place for her to run or hide.

When she was able to gain strength and courage, she devised an escape plan which meant risking her physical life. She left one day with a detailed plan to avert the followers who were always watching her when she went out. She took only a small amount of money, her jewelry, and little of anything else that would have raised suspicion.

Somehow, she got herself to another state far away from their home, got help, and was able to do the near impossible: get her name and social security number changed. She was unable to ever be in touch with anyone she had known from her former life. She lived every day, never knowing whether she would be located by private detectives or not.

Another sweet, petite woman lived with regular episodes of her husband verbally and physically beating her. Each time after the beating, he would sit in a rocker and sing hymns. He taught her that he was responsible for helping her overcome her weaknesses and that, of course, she deserved regular instruction and even discipline. One day, this lady fought back, though he was much larger than she was. She hit him back. He called the police, and she was the one who ended up in jail.

Yet another woman that I knew was unmercifully downgraded, corrected, and demeaned by her husband to the point where the stress ended with her getting cancer and dying. Her husband was a respected community leader, elder at their church, and others thought he was a terrific man. She did try to talk about her life, but no one believed her except her mother and another good friend, whom I also knew and who told me more after her death. Even at her funeral, he found a way to demean her.

THE TRAP AND THE CYCLE

The hard truth is that most people (usually women and children) remain trapped in their horror. Fear of leaving abuse overrides fear of staying to the point where about ninety percent of abused women never leave, or if they do, they usually return.

A similar phenomenon occurs with girls and women who are sex trafficked. They become so attached to their abusers that they cannot break free. Judges in courtrooms get confused when they try to help a woman by issuing a restraining order (when there is physical abuse). Then ten or so days later, the woman returns to court holding hands with their abuser, having been hooked back into the cycle of abuse in what is labeled the "honeymoon phase" when the abuser is sorry and promises things will be different. It rarely ever is.

NO ONE DESERVES ABUSE

No one—ever—deserves to be controlled, demeaned, or harmed in any form: verbal, emotional, financial, mental, or physical.

Freedom begins with truth: naming the abuse, breaking the silence, and accepting help. There are safe houses, counselors, and hotlines ready to respond. If you suspect you or someone you know is living in danger, please reach out.

THE NEW NAME
When God renames His children, it is not cosmetic—it is covenantal. A new name means a new beginning, a break from bondage, a reclaiming of dignity.

Changing my name did not erase my past, but it redeemed it. It marked the end of one identity and the beginning of another—one rooted not in fear or falsehood, but in freedom, truth, and love.

Like Abraham, Sarah, Peter, and Paul, I carry a name that tells a story:

Once lost, now found. Once silenced, now redeemed.

49

Non-Profits, Civics, Vocations

THE CALL TO PROTECT LIFE

Saturdays were the busiest days at the local abortion clinic. Outside, I joined others in the picket line—my oldest daughter was in the stroller bearing a sign that read, "Thank God my mother chose life."

Most of us were Catholics and Protestants standing shoulder to shoulder for the same cause. In those days, many Protestants were slower to awaken to the moral crisis brought by *Roe v. Wade*. American Protestants had lost the Christian consensus that once guided our culture. Far too many had forgotten the biblical mandate to bring God's truth to every sphere of life, including the civil arena.

Christians were never called to live quiet or private lives while the surrounding culture collapses into darkness. The Church is charged to hold the magistrates accountable and to speak unflinchingly for what God declares sacred, including the sanctity of every human life.

On many Saturdays, I served beside others as a sidewalk counselor, gently approaching women entering the clinic. We offered compassion, practical help, and hope—housing, medical care, clothing, food, money, and counseling. There was an army of people available to help the mother carry the baby to term and then support their decision about parenting or adoption. We showed brochures with pictures of unborn babies—tiny hearts that were already beating, pulsing brain waves, unique fingerprints, the capacity to feel pain and hear voices.

For a time, these compassionate outreaches were legal. Eventually, sidewalk counseling became a crime, and penalties were harsh. Some were jailed for their participation in *Operation Rescue*, the nationwide effort led by Randall Terry to defend the unborn. Yet from those very turbulent days, life-saving alternatives emerged.

I founded both the second and third pregnancy centers in the United States, modeled after the first in Washington, D.C., that was started by the Christian Action Council. Those centers became safe havens for women in crisis and their babies. It was rewarding to be part of the solution for women with unplanned or crisis pregnancies and their babies. Many who were scheduled for abortion in Baltimore are now grown adults with lives of their own.

COURIER ADVENTURE 1—CHINA, 1989

The *Tiananmen Square massacre* had just shaken the world. There was palpable tension and uncertainty in the region. Fear rippled through Hong Kong as the promised handover from England to Communist China loomed. Many people desperately sought to emigrate, but finding refuge in a free country proved very challenging.

ONE GIRL VS. A NATION ASLEEP

Bibles were legal in Hong Kong—but instantly became contraband upon crossing into Shenzhen. The potential of imprisonment for smuggling these illegal books was a constant threat.

I joined a small team of Bible couriers who began a perilous journey from Hong Kong, through a British colony, into mainland China. Led by a seasoned missionary, we set out with our meticulously concealed cargo. The instructions were clear: "Follow the leader. Stay calm. Do not draw attention." Bibles were hidden inside shoes, amongst clothing, and even in a baby's diaper.

The air in the Shenzhen security area was thick with apprehension as the group approached the conveyor belts. A sudden jolt of panic seized us when a few members were apprehended. Alarms blared as the scanners revealed the forbidden books within their luggage. Passports were seized, and the group was directed to a line where armed Chinese guards were systematically emptying bags, confiscating Bibles and hymnals.

Then, through the chaos, the missionary motioned urgently to me to start down a dimly lit corridor. Our eyes locked, and the unspoken command to *Run* resonated. Without hesitation, I clutched the large bag, heavy with the forbidden texts, and bolted towards the missionary. Shouts of "Hey!" erupted, punctuated by the menace of guards waving weapons. Breathless, I reached the missionary, his calm voice instructed, "Drop your bag!" The heavy canvas was released at his feet. In a flash, the guards thundered past, their pursuit fixed on the missionary as he bravely disappeared into the surging crowd. Though much of the precious cargo was lost that day, a significant portion was saved.

The journey continued, first by train, then by bus. After receiving an okay signal from the missionary, I slipped a *Gospel of John* from my shoe and quietly handed it to a young Chinese woman beside me.

She read it with rapt focus for the rest of the ride—as if I had handed her gold. The risks were real, the consequences severe, but the message of the Bible was deemed worth every danger.

When we reached the apartment safehouse, the curtains were drawn tight. We stacked the rescued Bibles, each one destined for pastors and congregations who had none. At the time, I felt nothing but peace—and awe that God had allowed me such a privilege. Only later did I grasp the danger.

1989 photo of me with my baby daughter in a hidden location inside mainland China.

COURIER ADVENTURE 2—CHINA, LATE 1990S

As if that adventure weren't enough, I returned on another Bible mission, this time by boat. The large suitcase was so heavy with the weight of books that its handle broke before I even got on the boat. I smiled through exhaustion, dragging it down the dock, pretending that it was all normal. It all had to appear effortless. There was no help available for handling my broken, heavy suitcase.

Disembarking the boat required repeating the earlier struggle with the broken suitcase. A bus ride followed, dropping everyone in front of a storefront where young Chinese woman opened the door, her English limited but her welcome warm. Our group was led through doors and hallways to a locked back room, away from the street. There, the stash of Bibles was unpacked, each designated for specific pastors and churches in China. The Bibles would travel further on, to remote villages.

The lovely Chinese hostess offered me a green, unripe banana. I hesitated, not wanting to take food she needed for herself not to mention that very green bananas were of no interest to my palette. A fellow courier whispered to me that accepting it would honor her. She wanted to bless me with her banana. I smiled, thanked her in Chinese and English, and ate my first and last green banana.

These adventures were a privilege. I often imagine the day in heaven when we will meet the countless Chinese believers who received and treasured those Bibles. In many villages, a congregation might own only one, so pages were torn out and shared. Individuals and families would memorize entire sections before passing them on, ensuring that God's Word was hidden in their hearts.

TEACHING ESL

Reading a book about Squanto with ESL international students on Thanksgiving in our home. Like children, they loved being in an American home and being read to.

My husband and I studied for internationally recognized TESOL and other ESL certifications so we could teach English as a Second Language. We taught mostly graduate students and visiting scholars from China who were looking to improve their English speaking and comprehension skills. For four years, we were part of a vibrant Chinese church community.

We loved opening our home to them for meals, the holidays, laughter, and cultural exchange. They loved being invited into an American home, something which few visitors from other nations get to do. We loved them and loved teaching English. Language and literacy have always felt sacred to me: tools of freedom, connection, and truth.

CIVIC DUTY AND PUBLIC ENGAGEMENT
My civic engagement began at the age of twelve, in 7th grade, when I quietly protested the removal of prayer and Scripture from my public school. I've never liked the word "politics"; I prefer "civics".

In elementary school, we were taught that each citizen has a "civic duty to preserve the liberty in their generation." I took that seriously and began writing editorials on local issues and later, I became a journalist covering the state legislature. I interviewed state legislators and attended events, earning small fees but great satisfaction.

I have always loved the United States Constitution, which was written not esoterically, but in plain language for the common man, so that all citizens could understand it. Every citizen should read and study the Constitution to know the laws of our land and our rights as citizens. It should be required for study in every school.

Over the years, I worked in local, state, and federal campaigns. I'm always enthusiastic about encouraging and registering citizens to vote. As a Christian, I believe that not voting in a nation where we have the coveted freedom to vote and elect those who represent us is a moral failure. Our liberty was bought at a very high price;

to neglect it is to dishonor those who pledged "their Lives, their Fortunes, and their sacred Honor to this country."

WOMEN'S LEADERSHIP TRAINING AND BEING "BORKED"

Before the birth of my third daughter, I was urged many times to attend law school. I chose instead to persue my goal of becoming a senator without law school. My activism caught the attention of political activist and commentator, Paul Weyrich, founder of *The Free Congress Foundation*. He invited me to the Women's Spokesman Training Conference that took place in Washington, D.C. The Conferences focused on equipping women with the necessary skills and strategies to articulate constitutional principles and effectively influence public discourse. I was living at that time in Columbia, Maryland, so it was easy for me to accept the invitation for this fully funded training in Washington, D.C.

If I had any fear remaining about public speaking, it was stomped on and extinguished by the rigors of this leadership training. We prepared and conducted a mock press conference. I learned to be comfortable with a microphone and camera in my face, to never let the media throw me off balance or sidetrack me off my intent, and to never get defensive but stick to what I am there to say!

We were grilled by nationally renowned media reporters (like George Will) who were there to train us for the most challenging time of our lives in public. When I took my seat after being grilled, one of my colleagues turned towards me. Looking at me intently, she said, "You became a different person. Nothing could dissuade you. You had fire in your eyes."

I was assigned to do my mock public debate with a super confident, articulate, recent law school graduate. I can sum it up by saying that she mopped the floor with me! I am not good at debating, but I am good at public speaking, even if thinking on my feet or planned en route to an event.

I observed and learned from President Ronald Reagan, whose

skill for dealing with opposition is incredible. He was masterful at not letting anyone put him on the defensive. One-time reporters began attacking him about his age on his birthday. Rather than getting defensive or fighting back, he skillfully turned the entire atmosphere around by getting the crowd to sing Happy Birthday for him!

Reagan was seventy-three when his opponent, Walter Mondale, ragged him about being too old for public office during the presidential debate. Reagan was an actor who became a politician, he was media savvy and had a quick wit. His statement back at Mondale was, "I decided I am not going to exploit, for political purposes, my opponent's youth and inexperience." Few could help but laugh; even Mondale was rendered speechless. Reagan won his second presidential term by a landslide. One of the biggest triumphs in election history, Reagan won forty-nine states, amassing 525 electoral college votes.

A month or so after my training in Washington, D.C. I was nominated for a county commission appointment. Now for public comments during the ratification of my appointment, a woman that was representing the National Organization for Women stepped to the podium and began attacking me and my character for articles I'd written years earlier in *The Baltimore Sun* newspaper. That triggered a media story, which landed me on the local newspaper's front page. Radio stations called me, and reporters shoved microphones in my face when I was out in public.

Michael Farris, legal counsel for Concerned Women for America, offered to represent me. I declined, pregnant and exhausted, though I later regretted not fighting.

I had been "Borked". My appointment was blocked solely because of my Christian beliefs—the first time such a thing had happened in that county.

The term "Borked" means illegitimately disqualified based on a political bias rather than sound constitutional or legal facts. It is a phrase that was coined by Judge Robert Bork in 1987. He was nominated by President Reagan to the Supreme Court. Judge Bork was put through terrible partisan opposition. When the Senate voted not to confirm Bork's nomination, the public was very shocked. Americans were aghast and found this to be extremely faulty and riddled with pure political bias rather than Judge Bork's qualifications. Reagan was attacked and forced to replace Bork with a different nominee.

Another example of being "Borked" happened a few years later. Clarence Thomas was narrowly confirmed to the Supreme Court in 1991, but only after extremely lengthy attacks on his life and character.

Clarence was accused of sexual harassment by a former subordinate of his at the Department of Education. The Senators grilled him to no end, though no evidence could be found to implicate Clarence.

Likewise, Justice Brett Kavanaugh endured similar attacks in 2018 during his Senate confirmation hearings but was able to prevail and now sits on the current Supreme Court along with Thomas, age seventy-seven.

A HEART FOR CIVIC RENEWAL

For a time, I considered running for state legislature in North Carolina. I prayed over it seriously, knowing the sacrifice that was required and that the need was great. State legislature requires a considerable financial and time sacrifice, along with constant badgering from those opposed to one's beliefs and views. Ultimately, a younger woman stepped forward to run, and I was relieved.

Too few citizens consider running for any public office, such as school board, state legislature, or any civic role, a serious shirking of civic duty.

Contrast this to our Founding Fathers, those who signed the Declaration of Independence, pledged "our Lives, our Fortunes, and our sacred Honor" to one another and to the liberty we still enjoy today.

VOCATIONS AND WORK

I started my first "jobs" in Junior High, they were small but formative—babysitting and ironing neighbors' clothes. When I turned sixteen, I was legally able to get a Social Security number, so I worked at movie theaters and bowling alleys. I also worked at a downtown Baltimore business doing boring filing on weekdays after school.

My $5 haircutting business. Notice the Hippie Huarache sandals. I wish I could find a pair just like them now.

During college and grad school, I cut guys' hair for five dollars, worked in a dormitory, and did regular house cleaning and housesitting jobs. I taught some summer elementary school art classes. I was a waitress at seafood restaurants in Maryland. I knew how to sell and serve Maryland hard crabs as well as other Chesapeake Bay seafood.

When I became a single mother, I would teach remedial reading to elementary students. Most of them came from homes without books. I had so much fun working with the children who struggled with reading. Most of them just needed some attention and someone to believe in them and that they were capable of being good readers and students. I was strict with my children by requiring them to read, write, eat vegetables, and not be caught lying.

I made sure to keep it fun by including daily surprises. I'd come into class carrying a basket on my arm. They were so eager to know "What's in the basket today?" One day, I had rulers and measuring tapes, so we set about measuring things all over the room and recording the measurements. They loved it. If they paid attention and recited their lesson, I showed them a card trick. One of the sweet little girls said one day, "I wish you were my mama!" I only wish my own children could be glad I was their mama.

Later, I launched an art business—painting walls, furniture, and light fixtures. I painted commissioned acrylic and watercolor art for customers, using their photographs. I also led nutrition workshops, skin-care sessions, makeover group sessions, and sold Shaklee products and essential oils.

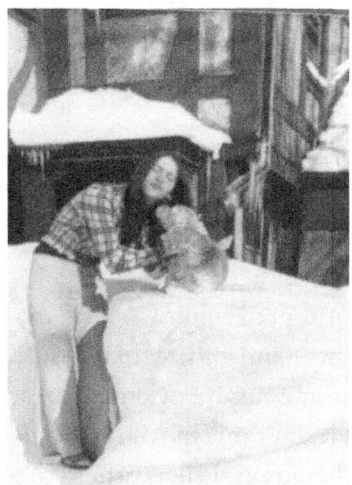

Taken while a college psychology teacher in New England

Over the years, I have been a top financial professional and manager, owner of a nutrition business, a lifelong health and wellness student, a runway and photography model, clinical counselor, college psychology professor, award-winning artist, homeschool mom, avid reader, published freelance journalist, long-standing business owner in non-mainstream financial services, and civically involved. My path was unconventional—non-mainstream, entrepreneurial, and faith-driven.

Through every season, whether ministry or marketplace, I have tried to live out one conviction: Every vocation is sacred when done for God's glory and the good of others.

50

Diving into Fear

I'm free, free fallin." Living the free-fall dream on a tandem skydive.

I've learned that, with God's help, it is possible to override fear and move into courage.

Fear threaded through my childhood and often gripped my days so tightly that it stole simple joys. I could write a whole book on the varieties of fear I entertained—but fear doesn't deserve that much attention. Facing, managing, overcoming, and talking about fear is the way forward. There is nothing to fear but fear itself. As Mark

Twain put it, "Courage is resistance to fear, mastery of fear—not absence of it." He also quipped that most of what we fear never actually happens.

The Bible says three hundred sixty-five times not to fear.

Scripture tells us "do not fear" repeatedly—enough for every day of the year. When I became a follower of Jesus, I learned that fear isn't to be entertained or coddled. Resist and overcome. Prayer became my reflex. And because I'm a bit of a non-conformist, I decided to practice leaving fear in the rearview mirror.

THE DAY I JUMPED

When my children were little, we took a field trip to Carolina Sky Sports to watch friends skydive. I started "interviewing" the divers; I peppered them with questions about why they would jump from an airplane. I knew for sure I would never ever skydive!

That day changed my life.

While listening to a devoted skydiver describe the experience, I realized that tandem skydiving with an expert—or jumping solo after training—might be statistically safer than daily driving. So, I made several decisions. First, I would skydive that day. Second, I would hire a diving photographer to record my whole adventure. Third, I would *not* let myself be afraid but just do it.

I thought it would help in my quest to leave fear behind. Carolina Sky Sports did a superb job preparing me. I watched the safety film, got suited up, met my tandem instructor who had thousands of jumps under his belt, and I learned that—even if I fainted—I would be securely attached to him, and he'd manage everything.

WHEELS UP

I did what my tandem instructor told me, one step at a time. We entered the landed plane along with a group of divers and were seated on benches around both sides of the plane. My diving photographer was nearby to photograph and video my entire experience.

Soon, the plane took off and slowly ascended until it reached 14,000 feet. The back of the plane was wide open. We stood and lined up at the back opening and one by one jumped. When it was our turn to stand at the edge of the plane, my partner yelled, "Let's go skydiving!" We tumbled forward, doing a somersault in the air, then descended belly-first toward earth.

FREE FALL
We were dropping at an exhilarating speed of 120 mph. I felt no sensation of "falling." It was more like hovering on a column of wind—like a bird suspended in the sky. The only clues there, were the roaring air and the push on my cheeks (imagine sticking your head out a car window at highway speed… then double it). This is the addictive part, the part that brings skydivers back.

UNDER THE CHUTE
At the altimeter's cue, my instructor deployed the parachute, and I felt a sudden drop. I wasn't prepared for that, so the fear hit me, but only for a few seconds. The increase in air resistance slowed us to a peaceful drift of 25 mph. When we landed, it was impossible to stay on my feet, so I tumbled over. There I sat on the grass for a long time with an unprecedented, indescribable adrenaline flow.

People say, that "There's God… and then there's skydiving." Nothing else compares. Sailing at sunset and a fast motorcycle ride are lovely—but skydiving felt otherworldly. For weeks afterward, I barely felt the ground.

My takeaway was simple: If I could jump out of an airplane, what else could I fear? I was proud of the courage I had shown by trying something new and unthinkable for me. Do I still have fears? Of course. I still get carsick on narrow mountain roads, and I've never made it past about the 20th of the 50 stories in the Washington Monument. That's okay. Wisdom is also knowing which fears don't need conquering today.

Diving into Fear

When I first landed on the ground after the skydive

51

Smoke in the Air, Sugar in the Cupboards

Eleanor in riding gear with a cigarette.

Eleanor pursued her love of animals and athletics well into adulthood. In this photo, she stands in her riding pants with a cigarette poised in her hand. That was normal. Most adults I knew smoked cigarettes. Not once did I hear anyone mention that smoking might harm one's health.

Smoking was a part of adult life. The only scandal was if a child smoked—not because it was harmful, but because it "wasn't for children." Adults smoked everywhere: living rooms, kitchens, offices, cars, and restaurants. Conversations took place through the drifting blue clouds. Women carried slim leather cigarette clutches the way one might carry lipstick or a compact mirror.

Cigarettes were fashionable. Cigarettes were sophisticated. Cigarettes were, quite simply, a part of adult life.

Hollywood made it glamorous. Lucille Ball and Desi Arnaz lit their cigarettes on TV; John Wayne had one hanging loosely from his mouth like a badge of rugged masculinity. My dad, George, smoked the unfiltered Pall Malls—"real tobacco." Camels were masculine too. Everyone knew the brands and everyone knew the ritual.

And then came the television marketing to women with the Virginia Slims cigarettes for women:

"You've come a long way, baby,

To get where you've got to today.

You've got your own cigarette now, baby.

You've come a long, long way."

Freedom, they said, looked like smoke.

Years later, lung cancer would be the number one cancer killer—especially for women. Baby Boomers grew up inhaling it as air.

And it wasn't just cigarettes.

THE FOG WE DID NOT QUESTION

As I got older, I began noticing something else: the harsh chemical smell in hotel laundry rooms, the overwhelming fumes in the "cleaning products" aisle at the grocery store. People called it "fresh." My body called it toxic. The dizziness and headaches from cleaning products spoke before the culture did.

The "smell of clean" was manufactured.

Since age nineteen, I have used nontoxic cleaning products—not because anyone taught me to, but because my body recognized what was harmful long before the world admitted it.

ADDICTED TO WELLNESS (BEFORE WELLNESS WAS A TREND)

It has always been my goal to die with all my original body parts except the tonsils and adenoids that the medical establishment removed when I was a child. (Again, may I please have them back?!) That was the routine of my generation. I wonder how many in my generation still have their tonsils. All my children kept their tonsils, an often-hard-fought victory with each child.

When one daughter suffered repeated ear infections, a doctor insisted that she needed tubes, tonsil removal, and "maintenance" antibiotics. I remember reacting with a loud "maintenance antibiotics!?" which prompted the physician to point me to his wall of framed medical degrees. I walked out. I did not have the answers yet, but I knew what I would not do. I was determined like a mother bear that if there was another way for my children, I would find it.

After researching and speaking with aware parents, I removed dairy from our diet and added nutritional supplements.

The earaches stopped.

When another child developed recurring kidney infections, I researched, studied, and built a nutritional support plan.

No antibiotics. No surgeries.

When one of my children had a severe reaction after an MMR shot, I read deeply from both sides of the vaccine debate. I also spoke with, questioned, and listened to parents on both sides of the fence. At that time, the idea of turning down childhood vaccines was scandalous if not crazy.

After extensive study, I made the personal decision to discontinue any further vaccines for our family. It was radical at the time and quite Lone Ranger-ish. I stood by it. I was responsible for the children entrusted to me.

When one of my children was diagnosed with ADHD, I turned down the medication remedies. I implemented diet, lifestyle, and other changes to help. Homeschooling was advised by a doctor for that child so that individualized instruction methods could be designed for the child's unique personality and learning style. It was challenging, but we made it work, including extra reading therapy to help this one learn to track words and sentences on a page.

Occasionally, we had to use pharmacological drugs in our family, but it was rare. Usually, preventive and natural age-old remedies worked very well.

I like what Thomas Edison said, though it certainly has not come true yet.

"The doctor of the future will no longer treat the human frame with drugs but will rather cure and prevent disease with nutrition."

And Hippocrates before him:

"Let food be thy medicine and medicine be thy food."

Germ theory focuses on the bacteria and virus pathogens that are causing the disease. Researchers propose that genetics is a major disease-causing factor. Are we predestined or pre-wired, to continue family ailments? Are we genetically, medically trapped?

These were not slogans for me. They became survival lifestyle guidelines.

THE SYSTEM TREATS ILLNESS. PREVENTION DOESN'T PAY

Our medical system is structured to treat illness—not prevent it. The allopathic medical model is problem-oriented, focusing on treating and managing symptoms. It boils down to sick care, not health care. Doctors themselves may care deeply, but the system they work within reimburses pharmaceuticals and procedures, not nutrition, rest, lifestyle change, or repair.

Insurance rarely covers:

- Chiropractic
- Massage
- Acupuncture
- Colon hydrotherapy
- Vitamin IVs
- Lifestyle-based disease prevention or reversal

I know this because I lived it.

Several years ago, after I had a gym accident that resulted in a partial elbow replacement, what I most needed was therapeutic massage, hydrotherapy, and chiropractic—was not covered. Some of these treatments after an accident are part of the routine care in other countries. They would blend well with physical and occupational therapy but are often unaffordable. But costly surgical and pharmaceutical treatments were readily available.

The priorities are clear.

I respect surgical skill, emergency medicine, and especially orthopedics. I am thankful for discoveries like antibiotics, which save lives. But true health begins with prevention and root-cause healing, functional medical care—not invasive methods or maintenance drugs for life. Billions could be saved.

Healing diabetes, heart disease, and even cancers is often possible through lifestyle change and natural medicine. Holistic practitioners are increasingly helping patients heal from chronic illness, yet many natural practitioners are ridiculed or persecuted. Dr. Stanislaw Burzynski in Texas, who has treated cancer successfully for decades, is one such example. His story, documented in a YouTube film, reveals the fierce resistance that has and still does occur.

AGE NINETEEN: THE TURNING

My childhood diet was sugar-based. Breakfast might be Instant Breakfast with milk, Tang (so-called orange juice that was colored sugar water), and some candy for the school bus ride. Mom sometimes sectioned a grapefruit the night before and covered it with sugar. Gran made hot Cream of Wheat with sugar and milk, and I devoured many chocolate donuts from her grocery store next door. Each morning, a bakery delivered baked goods made earlier that morning. I ate fruits like peaches and apples.

Lunches were cafeteria fare—fast food, milk, and ice cream, or, if I brought lunch, a bologna sandwich on white bread with cookies and cupcakes. At home, I ate TV dinners heated in a gas oven I had to light with matches. Naturally, I was hesitant every time I had to light the stove or oven, but I had to do it to cook my food. I heated cans of soup. I opened cans of stewed tomatoes and ate them cold. I ate obscene amounts of cookies, cupcakes, and all sorts of chocolate sugar items. I drank Coke and used it to make ice cream floats. Summer evenings included the sounds of the Good Humor truck and the Snowball truck. I loved anything chocolate, including chocolate snowballs with marshmallow cream on top.

Gran Anna fed me the best when I visited my dad and her. She cooked stuffed cabbage, sausage, sauerkraut, toasted bread with garlic and butter, and made cold cut sandwiches with meat she cut right in their grocery store. She always served a hot meal for supper with meat and vegetables. My dad sometimes brought home Maryland Blue Crabs steamed with Old Bay Seasoning. I was an aficionado at opening and eating Maryland crabs. It is a learned skill that I could teach. We feasted on crabs, corn on the cob, and ripe sliced Maryland tomatoes. Beer was the beverage to go with crabs.

Crab eating began with newspapers spread out over the entire kitchen table surface. The crabs were piled in the center, claws extending in every direction. Each person had their own tools—a wooden crab mallet, a knife, and a metal pick for removing the crab meat from small parts of the crab. One had to learn proper shell removal, avoiding the poisonous lungs. Removing legs, the claw, and easily obtaining the claw meat are precision tasks.

Gran Mildred fed me about the same fare as my mom. I had white bread toast with butter and jelly for breakfast. I remember her sour beef and dumplings, a traditional German dish. She added crumbled sugar snap cookies into the sauce for flavor. I never got any of her recipes. Nothing was written down on paper.

I ate extra ice cream to gain weight, but it did not help. A doctor said I was anemic, so Mom gave me Geritol. I had a toothbrush, but I do not recall if anyone taught me how to use it. Mom waited until I was a preteen to take me to the dentist. I required anesthesia to repair so much decay in my teeth. That experience cemented my lifelong commitment to preserving my teeth and health.

Children left to their own choices do not know what is good for them. I had no clue that sugar was dangerous. Had I not changed my lifestyle at nineteen, I might not be alive today.

My health changes marked me as radical and "weird." That has been the story of my life in everything. I embraced fruits, vegetables, and whole grains long before it was popular. From reading *Sugar Blues* (William Dufty, 1976), I learned that sugar is addictive and deadly.

At nineteen, while living and working at Phillips Crab House at the beach in Ocean City, Maryland, a surfer friend handed me a book on diet and health. I wish I could thank him today. It changed my life.

I became a lifelong student of wellness. I raised my children differently. I reclaimed my own health. I avoided major disease while my peers developed cancer, diabetes, and heart disease. That was not a coincidence.

I am not saying these maladies could never happen to me in a fallen, broken world, but I will say that most of my closest friends, older and younger, have already died of things like cancer. So far, it has been accidents that have hindered me, and usually they have happened in my efforts to maintain fitness and adventure.

Eating the standard American diet is not health-promoting. Sugar consumption in the U.S. today is staggering:

- ~57-150 pounds per person per year in added sugar

- Over 80 pounds total per person per year, including natural sources

Diabetes and Alzheimer's (recently termed "Type 3 diabetes") are epidemic. Our nation eats for taste, not nutrition or health.

FATIGUE, THYROID, MOTHERHOOD, AND NOT BOWING TO LABELS
As a preteen and teen, I was chronically exhausted. I had an eight o'clock a.m. high school U.S. history class about which I recall nothing. When I made it to school, I was often late because I could not get up on time, and I slept through every boring class. I dragged through the day, and when walking or riding the bus home, I often felt like I could barely shuffle along, putting one foot in front of the other.

This was after a fear-filled childhood where I was too scared to go to bed and never got adequate sleep. Later, I learned I had an overactive thyroid. Several doctors told me in my early twenties that I would not be able to have children unless my thyroid was removed and I went on multiple medications.

I declined and began studies on thyroid issues and alternative healing.

I studied. I nourished my body.

I went on to have ten (yes, 10) pregnancies and never had any abortions, challenging though they each were. It was all worth it. Not too many years later, my thyroid went from overactive to underactive. I do not consider this a major disease, but a health and lifestyle factor manageable through nutrition and compounded thyroid hormone supplementation.

Was I always perfectly balanced? No.

As a single mother and business owner, I was a workaholic—determined not to be poor, to provide for my children and mother. In hindsight, I wish I had rested more and been more present. My parents could not show up for the parents' open houses at school during the day. I was always disappointed when watching parents enter the room, but not mine. I did not do well in that area either. Workaholism is acceptable and encouraged in our culture, and I bought into it.

Running full speed left me drained. Occasionally, I slept most of a Saturday, and one child despised that. I still feel ashamed of my fatigue. I never used drugs, only natural thyroid supplements and briefly an antidepressant during divorce—something I regret after learning more about such medications.

One of my young adult children told me I was "mentally ill," a perpetuated myth. I remained silent, trusting that the truth would someday surface. It has not yet. Friends and acquaintances saw the reality. But I remained an army of one.

I stayed silent. I did not defend myself or try to explain how that false notion came about and how it was an alternate unreality. Truth should be patient.

Leadership is lonely. Motherhood is doubly so.

HOW I LIVE NOW

Today, I eat whole mostly plant-based foods—organic when possible—supplemented with grass-fed meats, raw dairy when I can obtain it, fish, nuts, seeds, greens, and legumes. I eat a wide variety of herbs, spices, roots, vegetables, fruits, and grains. Diversity feeds the microbiome, and the microbiome speaks to the brain through the Vagus nerve.

Fiber is crucial for gut and brain health. Research on the Vagus nerve or the "second brain" is new and intriguing. This nerve communicates between your brain and the rest of your organs. Americans barely eat 25 grams of fiber per day, while 100 grams is best for avoiding disease, including Alzheimer's prevention.

I do not think it is wrong or bad to eat animal products. I eat grass-fed meats and raw dairy when available. The amount of animal products and processed foods eaten by modern Americans is high and is deep fried, loaded with refined sugar, adulterated with hormones, antibiotics, and an increasingly extensive list of preservatives, coloring, and other additives. Tragically, modern factory farms offer us adulterated, tainted, highly drugged animals as food. Unnecessary animal cruelty is completely unbiblical.

"The righteous care for the needs of their animals, but the kindest acts of the wicked are cruel."

—PROVERBS 12:10

"If you come across a bird's nest... do not take the mother with the young. You may take the young, but be sure to let the mother go, so that it may go well with you and you may have a long life."

—DEUTERONOMY 22:6-7 NIV

Factory-farmed meat and fish often contain growth hormones, antibiotics, diseases, and vaccines, and they are fed cheap, easy grain-food that is not meant for them. Cows are designed to eat grass, not grains like corn. Feeding them corn makes them fatter faster. I will not even describe what happens to conventionally farm-raised fish.

All kinds of very toxic pesticides, such as glyphosates, are still widely used in the USA, but are unsafe in other countries. It is all about profit. Processed foods contain sugar in abundance, along with preservatives and a host of additives that are not food. Profit over people and animals. Profit over health.

I eat organically and exercise regularly to prevent disease. I make adequate sleep a priority. I work towards stress management. I love God's creations and love being closer to them. We are disconnected from nature, especially in cities.

Reading and studying never cease. Learning lifelong is my style.

I am not a natural kitchen person, so I must work all the time to do my best with food prep.

Many diseases are reversible and preventable. Even cognitive decline can often be slowed or prevented. The answers usually lie in simple lifestyle changes rather than drugs and surgeries.

Food and faith are intertwined.

Scripture commands humane treatment of animals. Factory farming violates that without apology.

Profit has replaced stewardship.

Profit has replaced health.
Profit has replaced community.
So, I choose:

- Real food

- Real rest

- Real movement

- Real connection to nature

- Real discernment

We must question everything.
I am grateful for medical care when needed, but:
M.D. does not mean "Mighty Deity."
God gave us a mind and a conscience for a reason.
Freedom of health choice is essential.

CLOSING

I grew up in a world where smoke, sugar, and chemicals were normal, unquestioned, and celebrated. I chose to wake up. I chose to live differently. I chose to guard my health—and the health of my children.

What we inhale.
What we eat.
What we believe.
What we trust.

These shape not only the body, but the community and soul of a nation.

52

Mortality

> "Even though I walk through the valley of the shadow of death, I will fear no evil, for you are with me; your rod and your staff, they comfort me."
>
> —PSALM 23:4 ESV

I attended funerals as a child, witnessing my grandparents' generation passing. Over the years, there were many more people of all ages.

When I worked as a clinical counselor and college psychology instructor in Massachusetts, a young woman that I knew—recently graduated and newly married—was in a tragic car accident. She wasn't wearing a seatbelt. Though the car was moving at only about twenty-five miles per hour, she suffered grave head injuries and slipped into a coma.

I watched only as a bystander while her husband and parents

were led toward organ donation, convinced by the medical personnel that she would not recover. Even then, I felt that the process was hurried—that her family was too quickly persuaded to give up hope. To this day, I believe her emotionally vulnerable relatives were influenced to surrender too soon, and that her life was sacrificed for her organs. This was in 1977, only a few years after the U.S. Supreme Court had rejected the Hippocratic Oath as a binding standard for medical ethics in 1973.

The Hippocratic Oath is a solemn promise taken by physicians to uphold the ethical standards—to do no harm, to treat the sick to the best of their ability. Once the oath was formally abandoned, medicine lost its absolute prohibition against abortion and its vow never to administer a "lethal medicine."

Years later, I attended the funeral of a pastor friend and his wife, who had lost their beautiful, healthy toddler boy to Sudden Infant Death Syndrome. I had studied SIDS and the controversies that surround it. Some researchers suggest that there is a potential link between vaccines and SIDS; others vehemently deny it. The debate remains unresolved, but the overlap merits honest inquiry. For that grieving family, debate didn't matter—only heartbreak.

It is easy, especially when young, to avoid pondering mortality. We imagine death is distant and irrelevant. Yet Scripture reminds us repeatedly of the brevity of life. Even though modern life spans are longer, they are still fleeting compared with early biblical history—Methuselah being the most famous example.

A few years ago, I experienced my own brush with mortality. I have been a lifelong "gym rat" and weightlifter; fitness always felt essential to longevity. But during a fitness challenge one day, I moved quickly across the gym floor when my new shoe caught on the faux surface. My body hurled toward a rack of heavy metal bars. If I had hit that metal frame, I could have been killed.

Instinctively, I twisted to avoid the impact and landed full force on my left elbow. The bone shattered into ten fragments—too many to repair. I required a partial elbow replacement. A year later another surgery was required to relieve an entrapped ulnar nerve. The surgeons did all they could, but I live with constant pain and significant weakness. My left arm and hand are visibly smaller from the muscle loss. The accident was sudden, overwhelming, and life-changing.

Chronic pain changes everything. Once strong and active, I now awaken each morning acutely aware of my frailty. There are days when I pray for endurance—and sometimes, for release. Yet even in pain, I thank God daily for the use of my arm and hand.

The accident itself is seared into memory: lying on the gym floor, pleading with the firefighters hovering above me for pain relief. They couldn't help. When the ambulance arrived, the "Charlie's Angels–looking" EMT crew got me inside. Suddenly, my blood pressure dropped rapidly and dangerously. As IV lines were inserted, my energy drained away. I could no longer speak.

In that silence, I prayed.

"Lord, are You taking me home now?"

I told Him I was ready.

What I felt next cannot be fully captured by words—only experienced. A peace beyond understanding. A serenity untouched by fear. I knew I belonged to Him. I knew He was there. There was no fear at all. I wish I could describe it better.

The paramedics raised my blood pressure just in time. By the time I reached the ER, I was speaking again, though I later learned I had gone into shock. That was my closest encounter with death, and the peace of that moment remains. I share it in hopes of conveying that when one knows the living God and walks in relationship with Him, there truly "is no fear in death."

As I age, mortality feels nearer, but it no longer frightens me. I believe older generations are meant to share that perspective with the young. Scripture says:

"Older women should teach the younger women to love their husbands and children."—(Titus 2:4)

That is a broad curriculum—and a sacred responsibility. But generational wisdom can only be passed down when families and communities can remain connected. The elderly must be willing to invest, and the young must be humble enough to receive.

I pray for a resurgence of family and community life—true "Blue Zones" of faith and fellowship—where generations honor one another and age is seen not as decline but as legacy.

53

The Tribute

When my mother was afflicted with cognitive decline and approaching hospice care, I reached out to an old friend from junior high. She had spent time in our home and knew my mother well. Her message to me was very honest and piercing:

> I'm not sure what you want to do. What does the doctor say? You've told me your mother sometimes treated you poorly, but the reality is that her cruelty was daily. I saw it firsthand. Are you making plans for her because you still want her love and

the relationship you always hoped for? Be careful. You might be setting yourself up for a crushing time after her passing. Please take care of yourself... realistically.

—LOVE, NADINE

Nadine's words stung and jolted me, but I knew they were true. She wanted to protect me from another heartbreak. Denial had been my coping mechanism for most of my life. When someone has lived feeling unimportant or unwanted, even a few crumbs of affection seem like a feast. Still, I remain deeply grateful for whatever love there was—and for the privilege of being her daughter. I prayed for her daily and tried all my life to honor her and love her, as God commands. I still do. I miss her voice and wish I could call her just once more.

One of the greatest helps I found during that season was *The Tribute* by Dennis Rainey (1994). His book showed me practical ways to live out the Fifth Commandment:

> "Honor your father and your mother, that your days may be long upon the land which the Lord your God is giving you."
>
> —EXODUS 20:12

Rainey teaches us that this commandment carries a promise—and without conditions. It does not depend on whether a parent "deserves" honor. We honor them because God says to. The book helped me realize that honoring a parent means acknowledging what they did right, however small it may seem. Even a mother who struggled deeply still deserves the respect for giving life. Carrying, birthing, and raising a child—even imperfectly—is worthy of gratitude.

For me, this truth was profound. My mother could have chosen an illegal abortion during her pregnancy with me. She didn't. She was brave. She endured hardship and lifelong consequences so that I

The Tribute

could live. For that alone, she deserved honor. Parents hold a sacred office—like a pastor or president, their position carries intrinsic respect, regardless of personal flaws or failures.

Rainey's book challenged me to make that respect tangible. In it he suggests creating a written "tribute," framing it, and presenting it publicly to one's parents. I took that suggestion to heart. After much prayer, I poured myself into writing the words, decorating and framing them with flowers, and preparing to read them aloud.

When the day came, all my children were present. I stood before my mother, read the entire document, and presented it to her. She wept uncontrollably—perhaps more deeply than I had ever seen. Her joy that day was radiant. Later, she hung the framed tribute on her wall, where it remained until her death. I will never forget her tears or the healing that moment brought to both of us.

If I had had a father in my life, I would have made a tribute for him too. But I do have a Heavenly Father—One I can never thank enough for His endless faithfulness and love.

This is what the framed Tribute to my mom says:

A TRIBUTE TO MY MOTHER

You're the only one in the world who holds the title of my "Mom."

I'm so glad I have you—there is no one else like you in my life.

You were there when I was born. You gave me life.

I could never thank you enough for giving birth to me and keeping me.

You were courageous. You did the best you knew how.

You've always shown courage through every tough time you faced.

I'm grateful for my fond childhood memories and all you've done for me.

It would take forever to express them all, but here are a few of my favorites:

- You cared for me when I had chickenpox.

- You held my hand on my first day of school—it was hard saying goodbye.

- You stayed with me in the hospital for tonsils and teeth. Thank you.

- You went to parent-teacher meetings and encouraged my studies.

- You helped me through Algebra, even paying for a tutor.

- You showed loyalty to family and made holidays feel special.

- You were only a phone call away when I got home from school.

- You became a Girl Scout leader just so I could join a troop.

- You welcomed every animal imaginable into our home (except, thankfully, elephants and alligators!).

- You encouraged my creativity—letting me paint, decorate, and dream.

- You worked tirelessly to provide for us, sacrificing so much.

- You taught me generosity, hospitality, and strength.

I once felt my childhood was hard—no father, no siblings—but now I understand it differently. As a mother myself, I know you can't be everywhere or fix everything.

You did the best you could, and that was enough.

The Tribute

Thank you, Mom, for giving me life and for being my mother all these years.

Thank you for loving my children and bringing joy to their lives.

I respect you for your courage to keep going when everything falls apart.

The sacrifices you made for me will ripple through generations.

I thank God for who you are and for all you've done for me.

I love you, Mom.

Honoring my mother helped bring peace to one side of my story. But the other side—the empty space where a father should have been—remained waiting to be faced.

54

Finding My Father

"When my father and my mother forsake me, then the LORD will take me up."

—PSALM 27:10

When I was thirty-five, I set out on a mission to stage an intervention for my dad, George, because of his alcoholism. He had been minimally involved in my life growing up, but he was still the only dad that I had ever known. As with my mother, I loved him deeply—no matter what—and always longed for his love in return.

My training helped prepare me for what I hoped to attempt. I knew how to do interventions with people living in denial about addiction.

Through my master's work in counseling and the years I spent

Finding My Father

as a clinical counselor, I learned a great deal about addiction, family systems, and recovery. I was also an ACOA—an adult child of an alcoholic—and had attended many ACOA and Al-Anon meetings. Twelve-step groups are excellent at helping people find the support they need to become and remain sober. We are not designed to do life alone. We are created for relationships and community.

I began calling people who knew my dad. I spoke to his brother, who was also in denial about Dad's alcoholism. I contacted friends and others with connections to the places where he was working at the time. Not one person was willing to help me orchestrate an intervention. It was deeply disappointing.

Eventually, I mustered the courage to speak directly to Dad.

I told him plainly that he needed help. He replied, "I know I am a drunk." And then, with painful clarity, he added, "Face all that reality? No thanks!"

He admitted he was an addict—but had no interest whatsoever in changing. I felt helpless. I wanted so badly to help him, but he had no desire to be helped.

Around that time, another concern weighed heavily on me. I had read much about "Grandchildren of Alcoholics," and as a mother bear, I wanted to protect my children from every possible harm. I had already begun homeschooling the older ones, and we were enjoying so many wonderful experiences together.

But I learned that the grandchildren of alcoholics are more prone to eating disorders and other struggles. This concerned me deeply, especially since all my children at that time were girls. One day, while I was talking to my mother on the phone, I was open about my fears. She tried to assure me that my daughters would not be affected, but I kept returning to facts and research she had not done. My mom loved my children more than she had been able to love me, for many reasons, and she was distressed by my concerns.

Finally, in exasperation, she blurted out, "He's not your father!"

I was stunned.

Then again: "He's not your father!"

I cannot describe the shock that went through me. The man I had believed was my father for thirty-five years truly wasn't.

That admission opened the floodgates. After thirty-six years of secrecy, my mother suddenly poured out everything. She had never told a single soul—not her mother, not a pastor, not a counselor. Not even George. She had carried it all alone for decades, afraid that if I discovered the truth, I would reject her. The only way to prevent that, she believed, was to tell no one.

Reject her? Never. What I felt was only compassion. I had started two crisis pregnancy centers and walked with women through unexpected pregnancies. I had always advocated compassion for both mothers and their unborn children. As Mom unfolded her story, my only response was compassion.

Still, I was in indescribable shock. I stared at my face in the mirror, trying to understand why I had never looked like my family. Who was I, really?

My mother became a living bundle of relief. She told me that even George had never known I wasn't his biological daughter. She had carried an immense burden of secrecy and shame for so long.

For days, she began reliving the hidden past: how she met Marv, how they began dating, where they went, what they did, their friends, the restaurants, the events. He was from New York, and she introduced him to steamed Maryland hard crabs. She told me about the Naval Academy Christmas dance and spoke of it as though she were there again—young, hopeful, and in love.

Mom had loved Marv deeply. She hoped to marry him. My conclusion was that he had liked her, but he had no such intention. His friends' descriptions of him in his Naval Academy yearbook painted him as a playboy. It is possible that he struggled with pornography—the modern pandemic that is found by many even when they are not looking.

I do not know the extent of his involvement, but I do know the world that he inhabited.

Their relationship continued, and I do not know whether he was involved elsewhere. As spring approached—the season of his graduation—Mom dreamed of the graduation dance and the long string of Navy weddings right after graduation. The graduate's weddings were held hourly in the beautiful Naval Academy Chapel.

She planned to tell him that she was expecting a baby. But before she could speak, he said he had something to tell her: "I'll be graduating soon and leaving Annapolis, so I won't be able to see you anymore."

She got up and walked away without a word. She wandered the streets until she found a bus. She was lost, overwhelmed, and without any plan.

She considered abortion. It was illegal, and for her, that was deterrent enough. She told me she had been too afraid to pursue it. I absolutely believe that when abortion is illegal, fewer unborn children die. I am living evidence.

ABORTION LAW IN THE UNITED STATES (1950)

- Abortion was illegal in every state except to save the life of the mother

- Doctors and anyone assisting could face felony charges, prison time, and loss of medical license

- The unborn child was legally recognized as a protected human life; abortion was classified as a crime against both public morals and the child

- In Maryland specifically, a woman seeking an illegal abortion could face:

  » Possible criminal charges for participating in the act

  » Pressure to testify against the abortionist

  » Police investigation and social stigma

  » Risk of being treated as an accomplice in a felony

  » Life-threatening medical danger, since illegal abortions

  » frequently caused infection, hemorrhage, sterility, or death

- No state permitted elective abortion; Roe v. Wade was still 23 years away

- Illegal abortion was widely recognized as dangerous, with high rates of complications and maternal mortality

- Cultural and legal norms affirmed that abortion intentionally ended the life of a child

While illegal abortions in the 1950s carried especially high risks of infection, hemorrhage, and death, the truth is that legalized abortion does not eliminate medical danger. Every abortion procedure—chemical or surgical—carries inherent risks. These include hemorrhage, infection, incomplete abortions that then require additional procedures, uterine perforation, cervical damage, complications from anesthesia, and long-term reproductive consequences for some women. These are not rare historical issues; they are documented realities of how abortion affects the female body.

Legal status changes the environment, not the biological reality. Even in the safest medical settings, ending a developing human life carries both physical and emotional costs. Many women report profound psychological and emotional trauma after abortion, including grief, guilt, depression, and long-term regret. Legality cannot remove these consequences. It can only disguise them.

Sometimes I wonder what I would have done had I been in my mother's shoes. I always thought abortion was unthinkable and instinctively knew it meant killing a baby. Mom could have gone away to a home for unwed mothers until my birth and then placed me for adoption. I wholeheartedly believe adoption is one of the most courageous, sacrificial acts a mother can make. I never asked my mom whether she considered adoption before marrying George.

But the truth is, my mother was very cornered—emotionally, socially, and culturally—and she devised the only plan she believed she could carry. It wasn't the story she dreamed of, nor the life she imagined for herself. Yet she stepped into a drama that would give me life while permanently altering the course of hers.

One of my favorite books, *The Waiting* by Cathy LaGrow, tells the story of Minka, who became pregnant after being raped in 1928. Like my mother, she faced the crushing stigma of being unwed. The struggles were enormous then—and still formidable when my mother later found herself in the same situation.

Once I finally understood my mother's fear and isolation, her next decision—the one that would define the course of both of our lives—made painful, heartbreaking sense.

My mother felt she could not have a baby without being married. So, she solved her impossible dilemma the only way she saw possible: she married George and led him to believe the baby was his. Less than nine months later, she gave birth to me by C-section. I was her and Marv's child. I am thankful she chose life—and thankful she later grew to love me, even though I had not been a "wanted" child.

Mom confessed that when I reached my teens, every day she

saw my face, she was reminded of the man who had rejected her. I resembled him—and I still do. The resemblance alone is proof of his paternity. Marv had rejected me too, though unknowingly. I have no conscious memory of how all this affected me as an unborn child, but I know it shaped me even then.

After listening to everything my mother poured out about my father, I made two decisions.

The first was to tell my dad George the truth. I had always believed that truth sets people free. I wanted him to know that none of this changed my love for him—not for a moment. In my mind, it would bless him to know how much I loved him. It felt like an honorable thing to do. I could never have predicted what followed.

He was furious with my mother. Understandably so. But then he rejected me completely because I was not his daughter. My attempt at unconditional love was met with absolute silence and the shutting of a door. The dye was cast; there was no rewinding the tape. What I had hoped would heal only fractured us further—him, my mother, and me. To this day, I regret telling him. I truly thought that I was doing the best, most honest thing.

My second decision was more instinct than logic: I had to find my biological father. Some people raised by non-biological parents feel no need to search for them. Others feel compelled. I was the latter. I longed for a father's presence—something I had never known—and hoped, perhaps naively, that he might want me. I yearned for some version of a happy ending, or at least a clear beginning.

Mom opposed the idea entirely. She said she hated Marv and wanted nothing to do with him. And yet, she remarkably knew a lot about him. She had followed his entire Naval career from a distance, all the way to his retirement as a Naval Captain on ships and submarines.

More than that, she was afraid of the outcome. She feared that if I found him, I would somehow replace her or reject her. I cannot fathom rejecting one's own mother—no matter what. I know adult children cutting off parents has become a modern cultural trend, but it goes against the grain of everything that is in me—everything I believe is good and right.

Eventually, Mom realized nothing would dissuade me. So, she reversed the course. She gave me the photos he had taken of her and finally revealed his full name. Astonishingly, she knew exactly where he lived.

A close friend of mine, a physics professor at the Naval Academy, made me a copy of Marv's photo and biography from an old Academy yearbook. Suddenly, I had everything: a name, a face, a history. Everything but a relationship.

Some people hire private detectives.

All I did was dial directory assistance.

After much prayer, I dialed his number on a Saturday afternoon. A woman answered. He wasn't home. I didn't leave a message.

Later, I called again. A deep, serious voice answered.

"Is this Marv?" I asked.

"Who is this?" he said.

When I finally heard his low, steady voice, I didn't know how to begin. I blurted, "Are you sitting down?"

Immediately, I regretted saying the most dramatic sentence of my life. Who was writing this script—me or a soap opera screenwriter?

"Who is this?" he demanded again.

"I am your daughter."

There was almost a click. I spoke rapidly, pouring out facts about his life—the Naval Academy, his sports, where he grew up, my mother's name—anything to keep him on the line. He listened. His voice softened. Suspicion slowly gave way to curiosity.

Finally, he said, "Send me pictures of your mother." Beyond that, he gave no other reaction. I agreed and said goodbye. The earth was moving underneath my feet. I was in shock.

I spent the next week preparing a letter, explaining who I was, assuring him I wanted nothing but the chance to meet him. I included the photos, as well as pictures of me and my three children. I proposed flying to his city so he could meet me for lunch at the airport. I sent the packet and waited.

The waiting was excruciating. Every day was like limbo. I wrestled with my identity. Having believed I was half Russian, I now learned that none of that was true. My father later told me his family was Austrian. I felt unmoored. Hope and fear wrestled in me constantly.

Mom gave me the photos he'd taken of her. I later learned he still had copies of the exact same photos of my mother, and he later showed his copies to me.

It's impossible to explain the emotional experience this was for me. Call it shock, trauma, or just utter perplexity. I wasn't exactly sure who I was. My feet weren't fully on the ground. My heart and mind overflowed with new hope for more in my life.

Each day passed slowly as it does when we are waiting. Would this man, who was my father, ever be in touch with me? Maybe. Maybe not. It rang too much like too many situations with boys and men. Will they call me? Do they like me? Will I see this person or speak with them again? What do they think? I always hated limbo land, as I called it.

One late afternoon, when my phone rang and I answered, I heard that very deep voice again. He said he had received my letter and photos and looked over them all. As he reviewed the details, I knew what was coming next—no thanks, this is not true. Then he said, "and I am persuaded it is true."

Can someone help peel me off the floor? I was speechless, feeling light-headed, close to fainting. There's no practice for responses in such situations. He then said he didn't want to meet me at the airport but wanted me to visit him, stay in his home, and meet his wife and two sons. He'd already told them. His wife accepted it as something that happened long ago, before she even knew him.

I made flight plans and had to take my nursing baby daughter along with me on this trip. My father was there to meet me at the airport. He was very warm, welcoming, and kind. I stayed two nights at his home listening to his wife, who was a non-stop talker but was kind too. I met his two sons, my half-brothers. I saw photos of my grandmother, aunt, and three girl cousins. One of the cousins looked like my twin.

My two brothers were nice to me. The younger one never had a bit of interest in me and never responded to me after that one meeting. The oldest son (but still a younger brother to me) has been kind enough to continue at least a minimal relationship. If I contact him asking to visit him, he'd likely agree. Long ago when I designed the house we were building, my brother came with his family to help for a few days with the early construction. This meant the world to me and was very kind and sacrificial of him. I hoped we could grow a real brother sister long term relationship. I especially love my brother because he is my brother.

Of course I had no experience with siblings, but I always wanted it as I observed friends and their families.

My brother, an introvert, does not usually initiate furthering our relationship though the times we have been together reveal to me an astonishing, powerful, cosmic sort of kindred factor. He elicits the best of my intellect.

The few times that I have seen him, we've connected in what to me was an unprecedented familial and intellectual way, though we have differing beliefs and different mothers. I felt more like who I am to the depths, to my core, when I was with my brother. I feel connected to him in unexplainable ways. Life would be much richer if my brother demonstrated need or desire enough to want me for me as his only sister.

My few days meeting my father and his family were beyond exhausting -- mentally, emotionally, and physically. His house was not baby-proof, and the entire time, I had to monitor my daughter, who could crawl and pull herself up and easily get into all the breakables in the surroundings.

It was hot and humid, and I was worn out. At one point, my father took me onto his porch, which became a guided photo tour of every ship and submarine he'd been on in the Navy. I was reeling with overload at that point.

Soon enough, it was time for him to take me to the airport for departure. He walked alongside me and my baby up to the plane entryway (which was till allowable at that time). Then he said goodbye and turned away. I stood there, watching my father walk away. I hoped he would turn around, delaying the good-bye, but he never looked back.

I wanted to cry out:
"Please come back.
Please say something.
Will I hear from you again?
Do you care?
Are you walking out of my life for good?"
He left me with only questions.

I put on my sunglasses to hide the torrent of tears. The downpour continued as I boarded the plane, found my seat, and sat numb.

We continued corresponding by letters. At one point, I asked to be allowed to meet his sister, my aunt and my cousins. He refused. He was never willing to let any of his extended family know about me other than his wife and sons. My grandmother died without ever knowing about me. I was denied ever meeting her. Same with my aunt, who I assume is now deceased, and my three cousins, who may be alive, but I have no way of knowing or finding them.

One early morning in 2021, I texted my half-brother asking if our father was doing all right. I had dreams about him that night. My brother said, "You must be prescient. He died last night." How could I explain that God had obviously revealed this to me? I wanted to attend my father's Navy funeral, but I wasn't invited, nor did I receive even a memorial flier about his funeral.

My father was a nice, gifted person, but sadly, too self-focused to make room for accepting me as his daughter. He was ashamed to let his family know about me as if I were a cause for shame. What he did had been decades earlier and was no fault of my own, yet he was ashamed of me. He had no use for me in his life and took little responsibility for the fact that he was my father.

When I first met my father, all he said about my mother was "I enjoyed being with your mother."

That was all.

I refer to Marv as "our father," when talking with my brother (whom I adore), he politely acknowledges it, but not in a way that includes me fully or as a genuine family member. He refers to my father as Marv not our father. I long for a closer relationship with my brother—it would mean a great deal—but relationships are not one-sided.

My father missed out on me as his daughter, my children as his grandchildren, and now my brothers miss out on the love available from a real sister. We cannot make someone else love us. Relationships are like the hotel suites with adjoining rooms. Both parties must be willing to open their doors.

My family story carried its share of ruins, yet even in that broken landscape, I was a child blessed to grow up in America—free, safe, and surrounded by possibility. That contrast shaped me. It taught me early that a life can be fractured and still be held by hope, that broken beginnings do not dictate the ending, and that God can build strength in the very places where foundations have cracked.

Though the wounds of my family ran deep, the blessings of my country ran deeper still: freedom, stability, opportunity, and the quiet assurance that I could grow beyond the sorrows I'd inherited. Those gifts allowed me to believe that restoration is possible—not only for individuals, but for families, and even for a nation.

For if a single life can be rebuilt, so can a home. If a home can be renewed, so can a country.

The story of my own journey—its losses and its graces—opened my eyes to the larger truth: the strength of a nation begins in the strength of its families, and the recovery of a people begins with the healing of one heart at a time.

That hope—that restoration—is not only possible. It is necessary. And it is within reach.

My father and I met for the first time

Marv stayed athletic his entire life, on and off the water.

55

O America!

> "We have no government armed with power capable of contending with human passions unbridled by morality and religion. Our Constitution was made only for a moral and religious people."
> —JOHN ADAMS

I loved America long before I understood her history—long before I could spell "Constitution," and just after I learned to spell "ice cream." Years later, a song I loved gave voice to that feeling:

"O America, you're calling / I can hear you calling me." It named what I felt long before I could articulate it—that love of country was a calling, not a slogan.

I have my elementary school teachers to thank for instilling in me a deep love and respect for my country. Each morning, we would stand, hand over heart, pledging allegiance to the flag of the United States of America and to the Republic for which it stands.

One of my teachers played the piano as we sang patriotic songs that she taught us to memorize. She exuberantly hit the keys with her entire being so that we learned rhythm, patriotism, and fear all at once. We recited the Lord's Prayer, and my teachers read a passage from the Bible. Every morning!

Those daily rituals planted seeds of patriotism that have never left me.

Growing up, I believed, and still believe that in a free society, the participation of each citizen is not optional. It is a duty.

Every generation must take part in the preservation of our liberty. Each of us is responsible for doing our part.

I hold this conviction wholeheartedly. Every citizen must take responsibility to vote in every election, local as well as national. Local elections shape our daily lives just as much as presidential ones. I am inconsolably grieved that so many Americans treat voting as optional. How can we take for granted what so many around the world have never known: the freedom to choose our laws and our leaders?

Our representative government means that those we elect are hired to serve the people. They are public servants, not self-seeking elites who chase power or money. It is our duty to hold their feet to the fire, to ensure they serve the people, not themselves.

We must remain very vigilant, limiting government control and holding it accountable to the Constitution and the rules of law. Its primary duties are to defend our nation from invasion and to punish evildoers. Beyond that, federal involvement in everyday life is hard to justify constitutionally, especially when regarding fiscal matters.

Neglecting our civic duty leads a nation from apathy to tyranny. Believing "someone else will handle it" is a dangerous myth.

During my high school and college years, I discovered countless ways to learn about and serve at the local, state, and federal levels. Every young person should seek such opportunities. Understanding the U.S. Constitution—is essential to knowing one's rights and responsibilities as a free citizen.

Every home should contain two books: the Bible and the U.S. Constitution. Children grounded in both stand on solid ground.

Two institutions that exemplify this are Hillsdale College in Michigan and Oak Brook College of Law and Government Policy in California. Oak Brook offers an affordable J.D. program delivered "principally by correspondence"—meaning students do the work remotely rather than attending a traditional brick-and-mortar campus. They teach the Constitution itself, not merely case laws. I think a law degree is a great idea regardless of what vocation one decides to persue. Knowing the law helps with everything. Most modern law schools have replaced constitutional instruction with case law—a travesty equal to medical schools abandoning the Hippocratic Oath. Physicians no longer pledging to "do no harm"! As William Penn, founder of Pennsylvania, wisely declared:

"Men must be governed by God, or they will be ruled by tyrants."

Our nation was founded on biblical principles—the Ten Commandments, moral law, and the belief that liberty requires virtue. Early New England laws were drawn directly from Old Testament statutes on theft, murder, and justice. History shows that when a nation drifts from biblical morality, it descends into moral anarchy.

And the later stages of moral anarchy always bring increasing chaos. When citizens lose the ability or willingness to self-govern by conscience, the state must step in to enforce order. The result is always the same: a police state leading to tyranny and rule by an elitist class. Freedom cannot survive long when separated from moral restraint.

I love patriotism. I have no patience for the claim that loving one's country somehow displaces loving God. Nonsense. God's supremacy stands above all things but love of country is not its rival—it is its reflection. Patriotism is a noble virtue, born of gratitude for God's blessings. Love for country stands in a class of its own, distinct from love of God and love of people.

I cannot pinpoint the first moment that I loved America. It grew quietly. I remember my teachers placing their hands over their hearts with reverence, not routine. I remember the swell in my chest whenever we sang The Star-Spangled Banner—a feeling of belonging to something noble and rare.

I remember Fourth of July fireworks lighting the sky and knowing, even as a girl, that we were celebrating something fragile and miraculous. As the years have passed, that love has only deepened. The older I become, the more clearly I see how delicate liberty is—how it must be cherished and tended, generation by generation.

America is a miracle in the history of the world—and each of us must do all we can to preserve her.

56

Social Insecurity

"No nation can remain strong if the home is weak. The cradle is the forge of a people."

—Adapted from early American sermons

Some children of the baby boomers—millennials—believe we had it easy. In certain material ways, life *was* simpler. One millennial friend once told me he views baby boomers with fascination, as a generation whose money "multiplied ten or twenty times," with easier paths to homeownership and financial growth.

What that view often misses is this: we worked.

Many baby boomers earned college degrees while holding full-time jobs, attending night classes, or working multiple jobs simply to afford tuition. Others delayed education for years while saving.

Think of George Bailey in *It's a Wonderful Life*, who labored tirelessly for a future he ultimately sacrificed so his brother could go instead. That ethic was not unusual.

Most young families lived for years in modest apartments, scrimping and saving before homeownership became possible. Today, many younger adults understandably want the stability their parents eventually achieved—but without the long, patient climb that preceded it. One of the greatest casualties of this shift has been children.

Few children now grow up with a parent at home full-time. Dual incomes are often assumed, and child-rearing is increasingly delegated to babysitters, institutions, or state-designed programs. Early childhood education begins earlier each year. The model begins to resemble the "womb-to-tomb" systems of communist societies, where the state, rather than the family, becomes the primary caretaker.

By contrast, baby boomers typically began school in kindergarten or first grade—and kindergarten itself was often optional. My own mother waited until first grade to send me. In hindsight, it was one of her wisest decisions. Young children flourish when given time to play, imagine, explore nature, and mature at a human pace.

Children need their homes—and their parents—as long as possible. Let children be children.

This does not mean neglecting instruction. History shows the opposite. I was deeply moved when I learned that John Newton's mother, who died before he turned seven, had so thoroughly taught him that by age four he had memorized the entire Westminster Shorter Catechism, including the Scripture references. Four years old.

Newton's later life veered tragically off course. He became a cruel ship captain and slave trader, openly mocking Christ. Yet when God seized his heart, Newton was transformed. Alongside his friend William Wilberforce, he helped bring about the abolition of the British slave trade in 1807. He later wrote *Amazing Grace*. Near death, Newton said, "My memory is nearly gone, but I remember two things: that I am a great sinner, and that Christ is a great Savior."

The seeds planted early mattered—even decades later.

In China today, women of childbearing age are required by the government to work outside the home. American women still have a choice, though many underestimate the formative power of motherhood and homemaking—roles once widely honored. As William Ross Wallace observed, "The hand that rocks the cradle is the hand that rules the world." Mothers shape nations.

Work began early for me. At eleven or twelve, I ironed baskets of laundry, babysat, and weeded flower beds. At sixteen, I applied for my own Social Security number and worked behind the candy and popcorn counter at a local movie theater. That marked the beginning of earning my own living.

My Social Security number was earned the old-fashioned way. Today, many receive one before leaving the hospital.

The Social Security Act of 1935 was designed to track earnings for retirement. The first recipient, Ida May Fuller, received $22.40 per month at age sixty-five. At the time, women's life expectancy was sixty-three. The system worked because most people never lived long enough to draw from it.

In 1940, there were 149 workers for every recipient. In 2025, there are fewer than three.

Enumeration at birth began in the 1980s. Most millennials received Social Security numbers almost immediately. Today they can log onto SSA.gov and view a lifetime ledger of earnings before adulthood has even begun. Insecurity is built into the system itself, raising unavoidable questions: Will benefits last? Will they be taxed away? Will the system survive?

These shifts in work, family, and security reveal more than generational differences. They expose a deeper longing—for stability, identity, and meaning. And those longings point us back to the truths we must recover if we hope to rebuild what has been lost.

57

My Husband

"A good marriage is the union of two forgivers."
—RUTH BELL GRAHAM

"Two are better than one... for if they fall, one will lift up the other."
—ECCLESIASTES 4:9–10

When I describe my husband, I often begin the same way: he is a ruggedly handsome, gifted, Renaissance-style man who loves books, guitars, and music in all its forms. A Navy veteran and a talented musician, he has performed for weddings, civic events, and community gatherings, written songs, and pursued creative work with a seriousness that mirrors how he lives. Watching his steady growth has been one of the great joys of my life.

From the beginning, I was drawn to his deep love for God, theology, reading, and lifelong learning. We share many interests, including fitness, ideas, faith, and conversation—especially conversation. Boredom has never been our problem.

Like most marriages worth keeping, ours was not without early struggle. Fatigue, stress, and the ordinary pressures of life once made small disagreements feel far larger than they were. Over time, commitment, patience, prayer, and a willingness to forgive taught us what endurance means. We are living proof that staying matters.

My husband has given me something I have lacked for much of my life: steady, unconditional love. When we speak publicly, we sometimes joke that we work together, live together, and spend most of our time together—and remarkably, we are still happy to do so. We genuinely value that partnership.

We are both artists, which means we are delightfully odd. He is a morning person with an energy level that should be regulated, while I remain a night owl at heart. He drinks coffee freely; I arrived late to that party. We laugh about these differences now, grateful for the balance they bring.

Faith has shaped our life together in quiet, faithful ways. Years ago, he introduced me to daily Scripture listening, a practice that has deeply formed me. His own work in prayer, music, and ministry has reached people far beyond our home, and I am proud of the good he offers the world. I am his most loyal audience—especially at performances—and yes, I still remind him about the tip jar.

We have shared hospitality with others, including international students and visitors who had never been welcomed into an American home. Around our table, cultures met, stories were exchanged, and community was formed in simple ways that mattered.

Life together has been imperfect and wonderful. Ordinary and extraordinary.

We don't live in a Jan Karon Mitford novel, but we do live a real, faithful life—complete with ordinary pressures, imperfect days, and grace that shows up anyway.

One ongoing challenge is the mysterious multiplication of

guitars, a matter on which I have not yet achieved victory—but I remain open to counsel.

In the end, our marriage is one of God's great kindnesses to me—a story still being written, marked by grace and loyalty, by two people who continue choosing each other. It is a love I once only imagined, and one I do not take for granted. My only real regret is that it did not begin sooner.

58

Commission

"If the freedom of speech is taken away then dumb and silent we may be led, like sheep to the slaughter."

—GEORGE WASHINGTON

"Despotism may govern without faith, but liberty cannot."

—ALEXIS DE TOCQUEVILLE, *Democracy in America*

Every story must lead somewhere. Every generation must decide what it will do with the truth it has been given. This final chapter is not a summary of what has been said, but a turning outward—a question placed gently, and firmly, into the reader's hands.

I am weary of empty diagnosis—books, sermons, and lectures that describe what is broken with precision, yet release the listener back into life unchanged. Insight without direction leaves people informed but helpless. Conviction without responsibility leaves them stirred but stranded.

The question before us is not simply *what should be done*, but **what kind of people must we be**.

Cultures do not collapse overnight. They erode when ordinary people grow numb to patterns, consequences, and moral cause and effect—when it becomes easier not to see than to see, not to feel than to feel, not to carry responsibility than to bear it. This numbing is understandable. It is also costly.

Action does not begin with instruction. **Action flows from identity.**

From what we love.

From what we believe is worth protecting.

From what we are willing to pass on.

If we wait for someone else to save what matters, we will wait a very long time. No generation is excused from stewardship. We inherit both blessings and burdens, and we decide—quietly, daily—what will endure.

This work does not begin in halls of power. It begins in homes, in speech, in habits, in courage practiced at human scale. A culture is healed one family at a time, one choice at a time, one conscience awakened and kept alive.

The older generations still carry memory, perspective, and hard-won wisdom. Do not retreat into silence. Your stories matter more than you know. Tell them. Share them. Pray with the young. Let your lives become living textbooks of what faithfulness looks like over time.

The younger generations are not without responsibility either. Seek those who came before you. Ask questions. Listen deeply. Learn from both their faithfulness and their failures. We were not made for isolation or cancellation, but for continuity—for the long work of belonging to one another.

What is asked of us is not perfection, nor heroics, nor visibility—but **attention, courage, and fidelity**. To speak truth without cruelty. To act without theatrics. To live in ways that quietly contradict what dehumanizes.

History turns when ordinary people refuse to drift.

We have been placed in this moment not by accident, but by Providence. Whether our sphere is large or small, one truth remains: we are stewards of what we have been given. The question is not whether change is possible, but whether we are willing to live as if truth still matters.

A PRAYER OF COMMISSION

Almighty God,

Author of liberty and Giver of life,

We come not with confidence in ourselves, but with gratitude for what You have entrusted to us.

Forgive us where we have chosen comfort over courage, silence over truth, and ease over faithfulness. Restore our sight where we have grown weary of seeing, and our hearts where we have grown tired of caring.

Teach us again to love what is good, to say what is true, and to do what is just—even when it costs us. Rebuild families where they are fractured. Turn hearts toward one another across generations. Give us courage equal to our convictions, and humility equal to our responsibility.

Make us people who live attentively, speak honestly, and act faithfully— not for applause, but for love of truth.

Like our ambitious forefathers, may we be faithful in seeking You, loving You, and doing Your will in the world. Equip us with creativity, ingenuity, courage, and determination to resist evil, to stand for what is good and right, and to labor faithfully in every sphere of life and culture.

And when our days are done, may it be said that we did not drift, that we did not look away, and that we stood our ground in our generation.

Amen.

    Go now—to live truthfully within it.
    Love gives. Love brings life. May we do the same.

Reflection and Discussion Questions

For deeper insight and extended reflection, download the full PDF at **MAVENPUBLISHINGMEDIA.COM** *in the Additional Resources section.*

PROLOGUE: I CAN'T SEE YOU ANYMORE

1. The Weight of Silence—Eleanor carried her secret and her child alone. What happens to the human spirit when truth is buried out of fear or shame? Can truth concealed ever truly heal?

2. Fatherhood Unseen—Marv was unaware he was a father, but that absence shaped two generations. What does this reveal about the sacred responsibility of men in a culture that too often treats fatherhood as optional?

PART 1: BREAKING THE SILENCE

1. INTRODUCTION

1. Documenting a Life, Recording a Nation—The author calls her story "a living museum." Why does preserving personal and family history matter—not just for one family, but for a nation's moral and cultural memory?

Reflection and Discussion Questions

2. Truth and Tenderness—The author writes as both journalist and daughter, researcher, and storyteller. How can truth-telling be compassionate—exposing error without demeaning people?

2. WHY ME?

1. What keeps people from asking meaningful questions of the older generation? How has the loss of generational storytelling affected American culture?

2. In an era of historical revisionism, what personal responsibility does ordinary citizens carry for preserving factual history?

3. THE MAKING OF A WRITER

1. The Gift of Literacy

The author calls literacy "a hallmark of civilization." How has reading this influenced your own thinking, relationships, or spiritual growth?

2. Books and Belonging

Reading offered the author refuge from loneliness and a bridge to other minds. What books or authors have served as companions for you during isolating seasons of life?

Reflection and Discussion Questions

PART II: ROOTS OF INHERITANCE

4. HASSELBARTH GERMAN IMMIGRANTS

1. Becoming American—Early immigrants adapted to a new language and culture while retaining pride in their heritage. What does it mean to become part of a new nation without losing your identity?

2. Preserving the Story—Much of the Hasselbarth family's early history was lost to time. How can we preserve and share our family stories before they disappear?

5. MILDRED

1. The Search for Roots—The author's quest to help her mother rediscover her father's story brought healing and closure. Why is it so important for us to know where we come from?

2. Love Across Generations—What does this story reveal about the power of one generation's love to redeem what another lost or buried?

6. TUBERCULOSIS

1. Isolation and Courage—Henry and Annette endured long separations while battling illness. What kind of inner strength does it take to face fear and loneliness?

2. Gratitude for Progress—The author marvels that antibiotics transformed what once was a death sentence. How often do we take modern medical advances for granted?

7. BALTIMORE, 1950S — LIFE IN MILDRED'S HOUSE

1. How do our childhood environments—whether warm, fearful, strict, or unpredictable—shape a person's sense of safety, trust, and identity?

2. What does this chapter reveal about the cultural life of mid-20th-century working-class Baltimore? How does it compare with today's expectations for childhood?

8. LIFE AND CHRISTMAS AT MILDRED'S HOUSE

1. Thrift as a National Ethic—How did Depression-era frugality influence American attitudes toward consumption and waste?

2. Cultural Civility and Respect—What social or economic forces eroded shared civility, and may it be renewed?

9. ELEANOR AND HER MOTHER

1. Working Women in Transition—How did mid-century women entering the workforce reshape American family life?

2. Cycles of Wounding and Repair—What does this reveal about forgiveness across generations?

10. MEN LOST TO WAR

1. Women in Uniform—What does Eleanor's Coast Guard service reveal about evolving roles for women during WWII?

Reflection and Discussion Questions

2. The Price of War Beyond the Battlefield—How do war's unseen legacies shape national identity after the guns fall silent?

11. DOMESTIC ABUSE

1. Silence and Social Blindness—What social norms made people reluctant to believe victims?

2. Cultural Memory and Responsibility—How can sharing stories of past injustice shape empathy and reform today?

12. ANNAPOLIS AND MARV

1. Marv's decision to abruptly end the relationship left Eleanor isolated and ashamed. What moral damage is done when truth and empathy are replaced by avoidance? How does silence compound sin?

2. Though Marv never knew Eleanor was carrying his child, his abandonment still left a lasting void for both mother and daughter. What does this reveal about the sacred duty of fatherhood—and the unseen, generational consequences when men turn away from life they helped create?

13. RUSSIAN—GERMAN WEDDING

1. In the 1950s, abortion was illegal because society recognized that it violated the fundamental right to life. What happens when moral law and civil law diverge—when what is legal may not be right, or what is right may not be legal? How does this apply to today's moral debates?

Reflection and Discussion Questions

2. Eleanor's hasty marriage to George arose from desperation, yet it became how an innocent life was protected. What does this reveal about the way God can bring redemption and purpose even from human mistakes and moral confusion?

14. NO CHRISTMAS BABY

1. What does Eleanor's determination reveal about the hopes and fears many mothers carry before a child is born or why she did not want a Christmas baby?

2. How have cultural attitudes toward childbirth shifted since the 1950s—especially regarding hospital births, family involvement, and expectations for mothers?

15. BRING ME MY BABY

1. The separation of newborns from mothers was common in the mid-20th century. How might such practices have shaped bonding, trust, or early emotional development? What does this say about the difference between medical procedure and maternal wisdom?

2. Anna stepping in to care for the newborn shows how earlier generations relied on extended family networks for survival. What does this say about the importance of intergenerational responsibility, and how has modern culture weakened or preserved these bonds?

16. ALCOHOLISM: THE POTENTIAL ROBBER

1. Addiction and Abandonment—What can this teach us about the roots of addiction?

2. Eleanor's Moral Courage—How does her perseverance embody the sacred duty of motherhood?

17. MY PARENTS

1. The Sacred Pattern of Family—How does God's design reveal His wisdom about human flourishing?

2. Forgiveness and the Healing of Memory—How can we remember without bitterness heal generational wounds?

18. GRANDMOTHER MILDRED

1. The Child's Hidden World—What happens to a child's sense of self when affection is absent?

2. Emotional Illiteracy as Inheritance—What is our duty to teach emotional as well as moral truth?

19. GRANDMOTHER ANNA

1. Business as Ministry—How can small acts of decency heal divisions more than slogans?

2. The Power of Innocence—What does childlike love teach about the image of God in every person?

20. COLOR BLIND

1. Righteous Anger—When is anger righteous, and when is it destructive?

2. When Laws Lag Behind Hearts—How long does it take for laws to catch up with God's justice?

Reflection and Discussion Questions

21. ART OF IRONING & WHERE ARE THE SIDEWALKS?

1. Homemaking as Holy Work—How can we recover reverence for stewardship in daily life?

2. Neighborhoods with Sidewalks—What have we lost by trading connection for isolation?

22. LEXINGTON MARKET

1. Home Remedies and Wisdom Lost—What truths have we lost by outsourcing health and self-care?

2. A Culture of Gratitude—How does gratitude protect against entitlement?

PART III: CAUGHT IN THE CULTURAL CROSSFIRE

23. BRIDES OF DRACULA & LIGHT

1. Television and the Imagination

Baby boomers were the first generation raised on screens. How did early media shape children's fears, desires, and worldview—and how does it compare to today's digital saturation?

2. Fear Without Comfort

What happens to a child who absorbs frightening images without an adult to help interpret them? Why does fear grow so powerful when a child must face it alone?

Reflection and Discussion Questions

3. The Power of Unchecked Media

The movie *Brides of Dracula* marked the author for years. What responsibility do adults have in curating what children see and experience? How has modern culture either protected or abandoned children in this area?

24. PREJUDICES AGAINST FLOWERS AND PEOPLE

1. History's Warnings—Why must each age reassert that human dignity is unconditional?

2. Faith and the Value of Life—How does belief in a Creator challenge ranking lives by convenience?

25. GREAT GRAN

1. Foundations of Independence—How do we balance preparing children for independence with making them feel secure?

2. Education and Moral Formation—What is lost when schools remove spiritual foundations?

26. FLOWER

1. The small grave, the popsicle-stick cross, the whispered prayer—these are acts of instinctive faith. What does it say about the divine image in human nature that even a child reaches for ceremony, meaning, and hope beyond death?

2. How might this early experience of love, loss, and undeserved guilt foreshadow the author's later conviction about the value of all life—especially the smallest and most vulnerable?

Reflection and Discussion Questions

27. CULTURAL TABOO

1. Death and Denial—How has removing death from homes changed how we value life?

2. Generational Shifts—How can we restore intergenerational living renew compassion?

28. WAKING MYSELF—SCHOOL BUSES AND RX DRAWERS

1. What role can imagination and play serve for a child living with instability? How did "playing school" become both refuge and rehearsal for future calling?

2. Children often carry adult secrets because they have no choice. What does being forced to lie to her mother's employer reveal about emotional burden placed on a child? How does secrecy shape identity? Why is childhood neglect so often invisible to outsiders? What signs in this chapter reveal unmet needs that teachers or neighbors might easily miss?

29. LATCHKEY

1. Small Responsibilities, Big Lessons—What does a house key symbolize about early self-reliance?

2. Love Without Affection—How do we interpret love expressed through provision rather than touch?

30. NATURE OR NURTURE?

1. Nature and Design—What does her story suggest about how much is written into our being?

Reflection and Discussion Questions

2. Inherited Wounds and Gifts—What family patterns or legacies have you inherited?

31. TOWERS OF JELLO"

1. Fragility and Survival—How do children adapt to instability?

2. Redemption of the Metaphor—What does emotional firmness look like when rooted in grace?

32. PENPALS

1. Creative Survival—What does letter-writing reveal about the human need for connection?

2. Faith and Wiring—How might restlessness be part of divine design?

33. POSSESSIONS CAN OWN US

1. Security or Suffocation?

How do possessions that once brought comfort sometimes begin to control us? What does "enough" look like in a culture built on accumulation?

2. The Inheritance of Habits

Depression-era scarcity shaped Mildred's mindset, while Anna's discipline modeled freedom from clutter. How do family patterns around money and possessions quietly shape our values today?

Reflection and Discussion Questions

34. AMERICAN DARK DIVE DAY (1963)

1. A Solitary "No"—What empowered a shy seventh grader to stand against cultural pressure?

2. The chapter notes that few adults mounted a national defense of prayer in schools. What does this reveal about cultural complacency? Why does silence often accelerate moral decline?

35. THE MURRAY CHRONICLES

1. What made this moment in the Baltimore classroom a turning point for the nation as well as for one young girl?

2. How did the removal of prayer from schools shape the moral trajectory of the next generation?

3. Why do some convictions become immovable, even in childhood?

4. What does William Murray's later conversion reveal about the long arc of truth and grace in history?

36. ASSASSINATIONS AND AFTERSHOCKS"

1. Why do truth-telling leaders so often face hatred—or death—for their courage? From Washington's miraculous survival to Kennedy's tragic death and Trump's near escape—how do you interpret divine protection or restraint in leadership and history?

Reflection and Discussion Questions

2. What happens to a nation that forgets the price of its freedom?

37. THE BEATLES—WHEN THE GROUND FIRST SHIFTED

1. How can music act as a barometer of cultural change? What made the Beatles uniquely positioned to transform—not just reflect—youth culture in the 1960s?

2. Most adults dismissed the Beatles as a fad. What cultural changes did they fail to recognize emerging beneath the surface? What similar signals do we miss today?

38. THE TEACHERS WHO SHAPE US

1. Why are children so likely to believe the negative assessments of adults, even when those assessments are inaccurate?

2. How can a single comment—like "You don't belong here"—reshape a child's understanding of their own intelligence and capability?

3. Which qualities made Mr. Stack the kind of teacher whose influence lasted a lifetime?

39. VIETNAM

1. Why were Vietnam veterans treated with hostility rather than honor when they returned, and what lasting damage did that cause?

2. What responsibilities do citizens carry to acknowledge and care for soldiers shaped by trauma they never chose?

40. WOODSTOCK NATION

1. How did the ideas embodied at Woodstock spread beyond the farm—into universities, media, politics, and eventually the courts?

2. How did the moral logic of the sexual revolution eventually make abortion appear necessary to preserve the new "freedom"?

41. PLANNED BARRENHOOD AND SLIPPERY SLOPES

1. How did fear of "overpopulation" become an excuse to devalue human life?

2. How have population fears historically been used to justify racism, eugenics, and coercive control?

3. Why are large families often met with hostility or disbelief, and what does that reveal about cultural priorities?

4. What did Anthony Comstock understand about the link between private vice and public harm, and how is that warning relevant today?

5. What can we learn from Gianna Jessen's survival—and her testimony—to help reawaken moral clarity in the current debate?

42. LOVE HUNGER

1. What false ideas about love and identity does our culture teach through media?

2. How can churches and families better nurture those scarred by fatherlessness?

PART IV: RESTORING WHAT WAS LOST

43. TRUTH SEEKING

1. What does Isaiah 5:20 reveal about the danger of moral confusion in any culture or individual life?

2. How might the search for truth today require the same courage, openness, and willingness to examine competing worldviews?

3. What does it mean, personally, to be "born again" into light and truth?

44. ROBBING GOD

1. **The Faith Test** Why do you think God invites us to "test" Him specifically in giving? How does stepping into generosity expose both our fears and our faith?

2. **Ownership vs. Stewardship** The chapter emphasizes that everything we possess already belongs to God. How does this shift—from owner to steward—change the way we think about money, resposability, and security?

45. CANNOT HAVE CHILDREN?

1. What does it mean to trust God with our fertility or infertility?

2. How does grief over child loss change a person's view of eternity?

3. Where have you seen God redeem what was once impossible?

4. How does modern culture's attitude toward children contrast with God's Word?

46. TEACHING FREEDOM

1. **Rewriting the Story for the Next Generation** What stands out to you about the author's intentional efforts to give her children opportunities she never had—swimming, music, athletics, creativity? How can parents rewrite harmful narratives they inherited?

2. **Living Books vs. Institutional Schooling** What impact do "living books" and rich ideas have on a child compared with standardized, test-driven schooling? How might returning to story-based learning restore curiosity and depth?

3. **Generational Literacy and Cultural Strength** How is America's loss of literacy (compared with early citizens who read the Federalist Papers, tied to today's confusion about truth, freedom, and citizenship?

47. MULTIGENERATIONAL DIVORCE

1. **Hidden Wounds and Invisible Performances** How does this chapter help you see the difference between what a family looks like from the outside and what may be happening behind closed doors? Why is emotional and nonverbal abuse so hard for others—even children—to recognize and believe?

Reflection and Discussion Questions

2. **Covenant, Safety, and Hard Choices** How does this chapter hold together two truths at once—that marriage is intended for life, and that sometimes separation is necessary for safety and sanity? What dangers arise when Christians apply simple formulas to complex, abusive situations?

3. **Children in the Crossfire** What are some of the ways the children in this story were affected—both by the marriage and by the divorce? How can we better support children who have lived through hidden conflict, favoritism, gaslighting, or divided loyalties?

48. A NEW NAME

1. **Recognizing the Subtle Signs** The chapter names clues of hidden abuse: fear of making mistakes, chronic stress, isolation, controlling behaviors, or forced secrecy. Why are these signs so often missed or dismissed? How can we grow in discernment and compassion?

2. **God's Renaming and Personal Redemption** Throughout Scripture, a new name signals transformation. How does the author's choice to take a new name reflect spiritual renewal, reclaimed dignity, and breaking generational bondage? Have you ever sensed God calling you into a "new name," identity, or chapter of life?

49. NON-PROFITS, CIVICS, AND VOCATIONS

1. How does courage in one area (faith, family, or vocation) strengthen courage in another?

Reflection and Discussion Questions

2. The Constitution was written in plain language so ordinary citizens could understand it. What happens to civic health when a nation forgets its founding documents? How might restoring civic literacy strengthen families and communities?

3. What risks are worth taking to defend the unprotected or stand for truth?

50. DIVING INTO FEAR

1. Where is fear quietly steering your choices?

2. What "training" (skills, counsel, prayer) would make your next brave step safer and saner?

3. What is your version of the jump—one bold act that would rewrite your relationship with fear?

51. SMOKE IN THE AIR, SUGAR IN THE CUPBOARDS

1. Adults smoked freely around children—at home, in cars, at restaurants—without the slightest concern. How does this contrast with today's awareness? What might future generations look back on in our time with similar disbelief?

2. The story of childhood sugar consumption paints a picture of a generation raised on convenience food and processed sweetness. How does early nutrition shape lifelong health, identity, and even emotional memory?

Reflection and Discussion Questions

3. Profit has replaced stewardship in the food and medical systems. What responsibilities do individuals bear when the larger culture fails to protect health? How might personal choices become acts of moral leadership?

52. MORTALITY

1. The abandonment of the Hippocratic Oath marked a major turning point in medical ethics. What happens to a society—and to patient trust—when a profession once grounded in absolute standards becomes guided by shifting cultural values?

2. When the author prayed, "Lord, are You taking me home now?" it expressed readiness, not dread. What does true readiness for eternity look like, and how might it reshape the way we live our present days?

3. Scripture says older women are to teach the younger. What wisdom about marriage, children, faith, or mortality is most needed in today's generation—and why is intergenerational connection so fragile in modern life?

53. THE TRIBUTE

1. What does it mean to "honor your father and mother" when the relationship has been painful or complicated?

2. How does forgiveness play a part in healing family wounds?

3. Why do you think God attached a promise ("that your days may be long") to this specific commandment?

4. What lessons about courage and compassion can younger generations learn from imperfect parents?

54. FINDING MY FATHER

1. The author responded with compassion rather than anger when learning her mother's secret. What enables a heart to choose empathy in the face of betrayal, fear, or decades of silence?

2. The chapter ends with a powerful contrast: family wounds alongside the blessings of growing up in a free and stable nation. How can gratitude and sorrow coexist without cancelling each other?

3. The author concludes that healing one life can ripple outward to heal families—and even a nation. What might this reveal about personal responsibility, generational restoration, and the role of individual transformation in cultural renewal?

55. SOCIAL INSECURITY

1. Younger generations desire instant stability—homes, careers, lifestyles—that earlier generations spent decades building. How does the loss of patience, apprenticeship, and long-term effort affect families, communities, and character formation?

2. The chapter raises concerns about young children being placed in institutional care from infancy. What are the long-term implications—for attachment, emotional security, and identity—when the state, rather than parents, becomes the primary caregiver?

Reflection and Discussion Questions

3. The author affirms the enormous value of motherhood and homemaking—roles often minimized today. Why does modern culture struggle to honor domestic work, and how might restoring honor reshape future generations?

56. O AMERICA!

1. What dangers arise when a society replaces Biblical morality with "case law" or purely human reasoning?

2. In what ways does the loss of self-governance and moral restraint lead toward tyranny?

3. How might William Penn's statement—"Men must be governed by God, or they will be ruled by tyrants"—apply to current American culture?

57. MY HUSBAND

1. Shared passions—faith, books, music, learning—became the foundation of their bond. How do common loves strengthen a marriage, and what happens when those shared pursuits deepen over time?

2. The author notes that unconditional love from her husband filled a lifelong void. What does this reveal about the healing power of faithful marriage—and how can love restore areas wounded long before the relationship began?

3. Humor, storytelling, and quick wit shape their everyday life. How does humor serve as a form of emotional resilience within long-term relationships?

Reflection and Discussion Questions

4. The chapter portrays marriage as a story still being written—full of forgiveness, growth, and shared purpose. What practices help a marriage remain a living story rather than a stagnant one?

58. COMMISSION"

1. Every generation must decide what it will do with the truth it has received. What truths has our generation forgotten, and what truths must be reclaimed if America is to remain free?

2. The author warns that waiting for "someone else" to save the nation is empty hope. What prevents ordinary citizens from recognizing their own part in preserving liberty, and how can that mindset shift?

3. Younger generations are called to seek out their elders and learn from them. What barriers—cultural, emotional, or technological—stand between generations today, and how can they be torn down?

4. The closing reflections insist that America can rise again—if families and individuals choose repentance, courage, and faith. What gives you hope that renewal is still possible, and where do you see signs of awakening?

5. The closing prayer asks that America once again become "a light set upon a hill" because of faith and virtue, not wealth or power. What would a nation shaped by humility, moral clarity, and reverence for God look like in daily life?

Appendix

Samples of Anne's Published Articles & Public Testimonies

Public Testimony Presented at Tyler, Texas library board public event at Town Hall, 1-26-2022

FACTS ABOUT PORNOGRAPHY

My name is Anne Odendhal. As a former college psychology instructor & clinical counselor, I have experience with people of all ages who battle addictive behaviors. Regarding the Tyler library collection policy, it is alarming that our public library has sexually explicit materials available in the children's section in the building and online.

The legal definition of a child or minor is anyone under the age of eighteen.

Our library allows access by legal minors to sexually explicit material. Local citizens pay the 1.8 million that funds our public library which exists to serve community values and interests. Library staff, local officials and the public must be informed of facts and effects that sexually explicit materials have on children.

The presence of such materials tells our children that we adults think sexual anarchy is okay!

Appendix

There are clear, unequivocally established facts (both scientific and criminal) that exposure to even a little bit of pornography often results in dangerous, addictive behavior akin to cocaine addiction. Pedophilia clearly starts with pornography. Violent crimes such as child molestation, rape, incest, and murder are undeniably rooted in pornography. Pedophiles know these facts and know how to lure and victimize children.

Scientific studies indicate that pornography results in impaired physiological brain functionality. The prefrontal cortex enabling complex brain function is not fully developed for sound decision making until age 25, meaning minors are at greater risk for addictive behaviors than adults. Pornography alters brain chemicals that hinder and can damage brain functionality the same as drugs such as heroin and cocaine. Adult moral integrity struggles usually begin at young ages. The results are broken lives, broken families, and even deviant criminal behaviors.

Pornography robs young people of healthy maturation and sound decision-making skills. Pornography increases risks of abnormal emotional, psychological, and social behaviors. Pornography exposure by undeveloped minors leads to impaired psychological, emotional, social, and academic maturation, individual and family breakdown and societal decay and ruin. Time does not permit but I have access to hundreds of peer-reviewed, science based clinical studies confirming all the above.

We citizens request the library board to protect our children and immediately remove access by minors to all hard copy and virtual sexually explicit materials. As citizens who value children, we need to know who and why anyone would endeavor to keep such materials available to children. We once again request that these books be immediately removed from the minor children's access and moved to the adult section. THANK YOU. *Anne Odendhal ©2022*

Appendix

"A REPUBLIC, MADAM, IF YOU CAN KEEP IT!"
Published in the Texas Scorecard, March 2023

Many great citizens currently use the term democracy when referring to our United States government. I respectfully request review and reconsideration in the study of American history. A democracy is precisely what too many elected and unelected bureaucrats are trying to accomplish. They are supportive when history is forgotten or rewritten. They discredit patriots who know history, applaud any who call our nation a "democracy." The United States has never been a democracy. This has become a commonly held, extremely dangerous myth.

"A Republic, Madam, If You Can Keep It!"

That was the response of Benjamin Franklin to a woman who asked him whether the newly formed United States of America was to be a republic or a monarchy. As he was leaving the last day of deliberation at the Constitutional Convention in 1787 Franklin was concerned about the future of the new nation. Like many of us today, others present at the Convention were also doubtful. In a letter to John Taylor, John Adams wrote "Democracy never lasts long. It soon wastes, exhausts, and murders itself. There was never a democracy that did not commit suicide."

Democracy is a fifty-one percent majority mob rule. Mob rule results in increasing chaos which can never be sustained. Such governments often end up in a police state to control chaos. Democracy means if there are three people voting and two of them decide the third fellow should be lynched, he can be executed by majority vote. We all know a majority can be wrong (and unconstitutional) as the Supreme Court was in the Dred Scott decision of 1857, stunningly declaring that Black people could be regarded as property, not persons.

The United States is *not* a democracy! I cringe and grieve when I often hear anyone in the USA or another nation refer to our beloved nation as a democracy. Lurking enemies within and without yearn to undermine the United States sovereignty and strength. Those seeking to tear down our constitutional Republic delight in reinforcing this erroneous, perilous democracy concept.

We are a Republic! We use (non-corrupt?) majority vote to elect representatives who are sworn in to uphold the Constitution. Too many of those we elect swear faithfulness to our rule of law, then cast it aside when in office. They aim to push their opinions and self-interest agendas instead of the law of our land.

We are a Republic! "I pledge allegiance to the flag… and to the Republic for which it stands…" A Republic is ruled, governed by the Constitution, not people or majority votes. The USA Constitution is what rules our nation and supersedes all bias or clamorous movements. Constitutional changes were designed by our founders to be an arduous process with many checks and balances preventing any mob rule or branch of government exercising runaway power.
Anne Odendhal M.A. © March 2023

Notes

THE MURRAY CHRONICLES & CULTURAL FOUNDATIONS

1. Murray, William J. *My Life Without God.* Harvest House Publishers, 1982. Autobiography of William Murray recounting atheistic upbringing, maternal abuse, and later conversion to Christianity.

2. United Press International (UPI), July 1983. News article quoting William J. Murray's claim that his mother, Madalyn Murray O'Hair, "was employed by the Communist Party when she initiated the Supreme Court case that ended prayer and Bible reading in public schools."

3. Court Cases:

   - *Engel v. Vitale*, 370 U.S. 421 (1962)—Banned official school prayer.

   - *Abington School District v. Schempp*, 374 U.S. 203 (1963)—Prohibited Bible reading.

   - *Murray v. Curlett*, 374 U.S. 203 (1963)—Case brought by Madalyn Murray O'Hair, merged with *Schempp*.

4. Beatty, Mike. Personal recollections of Woodbourne Junior High (Baltimore, early 1960s), confirming neighborhood proximity and reputation of the Murray family.

5. Marx, Karl & Friedrich Engels. *The Communist Manifesto* (1848); *Critique of Hegel's Philosophy of Right* (1843). Referenced quotations: "Religion is the opium of the masses"; "Communism begins where atheism begins."

MARGARET SANGER & POPULATION CONTROL IDEOLOGIES

6. Sanger, Margaret. *Woman and the New Race.* Brentano's, 1920. Referenced quotes regarding eugenics and discriminatory population control.

7. Sanger, Margaret. "The Negro Project" (1939). Referenced for its correspondence stating: "We don't want the word to go out that we want to exterminate the Negro population."

8. Rushdoony, R. J. *The Myth of Overpopulation.* Ross House Books. Critique of ideological overpopulation narratives.

9. Mosher, Steven W. *A Mother's Ordeal: One Woman's Fight Against China's One-Child Policy.* A firsthand account exposing coercive abortion and sterilization under China's population-control laws.

MISSIONARY COURAGE & CHRISTIAN WITNESS

10. Elliot, Elisabeth. *Through Gates of Splendor.* Tyndale, 1957. Story of missionaries Jim Elliot, Nate Saint, Ed McCully, Peter Fleming, and Roger Youderian.

Notes

11. Elliot, Elisabeth. *Shadow of the Almighty.* Harper & Brothers, 1958. Biographical reflections on Jim Elliot's life and faith

12. Davis, Dale Ralph. *My Exceeding Joy.* Christian Focus Publications, 2023.

13. Qureshi, Nabeel. *Seeking Allah, Finding Jesus.* Zondervan, 2014. Autobiographical account of a former Muslim's journey to Christianity.

14. Newton, John (1725–1807). Primary works referenced: *An Authentic Narrative…* (1764); *Cardiphonia* (1781). Author of "Amazing Grace"; influential in the abolition movement.

15. Wilberforce, William. *A Practical View of Christianity.* 1797. Classic work arguing that spiritual renewal precedes moral reform.

16. Metaxas, Eric. *Squanto and the Miracle of Thanksgiving.* Thomas Nelson, 1996. Recounts the extraordinary life of Squanto and his role with the Plymouth colonists.

CULTURE, MORALITY & CIVIC ORDER

17. Orwell, George. *1984.* Secker & Warburg, 1949. Referenced for parallels to modern cultural drift.

18. Solzhenitsyn, Aleksandr. *The Gulag Archipelago.* Referenced for insights into totalitarianism and human conscience.

19. Hoffman, Abbie. *Woodstock Nation*. Random House, 1969. Primary source on countercultural radicalism and 1960s social upheaval.

20. Grant, George. *Third Time Around: A History of the Pro-Life Movement*. Wolgemuth & Hyatt, 1991.

21. Trumbull, Charles. *Outlawed: How Anthony Comstock Fought and Won the Purity of a Nation*.

22. Mohler, R. Albert Jr. "The Case for Early Marriage." *Christianity Today*, July 2009.

23. DeYoung, Kevin. "The Case for Kids." Clearly Reformed, 2023. Reflection on declining birthrates as a moral issue.

DEATH, LOSS & MEANING

24. Kübler-Ross, Elisabeth. *On Death and Dying*. Macmillan, 1969. Origin of the Five Stages of Grief.

25. Lewis, C. S. *A Grief Observed*. Faber & Faber, 1961. Reflections following the death of his wife.

FOUNDATIONAL TEXTS & EARLY AMERICAN FORMATION

26. The New England Primer (1690). Colonial textbook combining literacy with Christian doctrine.

27. The U.S. Constitution. Full text available through the National Archivest.

28. Baltimore Historical Society. Immigration archives (1880s–1900s).

29. Hasselbarth Family oral histories and photographs (private collection).

INFLUENTIAL BOOKS & LITERARY THEMES

30. Lewis, C. S. *Mere Christianity*. Macmillan, 1952. Referring to Lewis's articulation of moral law and human nature.

31. Tolkien, J. R. R. *The Hobbit*. Houghton Mifflin, 1938.

32. Tolkien, J. R. R. *The Lord of the Rings*. Houghton Mifflin, 1954–1955. Referenced for themes of courage, friendship, and resisting evil.

33. Schaeffer, Edith. *The Hidden Art of Homemaking*. Tyndale, 1971.

34. Schaeffer, Francis A. *How Should We Then Live?*. Revell, 1976.

35. Schaeffer, Francis A. *True Spirituality*. Tyndale, 1971.

36. Schaeffer, Francis A. *A Christian Manifesto*. Crossway, 1981.

37. Schaeffer, Francis A. *No Little People*. InterVarsity, 1974.

Notes

MARRIAGE, FAMILY & RELATIONSHIPS

38. Gungor, Mark. *Singles and Stinking Thinking* (Video Series). Humorous, practical teachings about dating and marriage.

39. Graham, Ruth Bell. *It's My Turn*. Word Books, 1982. Source of the humorous quote: "Divorce, no—murder, yes!"

40. *The Waiting: A True Story of a Lost Child...* by Cathy LaGrow with Cindy Coloma. Tyndale, 2014. Referenced for parallels of maternal sacrifice and adoption.

About the Author

With roots in Maryland, Anne Odendhal has lived a life marked by wide-ranging experiences and a deep love for learning, truth, and culture. She holds a B.A. in English and Education from the University of Maryland, Baltimore County (UMBC) and an M.A. in Religion and Counseling from Covenant Theological Seminary. Her studies and travels have taken her across the United States and abroad, including to Switzerland, where she had the rare privilege of studying under Dr. Francis Schaeffer at the renowned L'Abri Fellowship.

About the Author

Anne is a wife, mother, and grandmother whose reflections on family, faith, and perseverance are grounded in real-life complexity and enduring love.

Her professional journey is as multifaceted as her worldview. She has worked as a clinical counselor, college psychology instructor, technical writer, journalist, nutrition and wellness entrepreneur, ESL instructor, art business owner, health podcaster, and award-winning artist. A lifelong civic activist and defender of America's Constitutional heritage, she brings historical perspective and heartfelt conviction to every project she undertakes.

Anne is the founder of Maven Publishing Media, a publishing imprint dedicated to awakening the soul of America through truth-telling, history, and redemptive storytelling. Her debut book, *One Girl vs. A Nation Asleep: Awakening the Soul of America*, blends narrative nonfiction, journalism, and cultural reflection to inspire readers toward courage and renewal.

CONTACTING AUTHOR, SPEAKING INQUIRIES:

MavenPublishingmedia.com

Info@MavenPublishingMedia.com

MAVEN
Publishing Media

Author Resources/ Continuing the Journey

Shawn and Anne Odendhal serve together as Managing Partners of Better Benefits Group, a financial literacy and consulting firm dedicated to helping individuals and families build secure, meaningful futures free from financial stress.

At Better Benefits Group, the Odendhals specialize in safe-money strategies—no-risk financial approaches designed to protect wealth while creating guaranteed, lifetime monthly income, much like a personal pension. Through principles such as the Infinite Banking Concept, they teach clients how to grow wealth while maintaining liquidity and control, without being financially strapped until traditional retirement age.

Their goal is to equip families with strategies that protect what matters most—enabling them to live well today and plan confidently for the future.

FOR ADDITIONAL RESOURCES AND INQUIRIES:
www.BetterBenefitsGrp.com
admin@BetterBenefitsGrp.com

Made in the USA
Coppell, TX
08 February 2026